1 Christ before Pilate (*see fig. 16 for the whole scene*) *From a fourth-century sarcophagus, Lateran Museum, Rome*

The Trial of
JESUS OF NAZARETH

S. G. F. BRANDON

Professor of Comparative Religion,
University of Manchester

STEIN AND DAY / *Publishers* / NEW YORK

First published in the United States of America by
Stein and Day / *Publishers*, 1968
Copyright © S. G. F. Brandon, 1968
Library of Congress Catalog Card No. 68–9206
All rights reserved
Printed in Great Britain by
William Clowes and Sons Ltd, London and Beccles
Stein and Day / *Publishers* / 7 East 48 Street, New York, N.Y. 10017

Preface

It is obvious that in a series of studies of Historic Trials the trial of Jesus of Nazareth must be included. Indeed, it would be difficult to resist its claim to be the most important trial in history, in view of the immensity and profundity of its consequences. If it were possible to assess the influence of Christianity on human culture and civilization, that would be the measure of the historic importance of the trial of Jesus. Yet, when mentioned together with other historic trials, it is seen at once to be uniquely different. The trial of Jesus was an historical event, having occurred at a particular place and time, and involving other historical persons besides the chief character.* But it is invested also with a religious significance, since the chief character has been regarded as a divine being, in fact as the Son of God. The records of the trial form part of a sacred literature, and are read on liturgical occasions. Consequently, any endeavour to evaluate the trial of Jesus involves consideration of theological ideas and interests, as well as the more obvious factors concerned in any human situation. How difficult and complex is this theological involvement will quickly become apparent in the study that follows.

In this study, although the approach is strictly historical, a sincere effort has been made to assess the theological issue with sympathetic insight. For a peculiar problem which besets the historian of Christian Origins is that he is dealing not only with an historical situation, but with issues that essentially concern beliefs sacred to many persons. Thus, whereas a few academics only may be disturbed by some new interpretation of the trial of Socrates or of Queen Caroline, an interpretation of the trial of Jesus which challenges the traditional presentation may deeply shock and profoundly grieve many Christian people. Yet it is the historian's inescapable duty to investigate the causes which led to the composition of the traditional presentation of the trial

---

* E.g. Pontius Pilate and Caiaphas, whose names and deeds are recorded by non-Christian writers of the period.

of Jesus, even if, in so doing, he is sadly aware that a critical evaluation of those causes must inevitably affect the prestige of a long-revered tradition. However, even if a re-assessment of that tradition is found to be necessary, it need not be feared. Our understanding of so significant a person as Jesus of Nazareth can only be enriched by an enquiry that can get behind the patently tendentious, if well-meaning, traditional interpretation of the events that led to his death on the Roman cross.

Attempts have sometimes been made by eminent lawyers to explain the trial of Jesus. Their forensic knowledge and experience seem to befit them preeminently for such an undertaking. Unfortunately such attempts have foundered on a primary misconception. It is supposed that the four Christian Gospels provide, severally, four accounts of the trial of Jesus which are basically authentic; allowance having to be made only for minor differences. But it is just here that the essential problem of the trial of Jesus lies. These four accounts are not only very meagre in content, as their paralleled presentation in the Appendix clearly shows; the elucidation and evaluation of their evidence also involves an extremely complicated investigation. For they constitute our only sources of contemporary, or near-contemporary, information about the trial of Jesus; yet none of them is an objective account. The author of each was primarily concerned to explain away the embarrassing fact that Jesus was executed by the Romans for sedition against their government of Judaea. Consequently, the first and chief task of the historian is the assessment of these writings. This inevitably entails a detailed analysis of each narrative, and much tortuous discussion of minute, but vital, points. Every endeavour has been made to present this investigation as clearly and concisely as possible. But the author remains uncomfortably aware that the argument will demand close attention in many places. However, he believes that any person who seeks to understand what caused that fateful crucifixion outside the walls of Jerusalem, on the first Good Friday, will also be prepared to make the necessary effort to master the complex evidence. The problem of the trial of Jesus is profoundly important, and it is fascinating; but it is not easy of solution.★

The author gratefully acknowledges the work of other scholars on the subject, especially of Hans Lietzmann, Josef Blinzler, and Paul Winter. His own approach has necessarily been shaped by his preceding studies of the political factor in Christian Origins. For the strange paradox of Christianity

★ The notes at the end of the book contain full references to the documentary evidence and discussion of all relevant points of critical concern. Such documentation is essential for the specialist scholar; but the book is planned to be read without reference to this material.

is that its founder, though regarded as the Son of God, was executed by the Romans for sedition against their government in Judaea.

I wish to record my thanks to Professor J. P. Kenyon of the University of Hull, who, as the Editor of the series, invited me to contribute a volume on the trial of Jesus. To Mrs Elizabeth Farrow I am indebted for her efficient typing of a difficult manuscript, and for her help with the Indices. I am grateful also to Mr G. A. Webb of the photographic department of the Arts Library, Manchester University, for his skilful assistance in the production of certain illustrations.

UNIVERSITY OF MANCHESTER
11 JULY 1968

Contents

The Illustrations

Acknowledgement

The Scripture quotations in this book are from the Revised Standard Version of the Bible, copyrighted 1946 and 1952 by the Division of Christian Education of the National Council of the Churches of Christ in the USA, and used by permission.

The Author and Publishers wish to thank the following for the kind permission to reproduce the illustrations in this book:
Trustees of the British Museum for fig. 15; Editions d'Art Albert Guillot, Paris for figs. 12 and 13; Hirmer Verlag, Munich for fig. 23; Israel Department of Antiquities and Museums, Jerusalem for fig. 2; Manchester Museum for figs. 3–10; Mansell Collection, London for figs. 11, 16, 17, 20 and 25; Foto Marlurg for fig. 24; Musée des Beaux-Arts, Ghent for fig. 26; National Gallery, London for the jacket illustration; Pontificia Commissione di archeologia sacra for figs. 1 and 14.

Figs. 18, 19, 21 and 22 are from the Author's collection.

CHAPTER ONE

History or Theology?
The Basic Problems of the Evidence of the Trial of Jesus

It can be claimed, without fear of serious contradiction, that the trial of Jesus of Nazareth is the most notable in the history of mankind. More people know of it, if only vaguely, than of the trial of any other person; its effect on human history has been incalculable. From its fatal outcome stemmed a religion that has become the faith of a large part of mankind and inspired the culture of the Western World; from it, too, has flowed terrible consequences for the Jewish people, held guilty by generations of Christians of the murder of Christ.[1]

History records other trials, equally tragic, in which religious issues have been involved. In 399 BC Socrates was tried and condemned in Athens for introducing strange gods and corrupting the Athenian youth. The case was presented by Plato and Xenophon as a travesty of justice, with Socrates as a martyr to truth against superstition and prejudice.[2] Mani, the founder of Manichaeism, a religion once of great influence in both the East and West, died in AD 276, after trial for his teaching, condemned by the Sassanian king Bahrām I.[3] The judges of Joan of Arc in 1431 sentenced her to be burnt for her belief that God had entrusted her with a special mission for her people.[4] Each of these trials is memorable for the moral heroism of the condemned, which inspired the veneration of their disciples and followers. But none of these trials, nor any other that might be cited, ever acquired a religious significance comparable to that attributed to the trial and execution of Jesus.

The religious significance of the death of Jesus is dramatically presented in the four Gospels which constitute the foundational documents of Christianity. The nature of this significance is difficult to define with exactitude, since the Gospels are narratives, not theological treatises; but it may fairly be described as residing in the evaluation of the death of Jesus as the vicarious sacrifice of the Son of God for mankind.

Such an evaluation of a historical event, for such is the crucifixion of Jesus, implies the use of criteria of a very peculiar kind and wholly different from those employed in historical judgment. This consideration faces the historian, who seeks to study the trial and death of Jesus as historical events, with a problem of peculiar gravity. For the Gospels constitute both the earliest and the only extant accounts of the events that resulted in the crucifixion of Jesus outside the walls of Jerusalem, probably in the year AD 30. And, since they are also Christian documents and thus may be suspect as *ex parte* accounts of the events they describe, these facts alone are sufficient to make the assessment of their testimony a task of extreme difficulty as well as one of basic importance. But the Gospels are also the work of men who believed that they were recording the earthly life of a divine being, whose death was the culminating episode in a divine plan designed to accomplish the salvation of mankind. Consequently, the historian must find himself asking whether the Gospels, although appearing to be narrative accounts of the career of Jesus, are really concerned with history or with theology.

Faced with this problem, one solution which at once suggests itself is that the Gospels may perhaps represent a later theological presentation of an original historical tradition about the career of Jesus. The fact that the Gospel narratives refer to historical persons such as Pontius Pilate and Caiaphas, the Jewish high priest, of whom we have independent information, indeed seems to indicate that a theological evaluation has been imposed on a primitive factual record. The problem, however, is more involved than this. The earliest of the Gospels, the Gospel of Mark, appears to have been written shortly after AD 70;[5] but some twenty years before its composition there is evidence that already the death of Jesus was being interpreted in a wholly esoteric manner, without any reference to its historical context. This interpretation occurs in a letter written about the year 55 by Saint Paul to his Christian converts in the Greek city of Corinth.[6] The passage concerned must be quoted, in order to show the extraordinary nature of the problem with which we are concerned. From what Paul says here it is evident that he assumes that his readers will understand his meaning without further explanation:

> among the mature we do impart wisdom, although it is not a wisdom of this age or of the rulers of this age, who are doomed to pass away. But we impart a secret and hidden mystery of God, which God decreed before the ages for our glorification. None of the rulers of this age understood this; for if they had, they would not have crucified the Lord of glory.[7]

The passage is quoted here in the American Revised Standard Version of the Bible, which certainly conveys something of the esoteric character of

Paul's statement; but reference must be made to the original Greek text to bring out its full significance. The key thereto lies in the words, 'rulers of this age'. Translated thus, these words naturally seem to refer to the Roman and Jewish authorities who were responsible for the crucifixion of Jesus, according to the Gospel record. But, in their Greek form (*archontes tou aiōnes toutou*), the words have a very different meaning. They denote the demonic powers that were believed to govern this present world-order, and their use in this passage reveals that Paul was thinking in terms of current Graeco-Roman astralism. This was a very esoteric system, based upon an ancient tradition of belief that the stars, particularly the planets, ruled the destinies of men. The planets were identified with, or were regarded as inhabited by, elemental spirits, whom Paul refers to elsewhere as the *stoicheia tou kosmou* ('elemental spirits of the universe').[8]

When the astral context of Paul's thought in this passage is thus realised, what he says about the Crucifixion assumes a strange significance. For, according to him, the Crucifixion was the work of these demonic rulers of the lower planetary world, which is the abode of mankind. But that is not all: the one crucified by the *archontes* is designated the 'Lord of glory', and is clearly regarded as a supernatural being. Moreover, Paul presents this curious transaction as due to the 'secret and hidden wisdom of God', and 'decreed (by God) before the ages for our glorification'. Further, this divine plan was evidently intended to involve the deception of the *archontes* about the real significance of their crucifixion of the 'Lord of glory'.[9]

In this truly amazing statement Paul is obviously referring to the crucifixion of the historical Jesus of Nazareth. But he has, in effect, lifted the event completely out of its historical setting and assigned to it a transcendental significance. Jesus is identified with a supernatural being described as the 'Lord of glory', and his crucifixion is really the work of the demonic *archontes*. And these *archontes* had been deceived by God into perpetrating the crime, evidently to their own detriment.

That such an esoteric interpretation of the death of Jesus should have been expounded, within twenty years of its happening, by one who appears to have been the leading exponent of Christianity is indeed surprising. The fact puts the Gospels in a new light. They would seem to follow, or be in agreement with, Paul in regarding Jesus as a divine being and attributing to his death a soteriological significance; but they differ strikingly from him in their evident concern to describe the career of Jesus in its contemporary historical setting. Whereas Paul makes the demonic *archontes*, without qualification, directly responsible for the Crucifixion, the event is presented by the Evangelists as the work of the Roman and Jewish authorities ruling in Judaea at the time, without the slightest suggestion that they were only agents of supernatural beings. Now, since the Gospels were written some two or more decades after Paul's statement, we must inevitably ask what was the source of the narrative tradition which they embody; for it implies a preoccupation with the historical context of the life of Jesus which is entirely lacking in Paul's interpretation.

The answer, or at least an important part of it, is to be found in a complicated situation which must be appreciated, if we are to be in a position properly to evaluate the Gospel accounts of the trial and death of Jesus. A prerequisite to this is to understand Paul's place in the development of primitive Christianity.

A casual perusal of the New Testament suggests that Paul was the Apostle *par excellence* of Christianity. His writings far exceed those of any other Apostle, and the Acts of the Apostles clearly presents him as the most important figure in the missionary activity of the infant Church.[10] Paul's subsequent reputation in the Church, and the enormous influence which his writings have had in the formation of Christian doctrine, naturally tend to confirm the impression created by the New Testament that Paul was, from the time of his conversion, the most influential figure in the Church and the recognised exponent of its doctrine. Closer examination of Paul's writings, however, reveals a very different situation; this situation can also be discerned by careful analysis beneath the idealised picture of Christian Origins presented in the Acts.[11]

In his letters to his converts in Galatia and Corinth, Paul shows himself to be profoundly concerned about the activities of other Christians who are both presenting a different version of the faith from his own and denying his right to be an apostle. He even accuses these persons of teaching 'another Gospel' and preaching 'another Jesus'.[12] The agitation, which he shows about their activities, indicates that they were seriously threatening his authority among his converts. Paul, curiously, never identifies these opponents; however, the fact that they can challenge his authority in his own churches, while he never questions theirs, suggests that their status, or that of the persons whom they represented, was too high for Paul to repudiate. Their identity, though it is a matter of inference, cannot be seriously doubted. They were the leaders of the Church of Jerusalem, which comprised the original apostles and other disciples of Jesus.[13] We know, from Paul's own evidence, that these leaders were actually James, the 'Lord's brother', Peter and John.[14]

That such men, or their emissaries, repudiated Paul's claim to be an apostle, and that they taught a version of Christianity so essentially different from Paul's that he denigrates it as 'another gospel' about 'another Jesus', is a fact of immense significance for our understanding of the beginnings of Christianity, and, in turn, for our evaluation of the Gospel evidence concerning the trial and death of Jesus. But, to appreciate this significance fully, it is necessary to know in what manner these rival interpretations of Jesus did differ from each other.

In seeking an answer, we encounter what is undoubtedly one of the greatest obstacles in the study of Christian Origins. It is the fact that the original Christian community at Jerusalem disappeared with the destruction of the city by the Romans in AD 70, and with it perished all its records and monuments.[15] Consequently, we have no direct, self-attested evidence of the teaching of the Mother Church of Christianity. What we know of it has to be deduced from the writings of Paul, from the Acts of the Apostles, which is a document dating from towards the end of the first century,[16] and from certain early traditions that have been incorporated in amended form in the later Gospels.[17] Some information may also be gleaned from the second-century Christian writer Hegesippus, from the so-called Clementine literature, and from the Jewish historian Josephus; but what is obtained from these sources is very meagre and problematic.[18]

Difficult though this situation is, it is not completely hopeless: and, for our particular purpose here, enough can be deduced from these secondary sources to indicate the real nature of the difference between Paul's version of Christianity and that of the Mother Church of Jerusalem. We will begin with Paul's version. This has to be reconstructed from his letters, since nowhere in them does he give a systematic exposition of his doctrine; but some very distinctive aspects of it can be discerned, as we have already noticed. Paul has fortunately left us a brief biographical sketch of his past, in which he recognises the distinctive nature of his teaching and endeavours to account for it in terms of the divine purpose. It occurs, significantly, in his letter to the Galatian Christians when he is seeking to defend his 'gospel' against that of his opponents, as we have previously seen. After admonishing his converts for their disloyalty, he writes:

> I would have you know, brethren, that the gospel which was preached by me is not according to man. For I did not receive it from man, nor was I taught it, but it came through a revelation of Jesus Christ. For you have heard of my former life in Judaism, how I persecuted the church of God violently and tried to destroy it; and I advanced in Judaism beyond many of my own age among my people, so extremely zealous was I for the traditions of my fathers. But when he who had set me apart before I was born, and had called me through his grace, was pleased to reveal his Son in me, in order that I might preach him among the Gentiles, I did not

confer with flesh and blood, nor did I go up to Jerusalem to those who were apostles before me, but I went away into Arabia; and again I returned to Damascus.[19]

This statement is very illuminating. It was designed to show the Galatian Christians, impressed by the authority of the 'gospel' of the Jerusalem Church, that his (Paul's) gospel was of divine origin and absolutely independent of the original apostles now resident at Jerusalem. In claiming that his interpretation of the faith 'came through a revelation of Jesus Christ', Paul also explains that God's purpose in making this revelation to him was that he (Paul) 'might preach (Jesus) among the Gentiles'. The explanation is of the greatest consequence. By implication, it shows that Paul believed that his presentation of Jesus was one specially designed to be intelligible to non-Jews. The implied comparison here with the 'gospel' of the Jerusalem Church is explicitly confirmed later on in the Galatian Epistle, when Paul designates his 'gospel' as 'the gospel of the uncircumcised', in contradistinction to the other which he describes as 'the gospel to the circumcised'.[20] This essay in differentiation also helps to explain Paul's strange accusation when writing to the Christians of Corinth, that his opponents there preach 'another Jesus':[21] his meaning must surely be that they presented Jesus in a manner intelligible to Jews, and not to Gentiles.

We reach, then, an important point in our enquiry. Paul witnesses to the currency of two different interpretations of Jesus within two decades of the Crucifixion. One of these, which Paul believed had been mediated to him directly by God, was conceived in a manner such as to make it intelligible or attractive to the Gentiles. The other interpretation, which presumably would not have been to Gentile taste, was that which the original Jewish disciples of Jesus had composed, evidently in Jewish concepts and terminology.[22] Now, since Paul's agitation over the propagation of the Jerusalem 'gospel' among his converts was so great, it must surely follow that there was some difference between these interpretations more radical than that of language or imagery. Can we discern in what this lay?

Paul seems to provide a clue in his *Second Epistle to the Corinthians*, in a passage where he appears to be defending himself against criticism that insinuated that he was not mentally sound:

For if we are beside ourselves, it is for God; if we are in our right mind, it is for you. For the love of Christ controls us, because we are convinced that one has died for all; therefore, all have died. And he died for all, that those who live no longer live for themselves but for him who for their sake died and was raised. From now on, therefore, we regard no one from a human point of view; even though we once regarded Christ from a human point of view, we regard him thus no longer. Therefore, if any one is in Christ, he is a new creation; the old has passed away, behold the new has come.[23]

Paul's diction here is admittedly obscure, but his general meaning is clear He was evidently rebutting the charge that his ideas were fantastic. The points at issue seem to be his belief that Christ's death was in some way universally vicarious, he had 'died for all'; that, because of the vicarious nature of his death, in some way all men had also died and become, or could become, incorporated in Christ; and that such incorporation made them 'a new creation'.[24] This mysterious transaction, although it was apparently related to the historical death of Jesus by crucifixion, is regarded by Paul as being so essentially mystical that he repudiates its connection with the actual historical event—'even though we once regarded (*oidamen*) Christ from a human point of view, we regard (*ginoskomen*) him thus no longer'. The expression 'Christ from a human point of view' means, in the original Greek (*kata sarka Christon*), 'Christ according to the flesh', and it surely designates Christ as a person of flesh and blood, or, in our modern terminology, the 'historical Jesus' who lived in first-century Palestine.[25]

This repudiation of knowledge of the historical Jesus, and the consequent assertion that 'the old has passed away, behold, the new has come', are of great significance when we recall Paul's relations with the Jerusalem Christians. Paul was a late-comer to the faith, not having been an original disciple of Jesus. He maintained that he had not learnt his Christianity from 'those who were apostles before me', but through a special revelation that God had made to him. It is understandable, therefore, that in defending his authority as an apostle against the authority of the Jerusalem leaders, who had been the original disciples of Jesus and 'eye-witnesses' of his life, Paul devalued knowledge of the historical Jesus in favour of mystical communion with the Risen Christ.[26]

This attitude found doctrinal expression, as we have already seen, in Paul's evaluation of the Crucifixion as a mystic event, wholly unrelated to its historical setting, which God had so contrived that the demonic *archontes*, unwittingly, had carried it out to their own detriment. Their victim was a divine being, designated 'the Lord of glory': no reference is made to him as a historical person, for that aspect of his being was temporary and irrelevant compared with his eternal nature.

Such an esoteric doctrine was not only un-Jewish, but it contradicted the basic principles of Judaism. It envisaged the whole of mankind, both Jews and Gentiles, as being in a state of spiritual perdition, enslaved to the demonic rulers of the universe. Deliverance from this condition had been arranged by God through the vicarious death of another divine being, the 'Lord of glory', and this deliverance was available to all men, irrespective of their race. Thus the doctrine violated the two most cherished beliefs of the Jews. For, by envisaging all mankind as needing salvation from a common doom, the fundamental distinction drawn by the Jews between themselves, as the Elect People of God, and the Gentiles was ignored, thus negating the basic premise of Judaism.[27] Then, the very idea of the existence of another divine being, called the 'Lord of glory', violated the principle of monotheism, which was also basic to Jewish religion.[28] Equally alien and offensive was the identification of a human person, Jesus, with this 'second god', the Lord of glory.[29]

It is understandable, therefore, that the Jerusalem Christians were shocked when they came to realise the full implications of Paul's 'gospel', and that they repudiated it, seeking to suppress it among the Gentile converts by rejecting Paul's claim to be an apostle and perhaps suggesting that he was insane. Their attacks seriously undermined Paul's position; for they had the advantage of him in that he could not challenge their authority as the original apostles of Jesus, while they could dismiss him as a late-comer to a faith which he had once persecuted.[30]

So far as the history of the conflict can be traced out from the extant evidence, Paul finally endeavoured to reach some *modus vivendi* with the Jerusalem Christians by going personally to the city. The result was disastrous. James, the brother of Jesus, being then leader of the Jerusalem Church, compelled Paul to prove his Jewish orthodoxy by performing certain rites in the Temple. Recognised there and attacked by other Jews, who regarded him as a renegade, he was saved from death by the intervention of the Roman garrison of the nearby fortress of the Antonia.[31] To avoid trial in Judaea, Paul appealed, as a Roman citizen, to have his case judged by the Emperor; the result of the Roman trial is unknown, and Paul disappears from history.[32] The memory of his teaching would doubtless have disappeared also, and the Jerusalem 'gospel' would surely have prevailed but for the Jewish revolt against Rome in AD 66.[33] After four years of disastrous war, the Jewish nation was overthrown and its holy city destroyed: in that catastrophe, as we have already noted, the Mother Church of Jerusalem also perished.

The consequences of the Jewish disaster of AD 70 for Christianity were immense, and we shall be concerned later in assessing them in relation to our subject; but now we must turn back to our immediate task of seeking to discover what was the teaching of the Jerusalem Church, from which Paul's teaching so profoundly differed. As we noted earlier, this can only be inferred from Paul's writings and the Acts of the Apostles, and from other minor sources; for the archives of the Jerusalem Church perished with it in the holocaust of AD 70. However, some deductions can safely be made of great importance for our purpose. The first and most crucial is that the original Jewish disciples, who came to form the Church of Jerusalem, did not regard their allegiance to Jesus as requiring the abandonment of their ancestral faith. Indeed, all the evidence points to their being exceedingly zealous in the practice of Judaism: they worshipped regularly in the Temple at Jerusalem, taking part in the sacrificial ritual, they kept the Jewish festivals, and observed the Jewish Law, even in matters of peculiar ritual custom such as the Nazarite vow.[34] Many priests and Pharisees joined their community,[35] and their leader James, the 'Lord's brother', was held in high repute for his piety among his fellow-countrymen.[36] The chief point on which they differed from other Jews was in their recognition of Jesus as the Messiah of Israel.

During this period there were many claimants to Messiahship,[37] and it is important to remember that, according to contemporary Jewish belief, the Messiah was not conceived as a divine being: the fundamental monotheism of Judaism rendered such a conception impossible.[38] The Jewish Christians' interpretation of the Messiahship of Jesus did not, however, deify him; it differed in another way. According to current Messianic expectation, the Messiah would be God's appointed agent to drive out the Romans and restore sovereign power to Israel.[39] Defeat and death automatically negatived the claims of any person to be the Messiah.[40] The Jewish Christians had surmounted the shock which Jesus' execution by the Romans had constituted to their faith in him as the Messiah, through their conviction that God had raised him from death. His resurrection they interpreted as divine endorsement of his Messiahship,[41] and they believed that he would soon return with supernatural power to complete his Messianic role—to 'restore the kingdom to Israel', as it is significantly described in the Acts of the Apostles.[42]

The Jewish Christians were primarily concerned to persuade their compatriots to accept Jesus as the Messiah.[43] To this end it was necessary that they should formulate a case which demonstrated his Messianic character according to contemporary expectation. This meant the recounting of actions, particularly of a miraculous kind, which proved that Jesus had the supernatural power expected of the Messiah.[44] The Jewish historian Josephus, incidentally, tells how miracles were attributed to other Messianic claimants.[45] Another need which the Jewish Christians had to meet is of special importance for our purpose. The Roman execution of Jesus, in which the Jewish national leaders had been involved, obviously demanded explanation, if their fellow Jews were to be persuaded that it had confirmed, not contradicted, his Messianic character. Here we meet an issue which will require some anticipation of our subsequent analysis of the accounts of the trial of Jesus preserved in the Gospels.

The Gospels devote considerable space to describing the trial and execution of Jesus.[46] These events naturally have an intrinsic interest which accounts for the attention devoted to them. However, in view of the fact that the Evangelists regard the death of Jesus as the vicarious sacrifice of the Son of God for the salvation of mankind, it is difficult to see how their descriptions of the historical circumstances of the event serve their theological purpose. Indeed, to the contrary, the attention of the reader becomes so focused upon the human drama that its supernatural significance tends to be forgotten. It is the actions and motives of the Jewish leaders, of Judas Iscariot, and Pontius Pilate, and the sufferings of Jesus that dominate; only the laboured exegesis of later theologians and preachers has sought to explain how this essentially human tragedy, described with so much realistic detail, had a supernatural relevance.[47]

These considerations, together with the obvious need of the Jewish Christians to explain how the execution of Jesus had endorsed, not contradicted, his Messiahship, consequently suggest that the Gospel accounts of the transaction derive from the records of the Jerusalem Church. It will be our task later to estimate how far this original tradition has been preserved in the Gospels or the reasons for its alteration. For our immediate purpose there is, however, one feature of the account of the trial in the Markan Gospel which now requires our attention, since it concerns the evaluation of the 'gospel' of the Jerusalem Church.

The Gospel of Mark, as the other Gospels, records what seem to be two trials of Jesus: the first by the Sanhedrin, the highest Jewish court,[48] and the second by Pontius Pilate, the Roman governor of Judaea.[49] Now, in the accounts of these trials only once is an attempt made to disprove a charge brought against Jesus. It occurs in the statement that at the Sanhedrin trial Jesus was accused by those who 'bore false witness' (*epseudomarturoun*) that he had threatened to destroy the Temple.[50] This accusation failed, it is asserted, because the witnesses contradicted each other.[51] The account goes on to describe how Jesus was condemned to death for blasphemy, because he had acknowledged himself to be the Messiah when questioned by the high priest.[52] In the subsequent trial before Pilate, where Jesus is accused of sedition against the Roman government, no argument is offered in the Markan account to disprove the charge;[53] the claim only is made that Pilate perceived the innocence of Jesus and sought to release him.[54] This claim will

2 Inscription of Pontius Pilate, found at Caesarea, 1961
This is the only contemporary monument of Pilate so far discovered. He is styled
'Praefectus of Judaea'

Israel Museum, Jerusalem

3 Silver denarius of Emperor Tiberius
The coin used in the Tribute episode was
probably of this type (*see p. 66*)

4 Bronze coin of Pontius Pilate
inscribed 'Tiberius Caesar'
The emblem is a *lituus* or augur's wand

COINS ISSUED BY THE JEWISH INSURGENTS DURING REVOLT OF AD 66–70

5 Silver shekel inscribed
'Jerusalem the Holy'

6 Bronze coin inscribed
'Deliverance of Zion'

Enlarged reproductions by courtesy of the Manchester Museum

7–8 Bronze *sestertius* of Vespasian, AD 71
Reverse shows victorious Emperor and mourning Judaea, inscribed *'Judaea Capta'*

9–10 Bronze *sestertius* of Titus, AD 80–1
Reverse shows mourning Judaea and Jewish prisoner, inscribed *'Judaea Capta'*
COINS COMMEMORATING ROME'S VICTORY OVER JUDAEA

Enlarged reproductions by courtesy of the Manchester Museum

engage our attention at length later; for the present it is necessary to appreciate the fact that the only charge that is specifically mentioned and refuted in the Markan account of the trials is that of Jesus' hostility to the Temple. This remarkable fact appears the more remarkable, when we note that Mark elsewhere in his Gospel believed that Jesus did foretell the destruction of the Temple, and there also existed a tradition to that effect.[55]

Since it is unlikely, therefore, that Mark would have invented an incident disproving that Jesus had spoken against the Temple, when he earlier describes him as prophesying its destruction, the trial account must surely go back to the Jerusalem Christians. That it should so do is also consistent with what we otherwise know of the veneration of the Jerusalem Christians for the Temple.[56] For it is understandable that they should have been at pains to refute a charge that their Master, whom they claimed to be the Messiah of Israel, had threatened the chosen sanctuary of the God of Israel.

We may, accordingly, discern something of an original Jewish Christian apologia concerning the trial and crucifixion of Jesus. The indications are that the first disciples formulated a record of the Sanhedrin trial which was designed to refute what they considered to be the most serious charge brought there against his Messiahship, namely, that he had spoken against the Temple. This apologia also recorded the condemnation of Jesus for acknowledging himself to be the Messiah. The fact that he was condemned for blasphemy on this admission by the high priest, who, as we shall see, collaborated with the Roman government of his country, would also have had its significance. Further, it is at least worthy of note, even if it be regarded as an *argumentum a silentio*, that Mark and the other Evangelists apparently found in this original Jewish Christian apologia no similar refutation of the charge of sedition brought against Jesus at the Roman trial. In other words, it looks as though the original Jewish Christian account of the trial of Jesus was concerned to rebut an accusation that could be used as an objection to his being the Messiah; but it showed no interest in disproving that Jesus was guilty of sedition against Rome.

It is not our purpose now to continue further with this analysis of the original Jewish Christian account of the trial. We have, instead, to turn back to our main theme in this chapter, namely, the significance of the theological factor in the earliest traditions about Jesus. Our investigation of the 'gospel' of the Mother Church of Jerusalem has shown that Paul's transcendental interpretation of the death of Jesus, which completely ignored its historical context, was Paul's own view; although it was being taught by him within two decades of the Crucifixion, it did not represent the teaching of the original disciples of Jesus, resident at Jerusalem. They, on the contrary, were essentially concerned with the life of the historical Jesus, whom they recognised as the Messiah of their people. Their desire to win their countrymen to their own faith in the Messiahship of Jesus caused them both to formulate accounts of Jesus' sayings and deeds which attested his Messianic character, and to compose an apologia concerning his trial which defended him against an accusation of hostility towards the Temple.

This evidence of an original tradition of the historical Jesus which presented him as the Messiah of Israel, while establishing a point of fundamental importance for our investigation of the trial of Jesus, inevitably faces us with a problem of exceeding complexity in evaluating the evidence of the Gospels, which provide the only accounts we have of the trial. We have seen that the Gospels evidently embody the original Jewish Christian tradition; but they also conceive of Jesus as the divine Saviour of mankind. In this conception they are decisively in the tradition of Paul's teaching, which was rejected by the Jerusalem Christians; yet, in their preoccupation with the historical Jesus, they seem to appreciate an evaluation which Paul considered irrelevant, if not actually mistaken.

The real dimensions of our task accordingly begin to become plain. Instead of proceeding straight to an examination of the Gospel records of the trial of Jesus, we find that we must first enquire how these records came to be composed of diverse traditions that point back to tensions and conflicts within the infant Christian movement after the death of Jesus and before the destruction of Jerusalem in AD 70. In other words, our study of the trial of Jesus can only properly begin after we have assessed the various, and obviously complex, factors that lie behind the composition of the four Gospels and their presentations of that tragic event.[57]

CHAPTER TWO

The Setting and its Enigmas: Judaea, 4 BC to AD 70

The four Christian Gospels, which record the trial and death of Jesus, are the products of four different Greek-speaking Christian communities, situated outside Judaea sometime after AD 70.[1] Yet each Gospel, through its own community, is indissolubly linked with Judaea and cannot be understood apart from what happened in that land between the years 4 BC and AD 70. The connection of each Gospel with the earlier part of this period, namely, that which coincides with the lifetime of Jesus, is, of course, obvious; but each Gospel was also decisively conditioned by events of the latter part, i.e. from the Crucifixion to the destruction of Jerusalem in AD 70.

The period, as defined here, covers the last and most tragic episode in the long history of the Jewish national state; for the catastrophe which befell Israel in the year 70 marked the end of the nation's life in the land of Yahweh's ancient promise, until its restoration in 1948 and its final repossession of its holy city in 1967. For our subject the year 4 BC has a special significance: it marked the death of Herod the Great, whom Christian tradition has so notably connected with the birth of Jesus of Nazareth.[2] The connection, though fortuitous, is important; for it means, if the tradition can be trusted, that the infancy of Jesus coincided with the close of one distinctive period of Jewish history and the beginning of another, which was fraught with tragedy and fateful consequence.[3]

The death of Herod in the spring of 4 BC, when Jesus was perhaps two years of age, ended the long reign of one of the most efficient and certainly the most hated of Jewish kings. The Jews hated Herod for his Idumaean origin, his pagan tastes and his ruthless suppression of all who opposed him or incurred his suspicion. Herod was, however, a shrewd and resolute ruler, whose ability was appreciated by the Romans, so that they supported him as a reliable and efficient client-prince of a land of great strategic importance to their dominion in the Near East. Herod, who knew the religious fanaticism of his subjects and its dangerous potentialities, seems to have pursued a

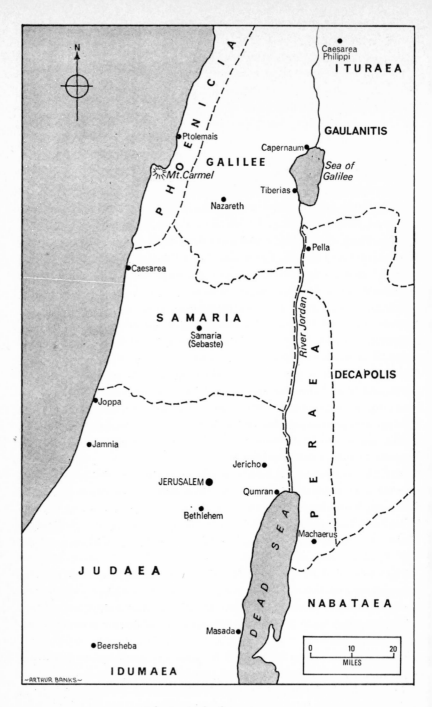

Palestine in the first century AD

policy designed gradually to integrate the Jews into the Hellenised society of the Roman Empire, in which their future inevitably lay. To this end he sought to placate their hostility by rebuilding the Temple at Jerusalem on a scale more magnificent than that of any of its previous constructions, while also promoting Hellenic institutions both in Palestine and abroad. Although his policy failed, Herod's long reign did have the effect of preserving the Jews from experiencing the realities of direct Roman rule.[4] For, however strong their hatred for Herod, in him they did at least have a professing Jew as their ruler, and not a heathen governor, representing the Emperor of Rome, who also claimed to be a god.[5] Moreover, the tribute, which they paid to Herod, went to support a Jewish national state, not a foreign empire; the money which they handled did not offend their religious scruples by its pagan symbols or the effigy of Caesar;[6] and they were not affronted by the presence of a foreign soldiery, whose standards proclaimed the might of heathen Rome and their subjugation to it.[7]

The death of Herod at once presaged the shape of things to come. It became immediately clear that the future of Israel was for the Roman Emperor to decide.[8] But, even before that decision was pronounced, an imperial procurator, Sabinus, had moved into Judaea to secure Herod's considerable fortune, presumably for the Emperor. The Jews were already in arms, and they demanded that Sabinus should withdraw from Jerusalem, declaring that it was their intention to recover their national independence.[9] The Jewish historian Josephus, who records these events, does not name any Jewish leader, and he gives no indication how 'national independence' was then conceived by the Jews: doubtless the aspiration was coloured by long-cherished traditions of the heroic days of David and the Maccabees, and it expressed the popular conviction that Israel must be free of the rule of any sovereign lord other than Yahweh, its god.[10]

Fighting broke out in Jerusalem, and there were risings in other parts of the country led by men whom Josephus does name: one of these was Judas, son of an Ezekias, whose execution by Herod, when a young man, had dangerously involved him with the Sanhedrin.[11] The gravity of the situation caused Varus, the Roman legate of Syria, to intervene with two legions. The risings were suppressed, and Sabinus, hard-pressed in Jerusalem, was relieved. Savage reprisals were taken: two thousand of the Jewish insurgents were crucified.[12]

Whether these risings influenced the decision of the Emperor Augustus is unknown. He set aside Herod's wish that his son Archelaus should succeed him in the kingship: instead, he divided the kingdom, appointing Archelaus to be ethnarch of Judaea and Samaria; over Galilee he set another son, Herod

Antipas, as tetrarch.[13] The arrangement had the effect of still holding off from the Jews the brutal facts of direct Roman rule. However, the fateful impact was delayed for one decade only. In AD 6 Augustus deposed Archelaus, who had proved himself an incapable ruler, and placed Judaea and Samaria under direct Roman government. To implement the new order, Augustus instructed P. Sulpicius Quirinius, legate of Syria, to which province Judaea and Samaria were now attached, to take a census of the people and the economic resources of the newly annexed territories for the assessment of tribute. A procurator, Coponius, was appointed to assist in the operation and to be the local governor, with full powers including authority to inflict sentence of death.[14]

A census was a normal administrative measure, to which other peoples of the Roman Empire were subjected; but for the Jews it was more than a token of their servitude to Rome. Of this other, and deeper significance of the census, they were quickly reminded by a rabbi, Judas of Galilee, whose protest was backed by Saddok, a Pharisee. According to Josephus, 'a Galilaean, named Judas, incited his countrymen to revolt, upbraiding them as cowards for consenting to pay tribute to Rome and tolerating mortal masters, after having God for their lord'.[15] In another version of the affair, Josephus states that Judas and Saddok stirred up sedition: 'They maintained that this census would lead to nothing less than complete slavery, and they called upon the people to vindicate their liberty. They argued that, if they succeeded, they would enjoy the consequences of their good fortune, and, if they failed, they would at least have the honour and glory of having shown greatness of spirit. Moreover, God would more surely assist them in their undertaking, if, inspired by such ideals, they spared no effort to realise them.'[16]

This presentation of Judas of Galilee comes from the pen of one who was bitterly opposed to the movement which stemmed from the example and teaching of Judas, as we shall see. Josephus, a well-born Jewish priest and a Pharisee, who went over to the Romans during the war for Israel's freedom that started in AD 66, blamed the Zealots, as the followers of Judas came to be known, for the catastrophe that overwhelmed the nation in the year 70.[17] Consequently, what he says in these passages has to be viewed with caution. However, even through what is thus the account of a hostile witness, the religious character of the ideals that led Judas to call upon his countrymen to oppose the Roman decree is apparent. For our understanding of Jewish affairs during this period it is essential that we rightly appreciate what these ideals were.

The fundamental principle, on which the exhortation of Judas was based, was that of the absolute sovereignty of God over the Jews. This was, of course, the very quintessence of Judaism: it underlay the peculiar Jewish belief that their god, Yahweh, had made a covenant with their forefathers that he would bless their descendants and settle them in the land of Canaan, if they would serve him loyally as their sovereign Lord. Hebrew literature embodies this belief in a rich variety of expressions, and it is the theme that runs through all the vicissitudes of Jewish history.[18] Josephus, ironically enough, coined the word 'theocracy' to describe the polity logically implied in Judaism: only a godly high-priest could rightly preside over the nation, as the vicegerent of Yahweh on earth.[19] Such an idealised conception of divine sovereignty meant that Judaea was regarded as Yahweh's holy land: hence to take of its resources and give them in the form of tribute to a heathen lord was an act of apostasy towards Yahweh. Moreover, the payment of such tribute involved the recognition of another lord than Yahweh—another lord who, though mortal, was worshipped as a god by his subjects.[20]

In view of the realities of political power in the contemporary world, such a doctrine was suicidal, and it was inevitable that those who held it should soon find themselves challenging the imperium of Rome.[21] But Jewish religion exalted the martyr-ideal, and its sacred writings abounded with stories of those who had suffered, and often triumphed, for their faith in Yahweh.[22] This readiness for martyrdom is clearly reflected in Josephus' account of the exhortations of Judas of Galilee. Like the prophets of old, Judas was uncompromising in setting the essential issue before his people, namely, the implications of the Roman census: to submit would be disloyalty to Yahweh; to resist would involve martyrdom, though divine succour might also come.

Many Jews followed Judas, rising in revolt against their new masters. Their resistance was crushed, and many died a martyr's death, doubtless among them Judas himself.[23] But their cause did not perish then, with their defeat: many survivors, including members of Judas's family, took to the deserts, whence they continued a guerrilla resistance against the Romans and those Jews who collaborated with them.

These Jewish collaborators were chiefly members of the priestly aristocracy, who held positions of prestige and affluence in the ecclesiastical organisation of the state.[24] Such men were primarily concerned with the maintenance of a stable government and ordering of society. They had no love for the Romans, but they were realists in recognising that their own security depended upon their cooperation with the new masters of Israel. Josephus mentions, significantly, that the high priest Joazar had sought to persuade his people to submit quietly to the census.[25]

Thus, already in the year 6, at the very start of the Roman rule, the pattern of Jewish reaction through the next six decades emerged. The Jewish aristocracy, though the official religious leaders of the nation, were concerned to keep their people submissive to their heathen overlord: it was a worldly-wise policy, and doubtless Israel's material interests, as well as their own, would have been best served by following it. But those who were zealous for the God of Israel would not thus compromise over the sacred principles of their faith. They refused to call Caesar 'lord', having one lord only, Yahweh; nor would they consent to giving of the resources of Yahweh's holy land in tribute to Caesar. As the ancient heroes of their faith, they preferred to risk martyrdom rather than apostatise. But theirs was not a passive resistance: inspired by the example of Phinehas, the original 'Zealot' for Yahweh,[26] and the Maccabees,[27] they resorted to arms, using whatever opportunity offered to damage or overthrow the Roman power and those who supported it.

Between these two groups of aristocratic collaborators and the Zealot resistance, the attitude of the mass of the people wavered, according to circumstances. Fundamentally, they hated the Romans, who gave them good cause both by their oppression and their frequent overt violation of Jewish religious sensibilities. Natural timidity and desire for peace generally ensured their submission; but secretly they admired the Zealots for their active resistance and supported them as and when they could.[28] Moreover, they shared in the apocalyptic outlook of their generation, and looked forward to the coming of the Messiah, Yahweh's Anointed, who would deliver his people and 'restore the kingdom to Israel'.[29]

It was in such an environment of alternating tension and violence, shot through with hatred for heathen Rome and its Jewish collaborators, and inflamed by apocalyptic hope, that Jesus lived through the formative years of his life and in which his mission was set. If the Gospel chronology is to be trusted, he was about twelve years of age when Judaea was directly incorporated into the Roman Empire and the census provoked the revolt of Judas of Galilee. Tradition locates the early life of Jesus in Galilee, over which Herod Antipas ruled as tetrarch.[30] But though not experiencing direct Roman rule there, he must have been keenly aware of the situation in Judaea. It was the custom of pious Jews to visit Jerusalem for the greater festivals, and the Gospel of Luke actually records a visit of Jesus there at the age of twelve.[31] As a precocious boy, he must have been keenly aware of the crisis that faced his nation. There can surely be no doubt where his sympathies would have lain—not with the hard insolent Romans, who now deprived Israel of its heritage; but with Judas and his followers, who had bravely ventured their lives in resisting the heathen oppressor and died the martyr-death.

Judas, himself a Galilaean,[32] would doubtless have been a hero of Jesus' boyhood, and it is likely that Jesus knew many of his followers, called *Kannā'im* because they were zealous for the God of Israel—men who had taken to the desert and whose exploits were eagerly recounted as the latter-day Maccabees.[33] Admittedly, these are inferences; but they are reasonable and necessary ones to draw from what we know of the historical situation of Jesus' life. However, to appreciate the full significance of that situation we have yet to consider the place which the Zealot movement had in contemporary Jewish life; for hitherto it has been greatly misunderstood.

Until the last decade, little attention was given to the Zealots in studies of the origins of Christianity. The reason for this neglect is undoubtedly to be traced to the fact that almost all our information about them comes from Josephus. This writer, as we have already noted, blamed the Zealots for the overthrow of the Jewish nation in AD 70. The seriousness of this charge, and the vehemence with which it was made, are evident in the following passage from his *Jewish Antiquities*, in which he describes the consequences of Judas' revolt and the movement which he founded:

> There was no evil that did not stem from them and from which the people were affected beyond description: wars, from the unceasing violence of which none was spared; loss of friends who might have lightened our sufferings; large-scale brigandage; the murder of important persons—it was all done on the pretext of the common good; but, in reality, it was motivated by personal gain. Whence arose seditions and political assassinations, sometimes of fellow-countrymen, who fell victims to their internecine fury and fanatical resistance to their enemies, and sometimes of their enemies; famine almost beyond endurance; the taking and destruction of cities, until this revolt finally delivered even the Temple of God to the fire of the enemy. So vast a changing and over-throw of national institutions brought destruction on those they in-volved. . . .[34]

It is a grim indictment, and in his various writings on these times Josephus purports to describe, with much lurid detail, the enormities of the Zealots, presenting them as wicked fanatics who drove a peaceful people, against the advice and efforts of their rightful leaders, into revolt against the might of imperial Rome and ultimately to the catastrophe of AD 70.[35]

Because no contrary account or indeed any other account existed, and because the spectacle of Israel thus plunging to its doom after crucifying its

Messiah was interpreted by Christians as the just vengeance of God,[36] Josephus' portrait of the Zealots was accepted without question, and it became, until recently, the established evaluation. Consequently, it was also accepted, without question, that Jesus could have had no dealings with such murderous fanatics; nor, too, could his original disciples, who formed the Mother Church of Jerusalem. This conclusion, moreover, was convincingly confirmed by the fourth-century Church historian Eusebius, who reported that the Christians of Jerusalem, warned by God, fled from the wicked city, which the Zealots held, before divine justice accomplished its doom in AD 70.[37]

A variety of factors have led, in recent years, to a re-assessment of the Zealots. The Second World War, when 'resistance' groups in many lands struggled fiercely, using guerrilla tactics often involving assassination and murder, against the occupying Nazi forces, induced willingness to look at the ancient Zealots with a new sympathy and insight. This new atmosphere also coincided with the establishment of the new state of Israel against what seemed in 1948 to be impossible odds. In their dedicated struggle, the Israelis found inspiration in the example of those Zealots who, in the year 73 at Masada, fought to the bitter end, preferring suicide to surrender to the Romans.[38] The excavation of this great fortress on the shores of the Dead Sea was undertaken by the Israeli government in 1963 not only as a piece of archaeological research, but as a gesture of national faith:[39] the results have been to demonstrate both the heroism and the essentially religious character of Zealotism.[40] In addition to this direct evidence, the discovery of the Dead Sea Scrolls and the excavations at Qumrân have revealed facets of Jewish religious life at this time hitherto unknown.[41] Their evidence has made more real the tensions then existing in Judaea, with much significant reference also to Rome[42]—evidence even more meaningful in view of a close connection that existed between Masada and Qumrân.[43]

This new evidence and re-orientation of sympathy have led to a more critical examination of Josephus' account of the Zealots. It can now be seen that the historian was moved by two very strong motives to denigrate these patriots. In the first place, his writings were addressed to Gentile readers and were intended to abate the hatred felt for the Jews, owing to the atrocities committed during their revolt.[44] He endeavours, accordingly, to exonerate the Jewish people by representing them as the victims of desperate fanatics who hounded them into revolt, murdered their proper leaders who were loyal to Rome, and compelled them to fight on hopelessly until utter destruction overwhelmed them.[45] The other motive was personal. Josephus needed to justify his own desertion of his nation's cause and secession to its enemies:[46] lacking the burning faith of the Zealots, whose whole-hearted dedication to Yahweh, the God of Israel, so signally rebuked his own apostasy, he sought to disparage the religious aspect of their movement by depicting them as lawless desperadoes, bent only on dragging the nation to ruin in the blind fury of their fanaticism. However, even in his own bitterly prejudiced account, Josephus unwittingly reveals something of the essentially religious character of Zealot inspiration. We have already noted that he does admit that Judas of Galilee called on the Jews to revolt because the payment of tribute was tantamount to disloyalty to Yahweh, as submission to Caesar also meant acknowledging another lord instead of Yahweh.[47] Another significant admission occurs towards the end of his *Jewish War*. Describing how a body of the Sicarii, an extremist group of the Zealots,[48] escaped to Egypt after the fall of Jerusalem, and, failing to stir the Jews there into revolt, were rounded up and finally executed, he witnesses to their amazing fortitude in refusing to deny the sole sovereignty of Yahweh:

> For under every form of torture and laceration of body, devised for the sole object of making them acknowledge Caesar as lord (*Kaisara despoten*), not one submitted nor was brought to the verge of utterance; but all kept their resolve, triumphant over constraint, meeting the tortures and the fire with bodies that seemed insensible of pain and souls that well nigh exulted in it. But most of all were the spectators struck by the children of tender age (*hē tōn paidōn hēlikia*), not one of whom could be prevailed upon to call Caesar lord. So far did the strength of courage rise superior to the weakness of their frames.[49]

It would seem that such heroic martyrdom caused even Josephus for a moment to forget that he was writing about his criminal Zealots, and, as a Jew, to commemorate such signal examples of Jewish religious faith.

It is important for our understanding of the historical environment of Jesus to notice that Josephus shows a curious reluctance to use the name 'Zealots' to describe those whom he thus blamed for the ruin of Israel. This name is the Greek equivalent of the Hebrew *Kannā'im*, meaning the 'zealous ones', and it evidently derived from the example of Phinehas, who is praised by Yahweh in *Num*. xxv:6–13 for killing a Jew and a non-Jewish woman, his paramour, 'in that he (Phinehas) was zealous with my zeal'.[50] The epithet had clearly become an honourable one among the Jews, and this fact probably explains Josephus' evident embarrassment about using it. His first use of it is revealing: he refers to 'the madness of the so-called Zealots (*tōn klēthentōn zelōtōn*)'.[51] When next he mentions the name, he comments illuminatingly on it: 'for so they called themselves, as though they were passionately concerned about the good and not excessively zealous (*zēlōsantes*) for the vilest deeds'.[52] The term he usually prefers to designate the Zealots by is *lēstai*, which meant 'brigands'. His preference is significant, for it doubtless was the term used by the Romans for these resistance-fighters who opposed their rule: equivalent designations have been applied by other occupying powers to those patriots who have resorted to armed action to regain their nation's independence.[53] Another epithet, obviously of Roman origin, which he also employs is *Sicarii*. The word derived from the Latin *sicarius*, a 'dagger-man' who murdered his victims with a *sica*.[54] Josephus' use of the word is somewhat ambiguous: in one passage he seems to indicate that the *Sicarii* were a special group of the Zealots, dedicated to the murdering of those Jews whom they deemed to be collaborating with the Romans;[55] but elsewhere he uses it as a general designation for the Zealots.[56]

From the evidence of Josephus, tendentious and distorted as it certainly is, it appears, therefore, that the first administrative act of the Romans on taking over Judaea in AD 6 provoked violent reaction and led to the formation of a resistance party, dedicated to maintain the absolute sovereignty of Yahweh over Israel, thus involving the rejection both of the lordship of Caesar and the payment of tribute to him. The movement, essentially religious in aim and character, took its name from that uncompromising zeal which ever characterised Yahweh, the god of Israel, and which found practical expression in the most devoted of his servants.[57] The profession of Zealotism was dangerous: its founder Judas of Galilee, died for it, and two of his sons were later crucified by the Romans.[58] Indeed crucifixion was a fate that every Zealot had to face.[59]

After the failure of the initial revolt, provoked by the preaching of Judas, the survivors of the movement operated from the deserts, seizing whatever opportunities came to injure the Roman government and its Jewish collaborators, and seeking always to stir the people to revolt. The fact that the Zealots were able to maintain themselves, from the founding of the movement in the year 6 until they led the fatal revolt in 66, must surely indicate that they had the continuous support of the people, generally covert but sometimes open.[60] This popular aspect of Zealotism is important in the context of our study, and there is one fact in connection with it that needs special note. When the Zealots succeeded in seizing Jerusalem in 66, one of their first actions was to burn the public archives, because, as Josephus complains, the destruction of the money-lenders' bonds encouraged the poor to rise against the rich.[61] It would, accordingly, seem that Zealotism, true to the prophetic tradition, had both a social and political aspect, and hence was regarded by the Roman authorities and the Jewish aristocracy as doubly subversive of the established order.

It was, then, among a people who thus reacted to the Roman government of their land, that Jesus was nurtured and lived his life. Of his relations with the Zealots it will suffice now to note that he included one of them among his band of apostles. The significance of this fact, and the problem which it raises, will concern us at length later.[62] For the present we continue with our task of tracing out the course of events in Judaea during the fateful years between AD 6 and 70.

So far as Josephus informs us, from the suppression of the revolt in the year 6 until the appointment of Pontius Pilate in 26, life proceeded peacefully in Judaea.[63] It is possible that the severity of Roman action in putting down the followers of Judas of Galilee had cowed the mass of the Jewish people into submitting to their new masters. However, Josephus' presentation of the pattern of Jewish affairs must be treated always with caution. His intention was apologetical, and, thoughout his narrative, he was concerned to present his fellow-countrymen to the Gentiles as a fundamentally peaceable people who were finally driven into revolt by the evilly-disposed Zealots, and also by the injustices of certain Roman governors. These Romans are, significantly, mostly notorious characters in Roman history, so that the sympathy of his readers would be readily enlisted for the Jews suffering under such men.[64] But there is often reason for wondering whether the apparently uneventful periods were in fact times of peace. For example, during the period AD 6–26, which incidentally covers the major part of Jesus' life, Josephus does mention without explanation, that Quirinius, the legate of Syria, deposed the high priest Joazar, against whom the people had revolted.[65] The action is puzzling, since Joazar should have stood well with the Romans in view of his cooperative action at the time of the census.[66] It is possible that his pro-Roman attitude had so incurred the hatred of the Jews that they had turned against him, and Quirinius decided that he was no longer of any use to Rome. But whatever may have been the reason, some disturbance or unrest did occur. The fact that the legate then appointed his successor, Ananus, must have been a humiliating reminder to the Jews that their high priest, who represented them before Yahweh, was really the agent chosen by their heathen overlord.[67]

Pontius Pilate, who was appointed by the Emperor Tiberius in 26 as praefectus or procurator of Judaea,[68] has acquired undying infamy for the decisive part he played in the crucifixion of Jesus. It will be our task presently to devote our attention at length to studying him, in an endeavour to appraise his position, ability and character relative to his fatal involvement with Jesus.

For the moment we must consider him in the context of Romano-Jewish affairs.

Josephus' account of Pilate's term of office is largely taken up with describing two occasions on which the procurator became embroiled with the Jewish people. The record creates the impression that the Jews, being peaceably disposed, suffered unfairly at the hands of Pilate; but, on analysis, this record is found to contain so many discrepancies that it would seem to be a tendentious presentation of the events it purports to describe. The first of these events seems to have occurred shortly after Pilate took up office.[69] It is necessary to explain, in this connection, that Jerusalem was garrisoned by a Roman cohort, stationed in the Antonia, a large fortress overlooking the Temple. The governor was normally resident at Caesarea, the Roman headquarters about sixty miles distant; he came to Jerusalem at the great festivals, when disturbances were to be anticipated. According to Josephus, it had been the custom of former governors to arrange that troops, on garrison duty at Jerusalem, should either dismantle their standards or leave them behind at Caesarea.[70] This was a concession to Jewish religious scruples; for Roman military standards were adorned with effigies of the emperor or of deities, and so constituted the 'graven images' condemned by the sacred Law.[71] The concession was a considerable one, since their standards were sacred objects to the Roman army, as well as symbols of their honour and pride.[72] It meant that the Roman government had accepted the Jewish evaluation of Jerusalem as a holy city, whose sanctity would be violated by the presence of the symbols of another religion within its walls. That such a concession should have been made suggests that, after the rising of AD 6, the Romans had carefully sought to conciliate Jewish feelings, which in their sight must have seemed unreasonable and even offensive to themselves. Pilate introduced a change. According to Josephus, he ordered troops, going to Jerusalem probably for garrison duty, to take their standards but to enter the city after dark.[73] The suggestion is that Pilate planned to face the Jews with a *fait accompli* when they saw the obnoxious standards displayed from the walls of the Antonia on the next day. The Jews were indeed outraged by the sight; but instead of violently demonstrating there against the sacrilege, Josephus tells how they journeyed in a large and orderly body to Caesarea to petition Pilate. An edifying account follows of Jewish passive resistance to the procurator's threats of death; at last, impressed by their readiness for martyrdom, he ordered the removal of the offending standards from the holy city.[74]

Josephus clearly presents the affair as one of Pilate's making. He introduces his account in the *Jewish Antiquities* with the improbable statement that Pilate 'led his army (*stratian*) from Caesarea and established it for winter-quarters in

Jerusalem, for the purpose of destroying the laws of the Jews'.[75] That Pilate should have taken such a step on his own initiative appears most unlikely. Since his action meant a reversal of former policy, it is more reasonable to assume that he was acting on superior orders. The concession about the standards was a considerable one for the Romans to have made, for it involved submitting to a subject people on an issue that was both insulting to the emperor and dishonourable to the army. It would seem more probable that what was an extraordinary concession, designed to reconcile the Jews to their new status after the initial troubles of AD 6, was regarded by the imperial government as a temporary expedient. The situation having been reviewed on the occasion of Pilate's appointment, instructions were then issued for a discreet withdrawal of the concession. Some indication that Pilate was acting under imperial orders is given by Josephus himself when he mentions that the procurator at first refused the Jews' petition at Caesarea, 'because it would be an insult to Caesar'.[76]

Whatever the true nature of the affair, which Josephus' apologetic obscures, it is evident that during the governorship of Pilate great tension had been caused by Jewish intransigence about the presence of the emperor's image on military standards in Jerusalem. We may note that it is odd that no mention is made of Zealot reaction over such an issue. Instead, we are given an edifying account of the orderly and peaceable petition of the Jews to a procurator allegedly bent on destroying their sacred laws—the contrast was an astute one in terms of Josephus' apologetical purpose, especially if his Gentile readers connected Pilate with Sejanus, the execrated favourite of Tiberius.[77]

The second incident also arose out of Pilate's alleged violation of Jewish religion. Again Josephus' two accounts of it, in the *Jewish War* and the *Jewish Antiquities* respectively, not only present somewhat varying versions but are both generally imprecise and problematic.[78] The cause of the trouble was Pilate's building of an aqueduct to bring water into Jerusalem. The project in itself, would seem a laudable undertaking, attesting Pilate's good government.[79] However, it profoundly upset the Jews. Josephus gives different accounts of their objections. In his earlier work, the *Jewish War*, he states that Pilate defrayed the cost of the construction out of 'the sacred treasury known as *Korbonas*'.[80] No mention of this implied sacrilege is made in the *Jewish Antiquities*, where it is related that the Jews objected, for some unexplained reason, to the operations involved [81]—possibly the cause of offence may have been the fact of Pilate's interference with the affairs of the holy city. Whatever the real point of contention, Jewish reaction was violent, and Pilate was himself personally insulted when he came to Jerusalem.[82] His counter-measures were odd. According to Josephus, he disguised his troops in

Jewish dress, and interspersed them among the mob, with orders to chastise the unruly with cudgels, not swords. The over-zealous execution of their orders by the troops resulted in many deaths; but the revolt (*stasis*) was quelled.[83]

From Josephus' curious accounts of this affair certain facts seem to emerge. It would appear that Pilate in carrying out an engineering project, designed to improve amenities in Jerusalem, incurred fierce Jewish opposition. If he did meet the cost by forcibly taking Temple funds, his offence would have been sacrilegious; but it is to be noted that Josephus does not accuse him of embezzlement for his own use. Whether the Temple money was in fact seized by force, and the sanctity of the Temple violated thereby, Josephus strangely says nothing. Doubtless a complicated administrative dispute lies behind the building of this aqueduct, over which Josephus preferred to pass in silence. Another significant point for future reference is that, whatever the real nature of Pilate's measures for quelling the disturbance, Josephus does record that he ordered his troops not to use their swords. Pilate's action thus shows remarkable restraint: he intended to control the mob, not slaughter it.

This incident, like the former one concerning the standards, reveals the extreme nature of Jewish religious sensibility and how easily it could be inflamed by action that the Romans would have regarded as necessary to firm and efficient government. Again, significantly, Josephus makes no mention of the Zealots, though both occasions would surely have invited their intervention, whether open or clandestine.

These two clashes of Pilate with the Jews over religious issues are the only ones recorded by Josephus.[84] Philo of Alexandria, however, describes another which is curiously similar to that concerning the standards. The account occurs in what purports to be a letter written by the Jewish prince Agrippa to the Emperor Gaius, in an attempt to persuade him from an act of sacrilege against the Temple, of which we must take notice later.[85] Agrippa finds occasion to recall how Pilate, some years earlier, had sought to annoy the Jews and how deeply he had incurred the anger of Tiberius thereby. According to Philo, or Agrippa, whom he claims to be reporting, the procurator had caused some gilded shields, inscribed with a short dedication to Tiberius, to be placed on the palace of Herod, which the Romans used for administrative purposes, in Jerusalem. It is expressly said that the shields bore no image or emblem that might have disturbed Jewish aniconic scruples.[86] However, Pilate's action did upset the Jews and a delegation, led by four Herodian princes, petitioned him to remove the shields, on the ground that they violated their native customs.[87] On Pilate's refusal, the Jewish leaders wrote to Tiberius, who is alleged to have been enraged at Pilate's conduct and ordered him to withdraw the shields from Jerusalem and place them on the temple of Augustus at Caesarea.[88]

This account equals those of Josephus, which we have noticed, in raising hosts of questions owing to imprecision on the many important issues involved; but on two points its testimony has a special interest for us. Since the shields had no images or emblems, their offence must have lain in the inscriptions: probably the dedication contained some reference to the divinity of the emperor.[89] If this were so, the fact might indicate that the teaching of Judas of Galilee was still influential concerning recognition of 'Caesar as lord'. The other point of interest is that, despite all that Philo says about Tiberius' anger, he did not dismiss Pilate, but only ordered him to put the offending shields out of range of Jewish susceptibility.[90]

These are the only three incidents concerning Romano-Jewish relations during the ten years of Pilate's governorship that are recorded by either Josephus or Philo. Philo's account, as we have noted, is only incidental, in that it occurs in a writing concerned with another and later issue. That Josephus, who was professedly writing the history of these times, should record just the two incidents described is curious. He does indeed tell of a clash with the Samaritans, which we must consider in detail when we attempt to assess the character of Pilate;[91] but of the procurator's further involvement with the Jews during his ten years of office nothing more is recorded, with one enigmatic exception. The extant Greek text of Josephus' *Jewish Antiquities* does contain a brief account of Jesus which, if it did indeed come from Josephus, would mean that he recognised Jesus as the Messiah and believed that he had risen from the dead.[92] Since such an acceptance of Jesus is inconsistent with all that is otherwise known of Josephus, the authenticity of the passage has long been doubted by scholars. The problem which it constitutes is a very complicated, as well as a very important one; for our purpose it will best be discussed when we consider what non-Christian evidence exists concerning the historical Jesus.[93] In the present context, however, we may note that it would not have served the apologetic purpose of his work for Josephus to have remained silent about Jesus. Christianity had already come to the attention of the Roman authorities as a revolutionary movement of Jewish origin.[94] On *a priori* grounds, therefore, it is likely that Josephus, in the interest of his apologetical theme, would have shown that the Jewish leaders took prompt action to suppress the movement. What was the original form of Josephus' evaluation of Jesus will be a subject for our later enquiry;[95] but now we must turn, with its problem in mind, to consider certain references and allusions in the Christian Gospels to political unrest and revolt during the procuratorship of Pilate.

It will be best to notice the most obvious evidence first. The Markan Gospel records that an insurrection (*stasis*) had taken place just before or during Jesus' last days in Jerusalem. The Romans had suppressed it, after suffering fatal casualties, and had taken prisoners, among them a leader named Barabbas.[96] Jesus had, moreover, been crucified between two *lēstai*, the term used by Josephus, and probably by the Roman authorities, for the Zealots: it seems likely that these *lēstai* were among the prisoners taken in the recent insurrection, thus indicating Zealot involvement.[97] In the Gospel of Luke (xiii: 1ff.), reference is made to certain Galilaeans, 'whose blood Pilate had mingled with their sacrifices'. The reference is tantalisingly brief, as is also its context, namely, that Jesus had been specially told about the incident.[98] The implication of the reference is that these Galilaeans had been killed by the Romans in the Temple on some cultic occasion. The incident, thus implied, would surely have been most grave in its significance, and calculated also to be in its consequences. We can only wonder why Josephus has recorded nothing of it; for its violation of Jewish religion went far beyond that caused by either the standards or the construction of the aqueduct. And who were these Galilaeans who had been specially selected for slaughter by Pilate in the Temple? If the name denotes inhabitants of Galilee, they would have been subjects of Herod Antipas; but that fact would not explain their slaughter, indeed it would more likely have caused Pilate to have been particularly careful in dealing with them.[99] The name could, however, be a designation for Zealots, being derived from their founder, Judas of Galilee: there is evidence of its use in this connection.[100] If it did thus mean 'Zealots', this reference in the Lukan Gospel would be of the utmost significance. However, although in view of the cryptic nature of the reference the identity of these Galilaeans must remain a mystery, that some such incident had occurred confirms the evidence of Josephus, selective though it be, of the tension and strife that permeated Judaism during the lifetime of Jesus.

Next, we may note, but leave for later investigation, the fact that the Gospels record that one of Jesus' apostles, Simon, was a Zealot,[101] and also that reference is made to the 'violent ones' (*biastai*), who would seize the kingdom of heaven by force.[102] Then, there is evidence of Jewish questioning: 'Is it lawful to pay tribute to Caesar, or not? Should we pay, or should we not?'[103] The very framing of the question implies seditious thinking, and it indicates the influence of Zealot teaching. That the question should be put to one acclaimed to be the Messiah, as the Gospels describe its being put to Jesus, is consistent with current Messianic expectation. With the significance of the Gospel account of Jesus' attitude to the Tribute-issue we shall be subsequently much concerned:[104] it is sufficient now to note that, according to the Gospels, the Roman tribute was an urgent issue among the Jews during the period of Pilate's administration.

Such, then, was the setting of politico-religious tension and unrest, exploding often in armed revolt, for the career of Jesus during the governorship of Pontius Pilate. We see it through the evidence of three different sources, none of which can be regarded as an impeccable witness; but the cumulative testimony is impressive in delineating a situation in Judaea in which few private persons, let alone public figures, could have pursued their way insulated from, or unconcerned by, the emotions and pressures generated by the basic conflict between the idea of Israel as a theocracy and the fact of Israel as the possession of the Emperor of Rome.

On the course of affairs in first-century Judaea, as recorded by Josephus, the trial and execution of Jesus left no perceptible trace. For the Jewish historian there was, soon after the death of Tiberius and the disappearance of Pilate from the Judaean scene, a threat to the sanctity of Jewish religion to record which was calculated to stir the sympathy of his Gentile readers for his unfortunate compatriots. In the year 37 Tiberius was succeeded as emperor by Gaius, or Caligula as he was popularly known.[105] To the Romans, Gaius proved to be one of the worst of their emperors, and the fact that the Jews suffered also from his insane megalomania served well Josephus' apologetical theme. The threat concerned was no less than that of the desecration of the Temple by the installation there of a colossal gilt image of Gaius in the form of Zeus.[106] Whereas the idea of the divinity of the Roman emperor had been fostered by the astute Augustus for political reasons, Gaius took his divinity very seriously.[107] This obsession appears to have been exploited by the Gentile inhabitants of Jamnia, a town in Judaea, to bring the imperial wrath upon their Jewish neighbours. Having contrived to cause the Jews to destroy an altar which they had erected for the cult of the emperor, they succeeded in getting the Jewish action reported to Gaius.[108] The information had the desired effect. To vindicate his divinity and to punish the contumacious Jews, Gaius ordered Petronius, the legate of Syria, to have the image made and put in the Jerusalem Temple.[109]

The Jews were thus faced with the gravest threat to their religion since the Seleucid king Antiochus Epiphanes profaned the Temple in 167 BC by setting up an altar to Zeus—the notorious Abomination of Desolation, foretold by the prophet Daniel.[110] Both Philo and Josephus describe the crisis.[111] Their accounts contain many mutual contradictions and improbable statements; but they agree in attesting the horror and dismay of the Jews, and their resolve to oppose the imperial order. Petronius, who had the unenviable task of carrying out the order, entered Palestine during the winter of AD 39–40 with a powerful force, comprising two legions and a strong body of auxiliary troops. He obviously anticipated fanatical Jewish resistance and played for time, while the Jewish prince Agrippa also sought to turn Gaius from his insane project.[112] Furious at Petronius' procrastination, Gaius finally decided to instal the statue himself; but his assassination in AD 40 saved both Jews and Romans from a fatal encounter.[113]

Although Josephus endeavours to represent the Jews as determined on passive resistance only, he lets slip the fact that Petronius expected war, which is also confirmed by the Roman historian Tacitus.[114] The nature of the threat, and its sudden removal by the murder of the heathen potentate who had thus threatened the majesty of Yahweh, must have created a profound impression on the Jews. The project of Gaius had made an awful reality what their subservience to Rome could entail, as Judas of Galilee had warned. What Gaius had been prevented from doing, another emperor might attempt. But, with this realisation of what Roman lordship could mean, there was the elation of deliverance through the foreign tyrant's death. The deliverance was naturally attributed to Yahweh, and it served to endorse the promise of Judas of Galilee that courageous faith would earn divine assistance.[115]

This portentous episode presents us, in our concern to evaluate the evidence of Christian writings relating to Judaea at this time, with a problem of puzzling import. The Acts of the Apostles is professedly an account of the fortunes of the infant Christian Church in Judaea during the period in which Gaius' attempt to place his image in the Temple convulsed the life of the Jewish people. In its narrative the Jerusalem Christians are depicted as assiduous in their worship in the Temple, which they revered as the house of God, and as including in their community many priests, who served in the Temple, as well as Pharisees who would have been devoted to its service.[116] Yet the narrative of Acts contains not the slightest hint that the sanctity of the Temple had been so signally imperilled by the megalomania of Gaius. The fact, moreover, that reference is made by Acts to other contemporary political events, none of which had anything like the significance of this threat to the Temple,[117] consequently causes suspicion about its silence concerning the attempt of Gaius and the effect of it on the Christians living in Jerusalem and worshipping in the Temple.

It is impossible to believe that the Jerusalem Christians could have continued living in the holy city, and worshipping in its Temple, wholly unconcerned at the impious act that threatened both the shrine and those worshipped in it. Such indifference is truly incredible, and we can only conclude that the apologetical purpose which runs throughout the Acts, namely, of showing that opposition to Christianity came from the Jews and not from Roman officials, also operated here.[118] It would not have served the cause of Christianity, as the author of Acts saw it, to record that the original Jewish Christians had reacted strongly to the Roman threat to desecrate the Temple —moreover, when he wrote, that Temple had already been destroyed by the Romans, and he had, in an earlier writing interpreted its destruction as divine punishment on the nation that had rejected Christ.[119]

But is there no positive clue in any of the Christian documents to the reaction of the Jerusalem Christians when the Roman menace overhung the Temple? The very need to ask this question is significant. For it reveals a further aspect of that problem which besets our enquiry, namely, that those Christian writings which purport to describe the beginnings of Christianity show a strange unconcern for, or elusiveness about, certain seemingly unavoidable involvements of the Jewish Christians with contemporary Jewish affairs. This problem is one of which we shall become increasingly aware, as we approach nearer to our use of these documents as evidence of the trial and execution of Jesus. However, it is possible that some reflection of the attitude of the Jerusalem Christians to the attempt of Gaius is to be discerned, in a different context, in the Gospel of Mark.

The thirteenth chapter of the Markan Gospel contains a long discourse by Jesus to his disciples when seated on the Mount of Olives, over against the Temple. The author of the Gospel has skilfully set the scene by describing how one of the disciples, emerging from the Temple with Jesus, had drawn his attention to the magnificence of this great shrine.[120] Jesus, in reply, prophesied its destruction: 'Seest thou these great buildings? there shall not be left one stone upon another, that shall not be thrown down.'[121] A little later, seated on that marvellous vantage point overlooking the Kedron Valley, with all Jerusalem and its Temple stretched out in its Herodian splendour before them, his disciples had asked Jesus: 'Tell us, when shall these things be? and what shall be the sign when all these things shall be fulfilled?'[122] Jesus then proceeds to foretell both the desecration of the Temple by the mysterious 'Abomination of Desolation' and the end of the world, with a wealth of apocalyptic imagery.[123]

We have already seen something of the problem which this ascription of a prophecy of the destruction of the Temple to Jesus raises, in view of the assertion, made in Mark's account of the Sanhedrin trial, that Jesus had been falsely accused of threatening the Temple in some such manner.[124] We noted that the rejection of such a charge as 'false witness' doubtless came from the original Jewish Christian account of the trial, on which Mark drew for his version. The explanation of Mark's contradictory statements about the matter is to be found in the situation which led him to write his Gospel. The identification of this situation is a basic problem for our understanding of the Markan account of the trial of Jesus, and its discussion will occupy us at length later. However, we can reasonably anticipate one conclusion that will emerge from that discussion, namely, that, in the apocalyptic discourse in chapter thirteen, Mark was concerned with the eschatological excitement caused among his fellow-Christians by the events of AD 70.[125] He identified, as we shall see, certain cultic acts performed by the Roman troops in the Temple, after its capture, with the mysterious Abomination of Desolation; then he turned to deal with the urgent question of when Christ would return to bring the existing world-order to its catastrophic end.[126] Now, in composing this apocalyptic discourse, which he attributes to Jesus when seated on the Mount of Olives, Mark evidently drew upon certain traditional apocalyptic material. Many scholars have recognised a distinctive unit of such material in the following passage:

> But when ye see the abomination of desolation standing where he ought not (let him that readeth understand), then let them that are in Judaea flee unto the mountains: and let him that is on the housetop not go down, nor enter in, to take anything out of his house: and let him that is in the field not return back to take his cloak. But woe unto them that are with child and to them that give suck in those days! And pray ye that it be not in winter. For those days shall be tribulation, such as there hath not been the like from the beginning of the creation which God created until now, and never shall be. And except the Lord had shortened the days, no flesh would have been saved: but for the elects' sake, whom he chose, he shortened the days.[127]

Behind the strange apocalyptic diction of this passage, a specific situation of great crisis, which had been suddenly terminated by an act of divine intervention, is clearly envisaged. The location is Judaea, and an impending act of sacrilege is equated with the notorious desecration of the Temple by the altar to Zeus which Antiochus Epiphanes set up therein in 167 BC.[128] As soon as the new Abomination of Desolation stands in the Temple ('where he ought not'),[129] those to whom the warning is addressed are admonished to flee at once into the mountains—doubtless the desolate hilly wilderness of Judaea. A time of great tribulation, which might occur in the winter, is foreseen. However, in some mysterious way God had suddenly ended the crisis, and he had done so for 'the elects' sake'—the identity of whom would have been obvious to those concerned.

Now, only twice, after Antiochus' original act of desecration, was the Temple menaced by an Abomination of Desolation: in AD 39–40 and in AD 70. The earlier occasion was when Gaius planned to erect his image there; but this threat proved abortive, as we have seen, owing to the assassination of Gaius, which was seen by the Jews as divine judgment on the impious tyrant. In AD 70 there was no divine intervention: the 'abomination of desolation' did stand 'where he ought not', as we shall duly see.[130] The passage must accordingly, in its original form, relate to the crisis caused by Gaius in AD 39–40: this identification is further supported by the reference to winter, for Josephus records that Petronius, the Roman commander, concentrated his forces at Ptolemaus in the winter of 39.[131]

It will be our task later to see how Mark adapted this apocalyptic passage, by certain significant touches, to the Roman profanation of the Temple in 70.[132] To have done this, of course, implies that Mark must have found the passage among the sources from which he compiled his Gospel. Such a conclusion is naturally of the greatest interest for our subject; for it indicates that an apocalyptic tradition associated with the attempt of Gaius was current in Christian circles in Judaea, and so may provide the evidence lacking elsewhere of the reaction of the Jerusalem Christians to the crisis of AD 39–40.[133]

If this inference be soundly based, valuable light is thrown on the attitude of the original Christian community at Jerusalem; it is, moreover, consistent with what we otherwise know of the attachment of the first Christians to the Temple. It means that, faced with the dreadful menace of the profanation of Israel's holy shrine by the image of the Roman emperor, they were ready to flee into the hills. And for what purpose? Obviously to get away from the Roman horror: although the setting up of the Abomination did not necessarily imply danger to the inhabitants of Jerusalem, if they had quietly accepted the situation. The area to which the Jerusalem Christians were exhorted to flee is, however, especially significant; for it was in the hilly wilderness of Judaea that the Zealots maintained their resistance, and the Qumrân sectaries prepared for the coming eschatological war of the Sons of Light against the Sons of Darkness.[134]

The passage also yields another valuable indication of the outlook of the Jerusalem Christians, if we are right in assigning it to them. For the concluding statement, that God had intervened 'for the elects' sake', discloses that the Christian community at Jerusalem regarded themselves as a distinctive group whom God so favoured that he had saved the Temple, presumably for their sakes, from Roman desecration.[135]

This interpretation is, admittedly, based on a very involved argument. But so is all interpretation of the New Testament documents; yet the task of interpreting them has to be undertaken, for we have no other evidence of the origins of Christianity. As we have previously seen, the complete silence of the Acts of the Apostles about the attempted desecration of the Temple by Gaius necessarily excites suspicion as to whether the Jerusalem Christians, who 'day by day, attended the Temple together',[136] could really have been thus so wholly unaffected by such a threat. If the Abomination of Desolation passage in the Markan Gospel, which has been called the 'Little Apocalypse' because of its evident unity and internal cohesion, does reflect the agitation of the Jerusalem Christians at this time, it provides an invaluable corrective to the silence of the Acts. It attests a reaction which on other grounds we might reasonably have expected: the Jerusalem Christians were on the point of fleeing from the Roman threat and joining their compatriots in the Judaean hills, where the Zealots had their hide-outs; the sudden death of Gaius they saw as a special act of divine intervention on their own behalf.

If this interpretation be sound, it affords not only a precious piece of information about the Christians of Jerusalem, but it also reveals an important fact about the author of Acts. For the complete silence of Acts about the episode can only mean that its author deemed it inappropriate to his purpose to mention that such had been the reaction of the Jerusalem Christians to the Roman threat against the Temple. In other words, in writing about the beginnings of the faith for Gentile Christians towards the end of the first century, the author of Acts suppressed information about the political attitude of those who formed the Mother Church of Jerusalem.

Turning back again to the course of Jewish affairs, we find that the accession of the Emperor Claudius, after the death of Gaius, ushered in a brief spell of Jewish independence from direct Roman rule. Out of appreciation for the part that the Jewish prince Agrippa had played in securing his accession, Claudius added Judaea to his other domains, so that he now ruled as king over the former kingdom of Herod the Great, his grandfather.[137] Agrippa, despite his Herodian descent and Roman contacts, won the approval of his Jewish subjects for his piety and zeal for Judaism.[138] However, in the Acts of the Apostles he appears as the persecutor of two leading members of the Christian community. The narrative of Acts is tantalisingly brief and uninformative about the motive behind Agrippa's attack. It merely states: 'About that time Herod [Agrippa] the king laid violent hands upon some who belonged to the church. He killed James, the brother of John, with the sword; and when he saw that it pleased the Jews, he proceeded to arrest Peter also.'[139] Then follows a long circumstantial account of the miraculous deliverance of Peter from prison by an angel, and his escape to 'another place'.[140] To this account is added a strange tale of how 'an angel of the Lord' suddenly struck Agrippa dead, after his subjects, impressed by his appearance and eloquence, had exclaimed: 'The voice of a god, and not of man!' The reason given for this deadly intervention is that Agrippa 'did not give God the glory'; consequently, 'he was eaten by worms and died'.[141]

The account, which is not only replete with miraculous incident and creates a serious problem about the status of Peter in the Jerusalem Church, is also clearly anti-Jewish in tone.[142] This revered Jewish king is represented as a capricious persecutor of Christians, whose cruelty pleases the Jews. The Jews are also depicted (an incredible touch this) as virtually according divine honours to Agrippa, who merits God's vengeance by accepting them.[143] Since the account is one of the few in Acts in which the life of the Jerusalem Church is linked with contemporary Jewish politics, it is important that we examine it more closely.

If we accept as authentic the bare fact that Agrippa executed James and would doubtless have executed Peter also, we have to seek for the reason, since the Acts does not give one. Such decisive action against two leaders of the Christian community marked a departure from the earlier policy of the Sanhedrin, as recorded by Acts. The action then taken against Peter and John was confined to beating and admonition not to preach Jesus as the Messiah.[144] The problematic execution of Stephen appears to have involved a different issue, and it is significant that Acts records that the apostles were excepted from the persecution that followed Stephen's attack on the Temple cultus and the people of Israel.[145] Why, then, did Agrippa change to a policy of exterminating these apostles?

There is evidence that this Jewish king, whatever his Herodian ancestry may have signified, was genuinely concerned for the future well-being of his people. His deep insight into the Jewish character, together with his intimate knowledge of Roman power which his long sojourn at Rome had given him, warned him of the fatal conflict that lay ahead and prompted him to do what he could to prevent or alleviate it. He doubtless hoped that his son would succeed him as king, and he sought to strengthen the kingdom by alliances with neighbouring states and by improving the defences of Jerusalem.[146] To further these ends, it seems likely that he also endeavoured to root out those elements in Judaea which he considered dangerous to the peace and well-being of the state. That Josephus does not record any action of Agrippa against the Zealots is doubtless due to the very fact that, under his rule, their chief grievances were removed: tribute was no longer being paid to Caesar, and the Jewish people were no longer obliged thereby to 'call Caesar lord'. But the quietening of the Zealots did not abate the Messianic aspirations of the

Christians. Messianic agitation, centred on Christ, caused Claudius to expel the Jews from Rome, and there is some indication of similar trouble in Alexandria.[147] It would seem probable, therefore, that Agrippa was also concerned about the seditious aspect of Christianity and decided to strike at the leaders of the movement in Jerusalem. That this was the motive of his attack is supported by the fact that Agrippa is reported to have executed James 'by the sword', which was the penalty for political offences as opposed to the religious sentence of stoning.[148]

In the light of these considerations, the account of the persecution in Acts is as significant for its reticence as it is for its anti-Jewish tone. It doubtless served the apologetic purpose of its author to present this Jewish king as a persecutor of the Jerusalem Christians; but it would not have helped that purpose to explain that the king regarded them, or their leaders, as politically dangerous. Thus, again, we see that the Acts of the Apostles, which purports to be a narrative record of the beginnings of Christianity in Judaea, and on which the traditional view of the movement has been built, is in fact a tendentious account, designed to present an idealistic picture of the infant faith, triumphing over Jewish opposition and pursuing its way in serene unconcern for the realities of contemporary Jewish politics. When we can, occasionally, penetrate behind this façade and catch a glimpse of the true situation, we find the Jerusalem Christians, as loyal and zealous Jews, deeply concerned for Israel's redemption from the yoke of heathen Rome and looking to their Master's imminent return to achieve it.

The relief that Agrippa's reign brought to the Jews was but brief. His death in 44 ended the four-years' reign of the last Jewish king; for Claudius, passing over his son, Agrippa II, probably on account of his youth, placed the whole realm under direct Roman rule.[149] This decision meant that not only was Judaea once again under the hated heathen government, but Galilee also now felt for the first time the reality of subjection to Rome. It is likely that the brief interlude of Agrippa's reign served rather to aggravate Jewish resentment at the re-imposition of the Roman yoke.

From this point onwards the histories of Josephus become largely catalogues of increasing clashes between the Roman authorities and Jewish resistance groups, who are invariably designated 'brigands' (*lēstai*). Sometimes these disturbances are caused by persons whom Josephus calls 'magicians' or 'wonder-workers' (*goētēs*), who promised their followers some final miracle of salvation: such was Theudas, who claimed to lead a new Exodus across the divided waters of the Jordan, or an Egyptian Jew, who, like a new Joshua, was to command the walls of Jerusalem to fall down so that his followers could slaughter the Roman garrison.[150] These more spectacular movements were quickly crushed by the Romans, but they were symptomatic of increasing popular fanaticism, which was continuously stimulated by Roman ruthlessness and inflamed by Zealot propaganda and action. Two incidents may be mentioned to illustrate the many others, perhaps not always so notable, that must have shocked and incensed all pious and patriotic Jews. Both incidents occurred during the procuratorship of Cumanus (48–52). One was caused by the obscene gesture of a Roman soldier, when on duty overlooking the Temple courts where Jews were engaged in worship. To quell the Jewish fury that ensued, Cumanus had to send troop reinforcements, and large Jewish casualties resulted—between twenty and thirty thousand were killed, according to Josephus' improbable figures.[151] On the other occasion, during reprisal action against villages suspected of supporting Zealots (*lēstai*), a Roman soldier desecrated and burnt a sacred Torah scroll. The outburst of Jewish fury was such that Cumanus deemed it expedient to sacrifice the offender.[152]

But how did the Jewish Christians react to such insults to their native faith, symptomatic as they were of the deepening tension between rulers and ruled? The record of the Acts again tells us nothing. This, in part, is due to the fact that from chapter thirteen to the end the narrative is concerned with the career of St Paul, although some reference is made to Judaean affairs about the years 60–62.[153] But there is an even stranger silence in Acts about James, 'the Lord's brother', who became the leader of the Jerusalem Church and was executed in the year 62, by the decree of the Sanhedrin at the instigation of the high priest Ananus. In later Christian tradition, James was regarded as a martyr for his faith, and held in high honour. The silence of Acts about his martyrdom is, accordingly, very strange; but it is part of a mystery that invests the whole manner in which James is treated in Acts. Unfortunately this mystery is paralleled by another that surrounds Josephus' account of the death of James in his *Jewish Antiquities*.

These mysteries now demand our careful investigation, for they hold an important clue to our understanding of one of the chief factors in the formation of the Gospel presentation of Jesus, and, consequently, of his trial. The task of unravelling each of these mysteries is exceedingly intricate. The nature of the issue involved will be best seen by starting with the mystery that surrounds James in the Acts. Our earliest evidence about James is provided by Paul in his Epistle to the Galatians, with which we have already been much concerned. In his references to him there, Paul distinguishes him as 'James, the Lord's brother'; he calls him an apostle, and he ranks him first in a triumvirate of 'pillars' (*stuloi*) of the Church, of which the other two members were Cephas (i.e. Peter), and John.[154] Of James' dominance, Paul provides significant evidence a little later in his Epistle. At Antioch, Peter had eaten together with Gentile converts, as Paul had also done. But, when 'certain men came from James', Peter, apparently admonished by them about his conduct in this matter, withdrew from table-fellowship and thereby incurred the vehement rebuke of Paul.[155] This evidence of James' primacy in the Jerusalem Church must be accepted as authentic, since Paul gives it incidentally in a letter written about the year 50, but referring back first to the situation at Jerusalem three years after his conversion: i.e. about the year 34.

The witness of Acts to this preeminence of James is most odd. In the earlier chapters, Peter appears as the Christian leader at Jerusalem.[156] There is no mention of the existence of another leader called James until the account of Peter's escape from the prison, after his arrest by (Herod) Agrippa, which we have already discussed. That account ends with the cryptic statement that Peter, having informed the brethren gathered in the house of Mary, the mother of John, and Mark of his miraculous escape, said: '"Tell this to James and to the brethren." Then he departed and went to another place.'[157] Peter's request clearly implies that in the Church at Jerusalem there was already a person of consequence named James, who had to be specially informed of the momentous news. But who was this James? The fact that the episode begins with the statement that Agrippa 'killed James, the brother of John with the sword' makes it clear that it was not the Apostle James, the son of Zebedee and brother of John, who, according to the Gospels, formed one of the inner band of Jesus' twelve disciples.[158] From later references in the Acts, it is evident that the James, to whom Peter refers, is the brother of Jesus, or, as Paul calls him, 'the Lord's brother'. But the author of the Acts never identifies him. He is suddenly introduced into Peter's farewell request as a very important person in the Christian community, yet without a word of explanation as to his antecedents. The two other subsequent mentions of James in Acts attest his supremacy in the Jerusalem Church, so corroborating Paul's testimony. Thus, in the so-called 'Council of Jerusalem', it is James who defines the decision, to which all the other members agree.[159] Then, in the account of Paul's last visit to Jerusalem, James is clearly presented as the head of the Mother Church, to whom Paul has to report: 'Paul went in with us to James; and all the elders were present.'[160] And it is obviously James who then required Paul to give the proof of his Jewish orthodoxy which cost him his liberty.[161]

But why this strange reticence to identify one who was head of the Church of Jerusalem? It is impossible to believe that it was due to some oversight on the part of the author of Acts, who specially prided himself on writing 'an orderly account'.[162] But, however that may be, why did he not call James 'the Lord's brother', as Paul does? The framing of this question inevitably raises another, essentially related to it. In the Gospels no mention is made of James having been a disciple of his brother Jesus. Indeed, the Gospel evidence indicates a completely different relationship. Jesus is represented as having been rejected by his family and relations, and as testifying to this rejection by saying that a prophet is not honoured 'among his own people and in his own house'.[163] The Gospel of Mark goes even further than stating this general attitude of rejection; it describes an occasion when members of Jesus' family actually tried to restrain him on the ground that he was insane.[164] Mark also records Jesus as replying, when informed that his mother and his brothers are seeking him: 'Who are my mother and my brothers?' And, looking around on his followers, he added: 'Here are my mother and my brothers! Whosoever does the will of God is my brother, and sister, and mother.'[165]

This amazing denigration of the family of Jesus in the Markan Gospel will require our special attention presently.[166] With regard to its witness to James, although he is not specifically mentioned, he is also not specifically excepted, so that it is reasonable to assume that he is included in the implied strictures on Jesus' family in the recording of these incidents. There is also another aspect of this Gospel evidence which is puzzling in this connection. Jesus is depicted as having an inner circle of three apostles, within the company of the Twelve, who alone witness certain episodes of his ministry. This triumvirate comprises Peter, and James and John, the sons of Zebedee.[167] Now, it is certainly curious that, according to Paul, there was also a triumvirate of leaders of the Jerusalem community with the same names; but the James was the 'Lord's brother', and not the son of Zebedee and brother of John.[168]

We find, then, a very strange, and surely a suspicious, situation in these Christian documents concerning the leadership of the Jerusalem Church. We have the early witness of Paul to the fact that James, the brother of Jesus, held a position of primacy among the apostles and that even Peter submitted to his authority in the incident at Antioch. The Acts of the Apostles tacitly agrees with this situation by telling of a James who presides over the 'Council of Jerusalem', to whom Paul has to report and take orders and whom Peter singles out as having to be specially informed of his escape and departure to 'another place'. There can be no doubt, therefore, that James, the brother of Jesus, was the recognised leader of the Church during this early and critical period. How he attained this position is unrecorded. It would seem that he must have displaced Peter, who, according to the Gospels and the first chapters of Acts, was the leading apostle of Jesus. Since there is no indication of a struggle for leadership, it appears reasonable to assume that blood-relationship to Jesus automatically gave James precedence. The recognition of such a factor would have been in accord with Jewish ideas, since Jesus had no son and James was his eldest male relative.[169] A significant parallel is provided by the Zealot movement, in which leadership was dynastic, with the sons of Judas of Galilee succeeding their father, its founder.[170] That the dynastic principle became established in primitive Jewish Christianity is further confirmed by the fact that Symeon, a cousin of Jesus, was elected to lead the movement on the death of James.[171] How James came originally to join the Church, seeing that tradition agrees that he was not an apostle of Jesus during his lifetime, is unknown, because it is unrecorded. But we may note the significant fact that Paul, not the Gospels, includes James as a special recipient of a vision of the Risen Jesus, in the list which he gives of Resurrection-witnesses.[172]

Having thus seen the strength of the evidence attesting to the leadership of James, we are brought back to consider the strange reticence which the author of the Acts shows both about James' blood-relationship to Jesus and his martyrdom. This problem is also closely connected with that of the shocking denigration of the family of Jesus in the Markan Gospel. One important fact in this connection, which we should now notice in passing and to which we shall later return, is that both the Acts of the Apostles and the Gospel of Mark were written after the destruction of Jerusalem in AD 70, when the original Christian Church there, over which James had presided, had also ceased to exist.

Our unavoidably complicated enquiry now leads us on to consider what evidence there is about the death of James, the brother of Jesus. As we have already noted, the event is recorded by Josephus. According to his account, during the interregnum of procuratorial government in 62 between the death of Festus and the arrival of his successor, Albinus, the high priest Ananus seized the opportunity to remove certain persons obnoxious to him. Josephus' description of his action, as it has come down to us, is very enigmatical:

> And so he (Ananus) convened the judges of the Sanhedrin and brought before them a man named James, the brother of Jesus who was called the Christ (*tou adelphou Iēsou tou legomenou Christou*), and certain others. He accused them of having transgressed the law and delivered them up to be stoned. Those of the inhabitants of the city who were considered the most fair-minded and who were strict in observance of the law (*tous nomous*) were offended at this.[173]

The account then continues to tell how some of those offended by Ananus' action complained to King Agrippa II, who had appointed him to the high-priesthood, while others went to meet the incoming procurator at Alexandria to inform him that Ananus had no authority to convene the Sanhedrin without his consent. The upshot of the matter was that Agrippa deposed Ananus and appointed another high priest.[174]

As with the other passages from Josephus' writings with which we have been concerned, this one both informs and baffles. It evidently records an event of some importance in Jewish affairs at this time, but one of basic significance for the study of Christian Origins. However, its brevity, and its vague allusions to the issues and persons involved, raise many and difficult problems for the historian seeking to understand its significance both in the context of Jewish and Christian history. But that is not the whole of the trouble which we encounter here; for there is reason to suspect that the passage in the extant Greek text, represents a 'revised' version of the original text which offended later Christian scribes.

To elucidate the very complex problem involved here, it will perhaps be best to start with the question of the possibility that the extant text represents a Christian censored version of what Josephus originally wrote. The fact that the passage makes reference to Jesus has caused it to be known as one of the two *Testimonia Flaviana*, or testimonies of (Flavius) Josephus to Jesus; it has naturally attracted much attention from scholars, who have generally been less critical of it than of the passage concerning Jesus himself, which we have already briefly noticed.[175] As the passage now stands, its description of James as 'the brother of Jesus who was called the Christ' would seem to imply that Jesus had already been mentioned earlier in the *Jewish Antiquities*, so that it strengthens the probability that Josephus did write something about Jesus, even if the present text concerning him does not preserve the original form of what he wrote.[176]

The chief reason for doubting whether the passage about James remains exactly as Josephus wrote it derives from the fact that Origen, a third-century Christian scholar of great ability, states, with reference to this passage, that Josephus interpreted the cause of the fall of Jerusalem and the destruction of the Temple as God's punishment of the Jews for killing the righteous James.[177] The extant version, of course, gives no indication of such an interpretation. Origen also complains that Josephus, while recognising the righteousness of James, did not accept Jesus as the Messiah.[178] In view of the care shown by Origen in referring to the exact book of the *Jewish Antiquities*, in which this passage occurs, we must, accordingly, conclude that the Alexandrian scholar read a version of the passage which connected the death of James in some way with the destruction of Jerusalem in 70. But, if such a connection was originally described by Josephus, why should a Christian censor have later removed it from the text? Such an interpretation by Josephus of the destruction of Jerusalem would surely have been very congenial to Christians, and useful for their apologetic. Faced with this enigma, we can only turn to interrogate the extant text for some clue of its original form and the reason for its subsequent alteration.

In recording the event, Josephus was obviously concerned primarily with Ananus, the high priest, and not with James. The Jewish historian had a high opinion of Ananus, a strong and dynamic character who endeavoured to put down the Zealots; he called him the 'leader of their (the Jews') salvation', and he dated the downfall of the Jewish state from the day on which Ananus was killed by the Zealots.[179] It is possible that Josephus' evaluation of Ananus in this connection explains his curiously ambiguous account of the affair which led to the deposition of Ananus from the high-priesthood. For, although he describes those who protested against the action of Ananus as men 'who were considered the most fair-minded and who were strict in the observance of the law', Josephus gives no hint that Ananus acted unjustly in trying James and his companions for transgressing the law and executing them.[180] And the only complaint specified against Ananus is that he had exceeded his authority in convoking the Sanhedrin. In what way James and the others were deemed to have transgressed the law is not stated; but their death by stoning suggests that they were condemned for some religious offence.

But why should Ananus have seized the opportunity of a procuratorial interregnum to accomplish the death of James, the leader of the Christian community? Since James had for many years led the movement in Jerusalem without molestation, it would seem that some new issue must have emerged to make him the object of this sudden attack by the high priest.

Certain evidence that Josephus gives in another connection suggests a likely cause. He records that about this time the sacerdotal aristocracy, which monopolised the chief ecclesiastical and civil offices in the state, and of which Ananus was a leading member, had become involved in a bitter struggle with the lower orders of the priesthood and other dissident factions in the city.[181] Josephus is vague in his references to these supporters of the lower clergy. However, the fact that a few years later the lower clergy were closely associated with the Zealots, as we shall see, may be significant. Although the strife was serious, according to Josephus, the Romans apparently did not interfere, which suggests that they regarded it as a purely domestic affair. The sacerdotal aristocracy was able to punish the lower priests severely by cutting off their income which came from tithes.[182] Now, we also know that many of these priests had joined the Christian community in Jerusalem, and there is even a later tradition that James himself had some priestly status in the Temple.[183] The inclusion of so many of the lower clergy among them would naturally have enlisted the sympathy of the Jerusalem Christians for their cause, and their hostility towards the priestly aristocrats would doubtless have been reinforced by their well-known animus against the rich and socially superior.[184] In the light of these considerations, and in view of James' obvious qualities of leadership and his zeal for the ritual law, it is likely that Ananus regarded James as the most dangerous champion of the cause of the lower clergy. Seeing in the procuratorial interregnum a unique opportunity of removing the leading opponent of his class, Ananus took it and accomplished James' death and probably that of others who had espoused the cause of the lower clergy. But he had not reckoned on the support that James had from the Pharisees, and possibly other patriotic groups, who hated the Sadducean aristocrats for their monopoly of ecclesiastical office and their pro-Roman policy.[185] Since Ananus had acted *ultra vires*, they in turn seized their opportunity of securing his deposition from the high-priesthood.

This interpretation of an essentially enigmatic situation helps in turn to explain why the original account of Josephus was altered by Christian censorship sometime after Origen had made his comments about it. If Josephus had recorded James' involvement with the cause of the lower clergy, who had revolutionary tendencies, he would probably also have noted that, by executing James and thus losing the high-priesthood, Ananus, the 'leader of Israel's salvation', unwittingly caused the catastrophe of AD 70 through losing control of the nation at the most critical juncture in its history.[186] Such a presentation of the affair would, moreover, explain Origen's statement that Josephus saw the destruction of Jerusalem as divine punishment for the execution of James. It would also be intelligible that James' involvement with the lower priests, together with Origen's comments, prompted Christian censors to emend the passage by excising what was deemed obnoxious; but that, in making the necessary alterations, they removed Josephus' words connecting the event with Israel's downfall in AD 70.

This long and intricate exegesis has been made necessary by the mystery that surrounds James, the brother of Jesus and leader of the Jerusalem Church. It is a mystery for which the strange depiction of James in the Christian sources, and the apparent tampering with Josephus' account of his execution, are responsible. At the expense of seeming to complicate the issue still further, attention must, however, also be drawn to another account of the death of James dating from the second century and apparently quite independent of that by Josephus.

This account was written by Hegesippus, a Palestinian Christian who was probably a member of the Church of Aelia Capitolina, the Roman city built upon the site of the ruined Jerusalem.[187] Hegesippus presents James as distinguished by his extraordinary zeal for the ritual practice of Judaism. According to him, James had taken the Rechabite and Nazarite vows, was constantly in the Temple, and had the unique privilege of entering the sanctuary itself.[188] The last statement, if true, would mean that James must have held some priestly office. Hegesippus goes on to tell that, so great was James' reputation for zealous attachment to the Torah, that among his compatriots he was known as the 'Just' and 'Oblias', a title supposed to mean 'Rampart of the people and righteousness'.[189] Because of his great influence over the people, the Jewish authorities when faced with an apparent increase of popular belief that the return of Jesus as the Messiah was imminent, strangely enlisted the help of James to damp down the excitement. Instead, James inflamed the political hopes of the people by publicly declaring his faith that the return of Jesus would indeed shortly occur. In their chagrin and wrath at James' action, the Jewish leaders hurled him from the battlement of the Temple and caused him to be beaten to death where he lay below.[190]

It is an extraordinary tale: not only does it completely diverge from the account of Josephus, it also contains many obvious improbabilities and internal inconsistencies.[191] It can be evaluated only as evidence of popular belief about James in Christian circles in Palestine about a century after his death, and also after the Mother Church had disappeared in the catastrophe of AD 70. Nevertheless, it has significance for our subject. It attests that a tradition still survived in Palestine of James' exceeding zeal for Judaism, and of the high reputation which he enjoyed among the Jews for it. The fact is remarkable in view of the antisemitism provoked by the Jewish revolts of AD 66–70 and 132–5, and it would seemingly attest its authenticity and strength.[192] Further, it is interesting that, in this account by Hegesippus of the death of James, the occasion is represented as one of intense Messianic excitement, which James accentuated by his witness and which the Jewish leaders were endeavouring to abate. Although the account appears to differ so completely from Josephus' version, it is not basically incompatible with it; for, from what Josephus tells us of him, Ananus would have sought to damp down Messianic excitement, and he may even have called upon James publicly to repudiate the Messiahship of Jesus, as Hegesippus seems to suggest.[193]

Out of this long and tedious discussion of such enigmatic evidence there does emerge, however, a picture of the Jerusalem Christians, in the context of

11 The Roman triumph over rebel Judaea

This sculptured panel on the Arch of Titus, Rome, shows victorious legionaries carrying the spoils of the Temple, including the Menorah, in the triumphal procession of AD 71 (*see p. 69*)

12 Jerusalem from the air

The Temple area is clearly visible, with the deep valley of the Kidron to the right. Gethsemane lies in the first grove of trees on the other side of Kidron. The dome of the Church of the Holy Sepulchre is seen among buildings to left of scene

13 The 'Lithostrotos' or 'Pavement' (John xix: 13) of the Antonia fortress overlooking the Temple. This is the possible site of the judgment by Pilate and the flagellation of Jesus (*see p. 191, n. 124*)

contemporary Jewish affairs, which is of the greatest importance for our subject. The importance is, in effect, a twofold one; we see both that the Jerusalem Christians were essentially integrated by race and faith with their nation's cause against Roman domination, and that the Christian writers, concerned with these times, were either silent or extremely elusive about this aspect of primitive Jewish Christianity. Thus the Acts of the Apostles, although it incidentally depicts the Jerusalem Christians as continuing the practice of Judaism, presents them as curiously insulated from the stirring events which were then happening in Judaea and which profoundly affected the life of its people, the most notable being the threat of the Emperor Gaius to desecrate the Temple. The fact that James, the brother of Jesus, emerged to lead the Church of Jerusalem, is also incidentally acknowledged in the Acts; but a strange reticence is shown about his antecedents, and no mention whatsoever is made of his blood-relationship to Jesus or of his martyrdom. Further, the Markan Gospel denigrates the family of Jesus in a most amazing way, considering the preeminence of James in the Jerusalem Church and the fact that the dynastic principle of leadership was preserved by electing a nephew of Jesus to succeed his brother James, when he had died as a martyr for the faith.

What was the cause for this evident embarrassment about such aspects of the original Jewish Christianity is, without doubt, to be found in the Jewish revolt against Rome, which started in 66 and ended with the destruction of Jerusalem in 70. Into the details of that fierce and fateful struggle we have no need to enter.[194] It will suffice for our purpose to notice certain facts which indicate the involvement of the Jerusalem Christians.

The revolt actually started in 66, when the lower priests refused any longer to offer the daily sacrifices in the Temple for the well-being of the Emperor and the Roman people.[195] These sacrifices had been a token of Israel's submission and loyalty to Rome, and the sacerdotal aristocracy were very concerned about their regular maintenance, for it assured their Roman masters of their loyal and efficient control of native affairs.[196] In view of the close association between the lower clergy and the Jerusalem Christians, it is difficult not to believe that the latter would have sympathised with this repudiation of what was tantamount to a prostitution of Israel's holy cultus for political ends. This gesture of the lower priests was effectively supported by the Zealots, who helped them to hold the Temple against the Sadducean aristocracy and the troops of Agrippa II.[197] As we have already noted, one of the first acts of the Zealots on gaining control in Jerusalem was to destroy the money-lenders' bonds by burning the public archives, in order to encourage the poor to rise against the rich, so Josephus complains.[198] In view of the

original communism of the Jerusalem Christians, and their evident
animus against the wealthy, this act would surely have had their ready
approval.[199]

The revolt against Rome, which thus came from the people, was a desperate act of faith against the overwhelming power of the mightiest empire
that the world had then known. No shrewd political leader, calculating the
odds, would have made it.[200] But the Jewish people, imbued with Zealot
teaching, were inspired by religious ideals, not political considerations. In
rising thus against Rome, they trusted to Yahweh, their god, not to the
material resources at their disposal, which were unorganised and meagre in
the extreme. They seem to have had no plan of campaign, beyond that of
offering the fiercest resistance to the Romans, when they came in force to
take vengeance for the act of rebellion and the consequent slaughter of their
garrisons in Judaea.[201]

The Roman punitive expedition duly came some three months after the
start of the revolt. It was led by Cestius Gallus, legate of Syria, who
commanded a strong force of legionary and other troops. They quickly swept
away whatever opposition the Jews had been able to organise in the country-
side, and laid siege to Jerusalem. Their operations were soon successful, and
they were on the point of breaking into the Temple, when their commander
suddenly ordered them to desist, and then to withdraw from the apparently
doomed city.[202] The reason for this amazing decision of Cestius Gallus
remains inexplicable, despite the investigations of many modern scholars.[203]
The beleaguered Jews, from utter despair were suddenly transported to the
exaltation of victory. Convinced now of the saving intervention of their god,
they furiously attacked the retreating Romans, turning their withdrawal
into a disastrous rout.[204]

No more signal demonstration of divine approval for their act of faith in
throwing off the Roman yoke could have been expected, even by the most
devoted of the Zealots. The seeming miracle confirmed the Jewish people in
their revolt, and even those who had counselled moderation now joined in the
national effort to meet further Roman attacks.[205] Of the reaction of the
Jerusalem Christians we have no direct information; but we can safely draw
our conclusions in the light of what we have already learned of their sentiments, and from the fact of the complete disappearance of the Mother
Church of Jerusalem after the destruction of the city in the year 70. The
repudiation by the lower priests of their obligation to offer daily sacrifice for
the heathen emperor and nation who oppressed them would surely have had
the sympathy and approval of the Jerusalem Christians, and so committed
them to that act of faith which the revolt against Roman suzerainty truly

was. The miraculous deliverance of the Temple from the army of Cestius Gallus, and the utter defeat of the Romans, must also have excited their apocalyptic hopes. As their compatriots, elated by the assurance of divine succour prepared for the greater test that must inevitably come from Rome the Jewish Christians would surely have looked with increasing confidence to the return of their Master, the Messiah Jesus, 'to restore the kingdom to Israel'. And so, inspired by such faith, many doubtless perished finally in the courts of the burning Temple, still hoping, with their fellow-Jews, for the saving intervention of their god.[206]

A late legend, deriving probably from the Gentile Church of Aelia Capitolina, the city which Hadrian built on the ruined site of Jerusalem, claimed that the Jerusalem Christians escaped from the doomed city and settled in the town of Pella, in Trans-Jordan.[207] But the legend not only is demonstrably a late fabrication on grounds of internal evidence, it is contradicted by the irrefutable fact that, after the catastrophe of AD 70, the Mother Church of Christianity, the original centre of faith and authority, completely disappeared.[208] This sudden extinction, coincident with the extinction of the Jewish metropolis, can mean only one thing: the Jerusalem Christians made common cause with their compatriots, and perished with them in the Roman fury that marked the last days in Jerusalem. There is much reason for thinking that the words which the author of the Matthean Gospel attributes to Jesus, when he orders Peter to cease armed resistance in Gethsemane, reflect the fate of the Christians of Jerusalem: 'Put your sword back into its place: for all who take the sword will perish by the sword.'[209]

CHAPTER THREE

The Gentile Christians and the Fall of Jerusalem in AD 70

One of the long-neglected mysteries of Christian Origins has been the effect of the fall of Jerusalem in AD 70 on the Gentile or non-Jewish Christians. The reason for the neglect was doubtless the fact that, since scarcely any reference is made to the Jewish catastrophe in the New Testament, scholars concluded that there had been no significant effect.[1] Such a conclusion, moreover, was in line with their theological presuppositions: Christianity was God's plan for mankind's salvation, and so could not have been conditioned by Roman-Jewish politics. It never seemed to have occurred to them, at least on *a priori* grounds, that it was strange that a religious movement, which had been directed and organised from Jerusalem for forty years, should have been unaffected by the sudden obliteration of its original source of faith and authority.[2] Yet, when the matter is considered as a historical phenomenon, it is indeed seen to be exceedingly strange and demanding of investigation. For our particular concern, the issue is also one of basic importance for understanding the factors that operated in the formation of the Gospel version of trial of Jesus.

If we reflect on what is known of the Christian movement in the decade preceding the destruction of Jerusalem in AD 70, it quickly becomes apparent that the non-Jewish Christians must have found themselves in a dangerous and difficult position as a result of the Jewish revolt against Rome. First, there is the obvious problem of their suddenly being cut off from the Mother Church of Jerusalem by its extinction after AD 70. In the thirty years after the Crucifixion, Christian communities had been established in Syria, Asia Minor, Cyprus, Greece, and Italy, including Rome, according to the Acts of the Apostles. The Acts also represents Paul as being chiefly responsible for thus propagating the new faith in these places;[3] and Paul's own writings witness to his activity in many of the places mentioned. This spread of Christianity is represented as a movement outwards from Jerusalem, which remained its venerated home and focal point. The Acts and Paul's Epistles show a strange silence about the spread of Christianity to Egypt, particularly to Alexandria, the second greatest city of the Roman Empire. However, there is reason for thinking that a flourishing church existed in Alexandria, having been founded by the Jerusalem Christians and being, consequently, un-Pauline in its form of Christianity.[4] All these daughter churches had been taught to regard the Mother Church of Jerusalem as the original source of tradition and authority, and to the maintenance of its members they were instructed to contribute financially.[5]

The nature of the relations between the Gentile churches and the Church of Jerusalem was profoundly conditioned by Paul's relations with the latter. As we have already seen, Paul had imparted to his Gentile converts that version of the faith which he maintained had been specially revealed to him by God for the evangelisation of the Gentiles; it was a version which differed seriously from that taught by the Jerusalem Church.[6] However, Paul was obliged, himself, to recognise the authority of the Jerusalem leaders, and to see that his Gentile converts duly contributed to the Mother Church.[7] But the Jerusalem authorities were not satisfied with this situation, and Paul's writings reveal that emissaries from Jerusalem operated among his converts, repudiating his claim to be an apostle and seeking to bring their faith into line with the Jerusalem 'gospel'. The disastrous defeat of Paul's attempt finally to effect some *modus vivendi* with James and the elders at Jerusalem resulted in his effective removal from personal contact with his churches.[8]

The author of the Acts of the Apostles, who knew the sequel to Paul's imprisonment in Rome, reveals, doubtless unintentionally in view of his apologetic concern, what happened in Paul's churches after his arrest at Jerusalem. The disclosure is made in the farewell speech which he attributes to Paul, when *en route* for his fatal last visit to Jerusalem. The speech is addressed to the elders of the church at Ephesus, who had come to meet him at Miletus; towards its end Paul warns them:

> And now, behold, I know that all of you among whom I have gone about preaching the kingdom will see my face no more. . . . Take heed to yourselves, and to all the flock, in which the Holy Spirit has made you guardians, to feed the church of the Lord, which he obtained with his own blood. I know that after my departure fierce wolves will come in among you, not sparing the flock, and from among your own selves will arise men speaking perverse things, to draw away the disciples after them.[9]

Whether Paul did utter these words or whether they represent a prophecy *post eventum*, they clearly indicate that Paul's work suffered seriously, after his removal, from external interference and internal disloyalty. And the situation depicted here is wholly intelligible in terms of what had gone before. Paul's communities would have heard that their champion had been obliged in Jerusalem to prove his Jewish orthodoxy by the Jerusalem Christians, and that he had been arrested in the Temple while so doing.[10] Such reports would doubtless have been puzzling and disturbing, and the disquiet of the Gentile Christians would soon have been increased as the Jerusalem leaders, in Paul's absence, stepped up their endeavour to eradicate his 'gospel' and replace it by their own doctrine as the true version of the faith.[11]

A period of bewilderment and perplexity must have followed for the Gentile Christians. They had no leaders capable of resisting the Jerusalem claims,[12] and many doubtless submitted, accepting a version of Christianity that was essentially Jewish in its ideas and outlook. A version, too, that assumed the spiritual superiority of Israel; for part of the offence of Paul's 'gospel', for the Jerusalem Christians, was its equation of Jew and Gentile in a common need of salvation.[13] The consequent eclipse of Paul's reputation and teaching is significantly reflected in what is called the Corpus Paulinum, i.e. the body of Paul's writings preserved in the New Testament. Whereas some of his Epistles, such as those addressed to the Christians of Rome, Galatia, Corinth (First Epistle), Philippi, Thessalonica and Colossae appear to be intact, what is known as the Second Epistle to the Corinthians is a mosaic of fragments of three letters; further, while the brief personal note sent to Philemon has been preserved, the letter which Paul addressed to Laodicaea has not survived.[14] Such evidence of damage and loss suggests that there was a period when Paul's writings were not treasured by his churches: later, when they were again valued, some had been completely lost or irreparably damaged.[15]

This period of Paul's eclipse probably lasted for about a decade, from AD 55 to 66;[16] it was terminated, in turn, by the eclipse of Jewish Christianity which ensued from Israel's defeat by Rome. Doubtless from the year 66, when the standard of Jewish revolt was raised, communication between the Jerusalem Church and the Gentile Christians outside Palestine ceased. As the war continued, and hatred of the Jews increased as reports circulated of their massacre of the Roman garrisons in Judaea and of the Gentile inhabitants of various places,[17] and of their fanatical resistance to the Roman armies, the Gentile Christians became increasingly alarmed about the Jewish connections of their faith. Neither their neighbours nor the authorities were likely to distinguish carefully between Jewish nationals and those who worshipped a Jewish messiah, whom a Roman governor had executed some years before for sedition. Indeed, it requires but little effort to imagine the danger and perplexity that must have been experienced by non-Jewish Christians, in different parts of the Roman Empire, during the fierce war of 66–70.

The final and catastrophic defeat of Israel, with the destruction of Jerusalem and its famous Temple, would have done little to lessen the danger of the Gentile Christians; but it probably did cause them to recall Paul's teaching about the inadequacy of the Jewish ritual Law. The destruction of the Temple, and the cessation of its cultus, had so signally confirmed his doctrine of the obsolescence of the Old Covenant of God with Israel.[18] Freed from the domination of the Jerusalem Christians, and with their faith in Paul's 'gospel' renewed, the Gentile Christians were doubtless eager to dissociate their religion from its Jewish origins.

But, above all other considerations, that which must, most sorely, have troubled and embarrassed the Gentile Christians at this time was the fact of the Roman execution of Jesus for sedition; for such a charge was politically dangerous and had nothing to do with religion. How the Romans would have regarded Christianity in this connection finds significant expression in the statement of the historian Tacitus. Describing the Emperor Nero's persecution of 'a class of men, loathed for their vices, whom the crowd style Christians', Tacitus briefly explains the origin of the movement for his readers:

> Christus, the founder of the name, had undergone the death penalty in the reign of Tiberius, by sentence of the procurator Pontius Pilate, and the pernicious superstition was checked for a moment, only to break out once more, not merely in Judaea, the home of the disease (*originem eius mali*), but in the capital itself, where all things horrible or shameful in the world collect and find a vogue.[19]

This contemptuous evaluation of Christianity was made by an educated Roman, with official connections, early in the second century, some eighty years after the crucifixion of Jesus.[20] It was contemptuous, and for Christians at that time it was also dangerous; for it meant that the ruling class then in Rome were mindful of the fact that Jesus had been executed by a Roman governor, and that the movement stemmed from Judaea, a land associated in the Roman mind with fanatical rebellion. How much more disturbing, therefore, must the realisation have been for Gentile Christians in AD 70, that their rulers held a similar view of their faith. For the Roman execution of their Lord for sedition was essentially a disturbing and dangerous fact, but one which the recent Jewish rebellion had then made even more disturbing and dangerous. Hence the urgent question that then faced them: how could the problem be explained and its danger removed?

These *a priori* considerations are reasonable and legitimate. They point to a predicament of the Gentile Christians, resulting from the Jewish war of 66–70, fraught with both danger and perplexity. But why, it must be asked, since this is so, is there no obvious evidence in the New Testament of Christian reaction to that war and its consequences? The answer seems to be that search has hitherto been made for the wrong things: 'obvious evidence' of reaction has been expected to take the form of clearly stated references and comments upon those notable events which are so vividly described by Josephus.[21] Attention has not been given to the possibility that the effect of the Jewish war and the destruction of Jerusalem on the infant Christian Church may have been so profound that it produced such a transformation that, after AD 70, Christianity became almost a completely new movement. Further, the possibility has not been explored that Christian writings after that date are really the products of this transformation, and present a new interpretation of Jesus and his mission.

In New Testament research the principle of what is called the *Sitz im Leben* has long been established. This means the recognition of the fact that the formation of the tradition about Jesus reflects the needs of the original Christian communities in Palestine.[22] But this principle has also to be applied in interpreting each Gospel, which embodies a selection of this tradition, as the product of the specific Christian community for which it was written. In other words, proper consideration must be given to the fact that a Gospel was not written as a piece of literature, namely as a biography of Jesus, for general publication, as biographies are written today. Instead, it was an interpretation of the life and teaching of Jesus, drawn from traditional material and designed to meet the needs of the community of which the author was a member. Moreover, these communities were situated outside Palestine after AD 70, and their needs were consequently different from the primitive Jewish Christians of Palestine, among whom the traditions about Jesus originated.

It is, therefore, the task of the historian of Christian Origins to seek in the Gospels for clues to the situation of the communities for which the documents were written. He is naturally helped in his task, if he can locate the community of any Gospel with which he is concerned. Now, of the four Gospels it is fortunate that there is a strong tradition, which has never been seriously challenged, for regarding the Gospel of Mark as a product of the Christian community at Rome.[23] The fact is fortunate, because the Markan Gospel is the earliest Gospel of which we have any knowledge, and its pattern was followed by the Gospels of Matthew and Luke.[24]

The Markan Gospel has, accordingly, the unique distinction of representing a new departure in Christian practice; no one had hitherto produced such an interpretation of Jesus set forth in narrative form.[25] Now, in view of the fact that the Gospels were, each, written to serve the needs of a specific community, we must ask what new, and evidently urgent, need had arisen among the Christians of Rome which the Gospel of Mark was thus designed to meet? The Gospel itself provides some very significant clues.

What is probably the most remarkable of these clues occurs in the list which Mark gives of the twelve apostles, whom Jesus appointed 'that they might be with him, and that he might send them out to preach the Gospel, and to have authority to cast out demons'.[26] Mark, in naming them, designates one 'Simon, the *Kananaios*'.[27] No explanation is given of the strange title of this apostle, although 'the *Kananaios*' would have been wholly unintelligible to Mark's Greek-speaking readers. This failure to explain a term of Jewish origin is strange, because Mark regularly explains Hebrew or Aramaic words and Jewish customs to the Gentile Christians, for whom he wrote;[28] indeed, just before mentioning Simon in his list of the apostles, he had explained the sobriquet '*Boanerges*' given to James and John, the sons of Zebedee.[29] Why, then, this silence about the meaning of '*Kananaios*'? The reason is not far to seek. If Mark had translated the Aramaic word, which he transliterates as '*Kananaios*', into Greek, he would have been obliged to write *Zēlotēs*, thus revealing that one of Jesus' apostles was a Zealot, a member of the Jewish national 'resistance' against Rome.[30] Rather than do this, he chose to depart from his practice of helping his Gentile readers in such matters, thus leaving them with the unintelligible title of 'the *Kananaios*' for the apostle Simon. His suppression of the fact that Jesus chose a Zealot for an apostle can surely have but one explanation. When Mark wrote in Rome, the disclosure of this fact was too dangerous or too embarrassing to be made. He must, accordingly, have written when the Zealots were 'in the news', which means a date about the year 70.

The significance of Mark's suppression of the fact that one of Jesus' apostles was a Zealot is further confirmed by another episode in his narrative. For among the issues which he selected for dealing with as matters of special concern to his fellow-Christians in Rome, was that of Jesus' attitude to the Jews' obligation to pay tribute to Rome.[31] The choice is remarkable; for the subject had no obvious spiritual significance. Indeed, it is possible to think of many other truly religious topics about which it might be supposed that the Roman Christians would rather have wanted to know the mind of Jesus. That Mark in his comparatively short Gospel, therefore, chose to devote space to the question of the Jewish tribute must mean that for the Christians of Rome it constituted an urgent and important issue. The fact, in itself, thus provides an important index to the situation of the Roman Christians. For it points, like the suppressing of information about the Zealotism of the apostle Simon, to a time when the Jewish payment of tribute and Zealotism were both questions of current concern for the Christians of Rome.

Mark's account of Jesus' ruling about the Jewish tribute also reveals in what way the issue did concern the Christian community at Rome. For it is found, on examination, to be so slanted as to present Jesus as endorsing the obligation of the Jews to pay tribute to Rome. Thus Jesus' ruling is tendentiously introduced as being given in answer to a question maliciously designed to compromise him with the Roman authorities: 'And they [the Jewish leaders] sent to him some of the Pharisees and some of the Herodians, to entrap him in his talk.'[32] Mark's Roman readers had already been given a bad impression of the Pharisees and Herodians earlier in his narrative:[33] it is possible also that the Herodians were known in Rome, and disliked as the followers of the Jewish prince Agrippa II; for the liaison of his sister Berenice with the Emperor's son Titus had caused much scandal in the capital.[34]

Mark's concern, in introducing the episode, to emphasise the malicious intent of the question which was to be put to Jesus, anticipates the nature of Jesus' reply.[35] The intent of his malevolent interrogators was obviously to entrap Jesus into some statement that could be construed as forbidding the payment of tribute to Rome. Mark's comment, therefore, thus assures his readers that Jesus avoided the trap of making an anti-Roman declaration on this vital issue.[36] His account of the incident must, however, be quoted in full, in order that its significance for our understanding of the situation of the Roman Christians, to which it relates, may be properly appreciated:

> And when they [the Pharisees and Herodians] were come, they said unto him, Master, we know that thou art true, and carest not for any one: for thou regardest not the person of men, but of a truth teachest the way of God: Is it lawful to give tribute unto Caesar, or not? Shall we give, or shall we not give? But he, knowing their hypocrisy, said unto them, Why tempt ye me? bring me a penny [*denarius*], that I may see it. And they brought it. And he saith unto them, Whose is this image and superscription? And they said unto him, Caesar's. And Jesus said unto them, Render unto Caesar the things that are Caesar's, and unto God the things that are God's. And they marvelled greatly at him.[37]

This passage has provoked much involved discussion down the ages concerning the meaning both of Jesus' action and statement; for the former is puzzling, and the latter ambiguous.[38] But we are concerned here with the significance of the passage in the context of Mark's Gospel: for it is there that this presentation of Jesus' ruling on the tribute first appears, and its meaning is surely to be sought there in terms of the situation in Rome which had provided the *raison d'être* of the Gospel.

Isolated from whatever was its original context, Jesus' pronouncement: 'Render unto Caesar the things that are Caesar's, and unto God the things that are God's', is ambiguous.[39] Its meaning requires definition of what are the things of Caesar and what the things of God. If the pronouncement was indeed made by Jesus (it has an air of authenticity), its meaning must have been clear to those to whom it was originally addressed. To argue, as some scholars have done, that Jesus intentionally made his answer ambiguous, to avoid involvement with a dangerous political issue, is neither realistic nor does it do credit to Jesus.[40] It is not realistic, because such an evasion would at once have been detected, and Jesus would have been pressed to define the contrasted 'things' of God and Caesar. Moreover, one who claimed to be, or was regarded as the Messiah, could not have hedged on an issue so fundamental for his fellow-countrymen. To assume that Jesus would have evaded such an issue stems from theological presupposition, not from historical probability: for the conception of Jesus as the Son of God, incarnated to save mankind, presupposes that he would not have involved himself with issues of current Roman-Jewish politics.

Such considerations require, therefore, that the saying must originally have been clear and definitive. Now, in the context of contemporary Judaea, there would have been no doubt what were the things of God, as opposed to the things of Caesar. As we have seen, the Zealot objection to the Roman tribute was religious: for it meant giving of the resources of the Holy Land, the 'things of God', to a heathen lord.[41] Jesus' pronouncement, therefore, was wholly in line with Zealot teaching, and so it must have been understood by those to whom it was originally addressed. In other words, Jesus ruled decisively against the payment of tribute. Caesar could, ironically, have what was his; but the Holy Land of Judaea, and its resources, were emphatically not his but God's.[42]

That this was Jesus' ruling on the issue is further confirmed by the Lukan Gospel in its report that the Jewish authorities charged Jesus before Pilate, saying: 'We found this man perverting our nation, and forbidding to give tribute to Caesar, and saying that he himself is Christ a king.'[43] The evidence, accordingly, builds up to a conclusion, which is consistent with the fact that the Romans executed Jesus for sedition: Jesus had ruled that the tribute was wrong on religious grounds, as did the Zealots. Into the significance of this conclusion we shall have to enter at length later;[44] for the moment we are concerned to evaluate Mark's presentation of the Tribute episode.

As we have seen, Mark carefully introduces the incident that leads up to the quotation of Jesus' ruling about the tribute, so that his readers will understand that ruling as endorsing the Jews' obligation to pay tribute to Rome. It is an astute move; but the fact that he has to make it has a twofold significance for us. First, it indicates that a saying of Jesus about the tribute ('Render unto Caesar . . .') was too well known among the Roman Christians for Mark to ignore it in his Gospel. Fortunately, isolated from its original context, the meaning was ambiguous to Gentiles, who had no exact knowledge of Jewish affairs some forty years before in Judaea. To Mark, however, it was obviously important that the saying should not cause perplexity to his fellow Christians in Rome; for its existence inevitably connected Jesus with this dangerous political question about the Jewish tribute. Consequently, he introduces it into his narrative, but in such a manner that it appears as attesting Jesus' loyalty to Rome. The other aspect of its significance is the evidence which the episode affords about the date of the Markan Gospel. Quite clearly a time is indicated when the question of the Jewish tribute was a lively and urgent topic in Rome. Such a time would seem to be the decade from AD 66, for one of the issues of the Jewish revolt that year was the tribute.[45] However, as we shall next see, it is possible to narrow down the period to about the year 71.

The reason for focussing on this year is that it was the year in which the Emperor Vespasian and his son Titus celebrated in Rome their triumph over rebel Judaea.[46] The Roman triumph was essentially a ritual act, solemnly decreed by the Senate and People of Rome. It took the form of a procession through the streets of Rome, in which the victorious troops paraded with their trophies and prisoners. Their general, wreathed with the laurels of victory, was acclaimed as he made his majestic way, in this procession, to the Capitol, to offer sacrifice to Jupiter Capitolinus in his great temple there: this act of sacrifice was preceded by the execution of the enemy commander in the Mamertine prison, below the Capitoline Hill.[47]

Such an occasion was one of impressive display, designed to thank both Rome's patron deity and her general for the victory, and to commemorate the city's imperial destiny. But the triumph celebrated in 71 had a further significance. The Jewish revolt had badly shaken the Roman people. It had started disastrously with the signal defeat of a Roman army, and it had dragged on for four years, marked by savage fighting. It had also had dangerous possibilities. Within two years of its start, the Empire itself had been convulsed by civil war and there were revolts in Gaul, Moesia and on the Rhine.[48] Rebel Judaea, moreover, lay athwart the lines of communication between Egypt and Syria, and the opportunity might have been seized by

Rome's perennial enemy, the Parthians, to invade the eastern provinces in support of the Jewish insurgents.[49] Consequently, Rome was grateful to Vespasian and his son for both bringing the civil war to an end and finally defeating the rebel Jews. But the triumph also afforded a unique opportunity to Vespasian who was founding a new imperial dynasty, following the death of Nero, to impress the Roman people with the achievements of his family.[50] Consequently the victory over Judaea was given great publicity in a new coinage;[51] but it was in the pageantry of triumph that special effort was made to demonstrate how great had been the achievement of the Flavii, as the imperial family was known.

It is fortunate that Josephus, who had returned to Rome in the retinue of Titus, has described in detail this Flavian triumph of AD 71.[52] He tells how, besides the prisoners and spoils of victory that were paraded through the streets of the city, specially constructed cars (*pegmata*) presented vivid tableaux of incidents of the war, so that it seemed to the onlookers 'as though they were happening before their eyes'.[53] Among the spoils were the treasures of the Temple: the magnificent *Menorah* or seven-branched lampstand, the golden table of shewbread, the silver trumpets, a great Torah scroll, and the purple curtains that veiled the sanctuary.[54] The Arch of Titus, in the Roman Forum, still preserves on its sculptured panels scenes of that triumph and the exaltation of Titus.[55]

In a world lacking our modern means of publicity, foreign events would normally have been little known to ordinary people. But the carefully mounted triumph of Vespasian and Titus, in the year 71, must have given the Roman people a most graphic impression of the Jewish war and the destruction of Jerusalem and its Temple. Josephus tells us that 'no one remained at home of Rome's countless population', and that every vantage point was taken from which to watch the mighty pageant of Roman victory over rebel Judaea.[56] In the streets of the city, on that day, many Christians also doubtless watched the spectacle; but it would have been with other feelings than those that animated their pagan neighbours. They would surely have gazed with a curious interest at the treasures of the Temple, symbols of a cult with which their own faith was linked, and now carried in the Roman triumph as tokens of Israel's overthrow and the Temple's destruction. But the scenes of fierce warfare and the Jewish captives, execrated by the Roman crowd, would have been disturbing reminders that their own religion had stemmed from a Jew whom a Roman governor had executed as a rebel. And the word 'Zealot' must have been on many lips, a well-known term of abuse for those fierce fanatics who had refused to pay the tribute due to Rome from all subject peoples.

It takes but little imagination, as one reads Josephus' account of the Flavian triumph or looks at the sculptured scenes on the Arch of Titus, to see how exactly the Markan Gospel reflects the situation of the Christians of Rome at this time. The concealment of the Zealot profession of one of Jesus' apostles, and the concern to show that Jesus had endorsed the Jews' obligation to pay tribute to Caesar are eloquent. But that is not all that so testifies. There is other evidence of Mark's preoccupation with the consequences of the Jewish war, and with its vivid presentation in the Flavian triumph.

Thus a significant reaction to the triumph is to be discerned in a curious incident recorded by Mark at the moment of Jesus' death.[57] The incident has often puzzled commentators, because it seems to be a legendary addition designed to present the death of Jesus as marking the end of the Temple cultus.[58] According to Mark, as Jesus died, 'the curtain of the temple was torn in two, from top to bottom'. The narrative continues: 'And when the centurion, who stood facing him (Jesus), saw that he thus breathed his last, he said, "Truly this man was the Son of God!" '[59] The two events appear to be connected in their significance; but it is evident that whatever that significance was, it must have been apparent to Mark's readers, since no explanation is given. Now, it may well be asked how would Gentile Christians, living in Rome, and doubtless poorly educated and untravelled, have known that the Temple in far-off Jerusalem had a special veil or curtain, and, moreover, how would they have understood its significance? The answer to this obvious question is surely to be found in Josephus' account of the Flavian triumph. For he records that the Temple curtains were among the spoils of the Temple, and that they were deposited afterwards, with other objects, in the imperial palace.[60] He does not inform us how these curtains were displayed in the triumph; but we may reasonably conclude, in view of the effort made to inform the Roman populace of the magnitude of the victory, that some explanatory description was given of the function of the curtains in veiling the Holy of Holies.[61] Hence, the Christians of Rome would have known about the Temple veil, and thus have understood the significance of its rending at the death of Jesus, as Mark now related in his Gospel. Indeed, it would not be too imaginative to suppose that the evidence seen in the Flavian triumph of the desecration of the Temple, and of the end of its cultus, had caused much discussion among the Roman Christians. Being acquainted with both the teaching of Paul and the Jerusalem Church, for them that evidence would have been invested with a peculiar significance.[62] For, seeing such proofs of the overthrow of Judaism, they would doubtless have recalled Paul's doctrine that the death of Christ had marked the ending of the Old and the institution of a New Covenant.[63] What the Roman victory had thus rendered an historical fact, Mark now showed in his Gospel to have been divinely proclaimed by a rending of the Temple veil at the final moment of the Crucifixion.

Mark's connecting of this signal demonstration of the abrogation of cultic Judaism with the Roman centurion's recognition of the divinity of the dying Jesus was a masterly stroke. For it assured his Gentile readers that it was a Gentile, not a Jew, who first perceived Jesus to be the Son of God. It was, moreover, a Roman soldier who had this insight at the very moment that the miraculous rending of the Temple veil had proclaimed the ending of the Temple cultus, which the Roman army, under Titus, had now rendered an accomplished fact. Thus the Roman Christians were encouraged to see in the Flavian triumph not a disturbing reminder that they worshipped a Jew executed for sedition against Rome, but inspiring evidence that Rome had fulfilled God's purpose, adumbrated in the rending of the Temple veil and the centurion's confession.[64]

There is another indication of Mark's preoccupation with the destruction of the Temple, which the triumph had undoubtedly emphasised. It has a special significance for us, since it helps to solve a problem of Mark's account of the trial of Jesus. We have already seen that Mark represents the charge brought against Jesus at the Sanhedrin trial, that he would destroy the Temple, as 'false witness'; yet, earlier in his narrative, he records how Jesus had foretold the Temple's destruction.[65] In our previous discussion of this apparent contradiction, we concluded that Mark followed an original Jewish Christian account of the Sanhedrin trial, which was specially concerned to rebut the charge that Jesus had threatened the Temple.[66] We come now to consider why Mark was thus led into making this apparent contradiction of statement in his Gospel.

The clue to the problem is given in certain words, in parenthesis, which Mark curiously adds to the Abomination of Desolation passage in the so-called Little Apocalypse. We have already discussed the passage in another connection, and found reason for believing that it relates to the reaction of the Jerusalem Christians to the attempt of the Emperor Gaius to desecrate the Temple.[67] The particular verse which concerns us now needs to be quoted, so that its curious construction may be appreciated: 'But when ye see the abomination of desolation standing where he ought not (let him that readeth understand), then let them that are in Judaea flee unto the mountains.'[68] Mark thus represents Jesus as foretelling, about the year 30, a coming desecration of the Temple in terms of Daniel's reference to the desecration perpetrated by Antiochus Epiphanes in 167 BC.[69]

On analysis, the verse contains, besides the words in parenthesis, a small, but significant, alteration which Mark must also have added to the original form of the statement. This alteration is best appreciated in the original Greek. The word 'abomination' (*bdelygma*) is a neuter noun, so that its dependent participle 'standing' should also be neuter. Consequently the verse should read: 'When ye see the abomination of desolation standing where *it* ought not. . . .' But Mark has made the participle masculine, so that it reads: 'standing where *he* ought not . . .'. In other words, Mark has identified the Abomination of Desolation, which originally referred to an altar or statue, with a man.[70] But who was this man? The words that follow in parenthesis are of the greatest significance: '(let him that readeth understand)'. Quite clearly Mark thought it indiscreet to make an exact identification in his Gospel; but he had given a sufficient hint for his readers to enable them to make the identification for themselves.[71]

We perceive, then, a most interesting and revealing situation. Mark represents Jesus as foretelling the desecration of the Temple by a man whom the Christians of Rome would easily be able to identify, but whom he preferred not to name. Now, we know of only one desecration of the Temple to which the alleged prophecy of Jesus could apply. It occurred in AD 70, when the Romans captured the Temple, and it is recorded by Josephus.[72] According to his account, while the sanctuary (*naos*) itself was in flames, the victorious legionaries erected their standards in the Temple court, opposite the eastern gate, and sacrificed to them and hailed Titus as '*imperator*' (*autokrator*). Both acts had religious significance, but the latter specially concerns us. The original religious element in the Roman title of *imperator* had become greatly enhanced by its association with the Emperor-cult, so that the legionaries' salutation was tantamount to a recognition of the divinity of Titus.[73] Thus, in the year 70, the Temple was not only desecrated by the act of sacrifice made to the military standards, but by the presence of a man, in Christian eyes impiously regarded as divine, who stood 'where he ought not'.

It is very probable that this cultic gesture of the victorious legionaries had been portrayed in one of the tableaux, which Josephus so enthusiastically describes in his account of the Flavian triumph. Thus the Roman Christians would have known that the Temple had not only been destroyed, but that it had also been signally desecrated. Now, it is evident that these portentous events had also greatly excited the apocalyptic hopes of the Roman Christians. They were seen as the culmination of a series of portents heralding the Return of Christ and the end of the world.[74] In the thirteenth chapter of his Gospel, Mark deals with this situation of expectancy among his fellow-Christians, being intent on both confirming their belief and controlling their excitement. His treatment of the subject is of great importance to us.

14 The crowning with thorns
Oldest-known depiction of the Passion of Christ from the Catacomb of Praetextatus,
third century (*see p. 157*)

15 Pilate washing his hands, Christ bearing the cross, and Peter's denial
Ivory pyxis from southern Gaul, fifth century (see p. 158), British Museum

16 Christ before Pilate (*see frontispiece*)

17 Simon of Cyrene bearing the cross (Mk. xv: 22) and the crowning with thorns

Panels from a fourth-century sarcophagus (see pp. 157–8), Lateran Museum, Rome

It would seem that the impression left on Mark by the Flavian triumph was too strong to be denied, despite his acceptance of the Jerusalem Christians' account of the Sanhedrin trial which maintained that Jesus had not spoken about the Temple's destruction. For Mark the catastrophic overthrow of cultic Judaism must surely have been foretold by Jesus; so he set about adapting the 'Little Apocalypse', originally inspired by the attempt of Gaius in AD 39–40,[75] to suit the current situation. His *mise en scène* to the prophecy is striking in its vivid detail, and we may well wonder whether it had not been inspired by one of those graphic tableaux which, according to Josephus, portrayed 'walls of surpassing compass demolished by engines': [76]

> And as he came out of the temple, one of his disciples said to him, 'Look, Teacher, what wonderful stones and what wonderful buildings!' And Jesus said to him, 'Do you see these great buildings? There will not be left here one stone upon another, that will not be thrown down.'[77]

The sequel, which is located on the Mount of Olives, significantly reveals how the destruction of the Temple was connected, in the mind of Mark, with the Second Coming of Christ and the end of the world. Although Jesus had spoken only of the destruction of the Temple, the disciples are represented as asking:

> 'Tell us, when will this be, and what will be the sign when these things are all to be accomplished?' And Jesus began to say to them, 'Take heed that no one leads you astray. Many will come in my name, saying "I am he!" and they will lead many astray. And when you hear of wars and rumours of wars, do not be alarmed; this must take place, but the end is not yet!'[78]

Jesus then goes on to recount various trials which the disciples must undergo, and which probably represent the experience of the Roman Christians during the Neronian persecution in 66.[79] This recital leads on to the Abomination of Desolation passage, which, as we have seen, so strikingly relates to the desecration of the Temple in AD 70. The chapter continues in an ambivalent vein: on one hand, endorsing belief that the Second Coming of Christ is imminent,[80] while, on the other, warning that no one can tell the exact time and that the disciples' duty is unceasing vigilance: 'Take heed, watch; for you know not when the time will come.'[81]

The situation of the Roman Christians thus becomes clear and intelligible, and with it the Gospel of Mark was intended to cope. Under the impact of the Flavian triumph, the Jewish war and the destruction of Jerusalem became realities that caused these Christians both danger and perplexity; but the end of the Temple cultus also reminded them of Paul's teaching and stimulated their apocalyptic hopes. Mark, suppressing the awkward fact of Simon's Zealotism, had adroitly presented Jesus to them as endorsing the Jewish obligation to pay tribute to Rome. He exploited the evidence of the triumph to prove the obsolescence of cultic Judaism, and he discreetly identified the Temple's desecration with the presence of Titus there. But there were other problems, caused by the Jewish revolt, for which he had to find other answers.

First and foremost, and to which all other considerations were ancillary, was the problem of the Roman execution of Jesus for sedition. As we have already seen, the Roman historian Tacitus traced what he regarded as the pernicious character of Christianity to its founder, whom Pontius Pilate had executed—the implication being that he merited the penalty.[82] It is unlikely that Tacitus was alone among Romans in his view of Jesus; for, as the Neronian persecution shows, the Christians were obvious scapegoats because they were popularly regarded as subversive in their attitude to the established order.[83] Their connection with Judaism was also well known, though misunderstood.[84] Consequently, in Rome, excited by the Flavian triumph, the knowledge that Jesus had been executed as a rebel against the Roman government of Judaea, was both embarrassing and dangerous to the Christian community. Hence, Mark's chief task was to explain, or, rather perhaps, to explain away, how Jesus had come to be so condemned by Pontius Pilate. He seeks to achieve this in his account of the trial of Jesus, which he so presents as to make Pilate testify to Jesus' innocence.[85] This presentation we must duly subject to a searching analysis;[86] but, in order to be in a position to do this properly, there are still certain other aspects of his Gospel that we must first evaluate.

When the Gospel of Mark is considered as a narrative account of the career of Jesus, it exhibits some curious traits. Although, as we have already noted, it claims to be 'the gospel of Jesus Christ, the Son of God',[87] its theological presuppositions do not appear to lessen its concern to present Jesus in his contemporary Palestinian environment. This preoccupation with what may be described as the 'historical Jesus', as opposed to Paul's repudiation of 'Christ according to the flesh', must derive, as we saw, from the tradition of the Jerusalem Church.[88] However, this dependence upon the Mother Church is not matched by any sign of appreciation for its leaders. Indeed, far to the contrary, a distinct denigration of them characterises the Gospel. Thus the apostles are presented as a dull vacillating band, who are only able to recognise Jesus as the Messiah of Israel, and fail dismally to perceive that he is the divine saviour[89]—in fact, it is the Roman centurion who is the first human being to discern the divinity of Jesus.[90] The apostles, moreover, do not only fail to comprehend the true nature of their Master, but one of them betrays him to his enemies,[91] their leader, Peter, denies knowledge of him,[92] and they all desert him in Gethsemane.[93] It is, indeed, a shocking record, and we may well wonder why these men, who had until recently been the leaders of the original movement, are so cruelly presented by Mark. But that is not all. There is also the parallel denigration of the family of Jesus, which we have previously noticed.[94] Again our curiosity is legitimately excited, especially when we recall that James, the brother of Jesus, had presided over the Jerusalem Church, and, on his death, had been succeeded by another member of Jesus' family.[95]

What, then, can have been the cause of this strange animus against persons whom we might naturally expect Mark and his fellow-Christians to have revered? For an answer, it is necessary to recall that, when Mark wrote, the Jerusalem Church was no more, having disappeared in the holocaust of AD 70. The fact is surely significant; and it may be that we are seeing in the Markan Gospel a reaction, inspired by an intelligible resentment, against the control which the Mother Church had exerted over the Gentile communities. It is a legitimate inference: and such animus, moreover, would have had further cause, if the Christians of Rome had also known, which seems likely, that the Jerusalem Christians were strongly nationalist and had perished in the revolt against Rome.[96]

This hostile presentation of members of the Mother Church has the effect, in Mark's Gospel, of isolating Jesus from his Jewish origins: his Jewish disciples cannot understand him, and his family think him to be mad. A similar effect is also produced in the accounts of Jesus' relations with the leaders and people of Israel. The Pharisees, the Herodians, and the 'chief priests' are depicted as opposed to Jesus and plotting to destroy him from the very beginning of his ministry.[97] It is the Jewish leaders who arrest him, condemn him, and force a reluctant Pilate to crucify him.[98] The Jewish people reject him, and call forth from Jesus the bitter comment: 'A prophet is not without honour, except in his own country, and among his own people, and in his own house.'[99] And, finally, comes the amazing contrast. On Golgotha, while the Jewish leaders and people deride their dying victim, it is the Roman centurion who testifies to his divinity.[100]

In other words, a definite anti-Jewish theme can be traced through Mark's Gospel, and it has the effect of presenting Jesus as rejected by, and in turn rejecting, all those natural ties that connected him with the Jewish nation. Thus the lineaments of an apologetic emerge, of basic importance for our evaluation of Mark's account of the trial of Jesus, which, as we have noted, provided the pattern for the Gospels of Matthew and Luke. It was an apologetic designed to cope with the dangerous and perplexing situation in which the Christian community at Rome was placed by the Jewish revolt and the publicity given to it at the Flavian triumph. Mark wrote his Gospel with a twofold intent: to explain away the problem of the Roman execution of Jesus and present him as loyal to Rome; and to show that Jesus, though born a Jew, had no essential connection with the Jewish people and their religion, and that a Gentile was the first to perceive the truth, to which the Jews were blind, that Jesus was the Son of God.

The Markan Gospel is, accordingly, to be evaluated as the product of the reaction of the Roman Christians to the Jewish revolt against Rome and the catastrophe that followed. It was too involved with the consequences of those events to assume the detached interest towards them expected by some scholars. And the fact of this involvement is the foundational datum for any proper investigation of the trial of Jesus. For Mark's account is the earliest we have of the trial, and it has been followed in its essential pattern by the other Gospels. Why this has been so, and the immense effect it has had on the formation of the Christian conception of Jesus, must now be considered before we pass on to examine the Markan presentation of the trial.

The fact that Christianity was suspect to the Roman government as a subversive movement provides one of the major themes of Early Church history. It caused outbreaks of persecution for nearly three centuries, until Constantine's 'Edict of Milan' in 313 announced the Church's victory over the Roman Empire.[101] In the early decades of its existence, Christianity's Jewish origins inevitably prompted suspicion, as we have seen. And this suspicion continued for some time, even after the instinct to regard the Christians as 'fellow-travellers' with Jewish nationalism gradually faded as the strong emotions caused by the events of AD 66–70 subsided. Tacitus' view of Christianity was most probably representative of Roman opinion in the early second century.[102] Consciousness of this view, and the desire to remove it, are evident in many New Testament writings. The Acts of the Apostles is clearly designed to show that opposition to Christianity, both in Judaea and other places in the Empire, came from the Jews, who sought to misrepresent the new faith to Roman magistrates.[103] The authors of the Gospels of Matthew, Luke and John were similarly concerned to show that Jesus' execution for sedition was due to Jewish malice. They followed Mark's lead; but, whereas he was primarily concerned to show Jesus as pro-Roman, they developed the theme of his pacifism.

It is unfortunate that tradition does not associate these other Gospels with specific Christian churches, as it does Mark with the church at Rome. Scholars have sought to find evidence of locations, and various suggestions have been advanced. A strong case, however, can be made out for locating the Gospel of Matthew at Alexandria, the great city on the Egyptian coast.[104] On grounds of internal evidence, the Gospel of Matthew appears to have been written for a Greek-speaking Jewish Christian community. And nowhere else, after AD 70, did such a flourishing community exist than in Alexandria; moreover, there is much reason for thinking that the church there had been founded by the Jerusalem Church, with which it had strong ties until the destruction of Jerusalem.[105] That catastrophe evidently had serious repercussions for the Alexandrian Christians, which found reflection in Matthew's Gospel.

Important evidence of the current situation in Alexandria comes from Josephus, who tells how a body of the Sicarii, the extremist wing of the Zealots, escaped from doomed Jerusalem to Alexandria, and tried to incite the Jews in Egypt to revolt against Rome.[106] A serious situation was created, and it would seem that the Jewish temple at Leontopolis was in danger of becoming the focus of a revolt.[107] But the Jewish leaders in Alexandria had been sufficiently warned by the disasters in Judaea not to allow such a desperate attempt in Egypt, and they cooperated with the Roman authorities in rounding up and exterminating the Sicarii.[108] Significant signs of the reaction of the Alexandrian Christians to this situation may be discerned in the Gospel of Matthew. The most notable, from our point of view, occurs in additions which Matthew makes to Mark's account of the arrest of Jesus in Gethsemane. Mark, for reasons which we can now well appreciate, found it prudent to conceal the fact that the disciples of Jesus were armed and that his arrest had been violently resisted. Consequently, he vaguely mentions that 'one of those who stood by (*tōn parestēkotōn*) drew his sword, and struck the slave of the high priest and cut off his ear'.[109] He makes no comment on Jesus' reaction to this act, which, significantly, was inflicted on a Jew and not on a Roman. Matthew, however, expands Mark's account of the incident so that it becomes a carefully presented reproof by Jesus of Christians who resort to armed conflict:

And, behold, one of those who were with Jesus (*heis tōn meta Iesou*) stretched out his hand and drew his sword, and struck the slave of the high priest and cut off his ear. Then Jesus said to him, 'Put your sword back into its place; for all who take the sword will perish by the sword. Do you think that I cannot appeal to my Father, and he will at once send

me more than twelve legions of angels? But how then should the scripture
be fulfilled, that it must be so?'[110]

To appreciate the full significance of Matthew's expansion of Mark's record
here, we must bear in mind that the Jewish Christians of Alexandria, to
whom the Gospel is addressed, would have understood the reference to those
who had taken the sword and perished by it.[111] For from the refugees from
Judaea, some probably being Jewish Christians, they would have learned
what had been the penalty of seeking to establish the kingdom of God by
war.[112] They are, accordingly, reminded here by Matthew that Jesus, when
on earth, could have opposed the legions of Rome by legions of angels; but
he would not. Thus, instead of the martial Messiah of current apocalyptic,
Jesus is presented by Matthew as the pacific Messiah who forbids his followers
to resort to violence on his behalf.

Other aspects of Matthew's Gospel of similar significance, relating specifically to his presentation of the trial of Jesus, we shall consider later.[113] From his
depiction of a pacifist Jesus we must now turn to assess Luke's version. Luke
evidently wrote at a place where, unlike Mark at Rome and Matthew in
Alexandria, he could safely record that one of Jesus' disciples was a Zealot.[114]
There are other indications also, which we shall presently note, that he could
write with a certain detached interest about the destruction of Jerusalem. It is
significant also that he, imprudently, reveals that the disciples of Jesus were
accustomed to carry swords.[115] However, he depicts the birth of Jesus as
inaugurating an era of peace—the 'herald angels' sing: 'Glory to God in the
highest, and on earth peace among men with whom he is pleased.'[116] This
note characterises Luke's portrait of Jesus, and it finds significant expression in
his presentation of Jesus mourning over the obduracy of Jerusalem and its
coming destruction. Thus, in a poignant scene unparalleled in the other
Gospels:

And when he (Jesus) drew near and saw the city he wept over it, saying,
'Would that even today you knew the things that make for thy peace!
But now they are hid from your eyes. For the days shall come upon you
when your enemies shall cast a bank about you and surround you, and
hem you in on every side, and dash you to the ground, you and your
children within you, and they will not leave one stone upon another in
you; because you did not know the time of your visitation.'[117]

So Luke sets Jesus over against rebel Jerusalem, which had gone down in
blood and flame, as one who had vainly sought her peace. In his subsequent
work, the Acts of the Apostles, Luke imputes the crucifixion of Jesus wholly

to the Jews, in accordance with his anti-Jewish apologetic theme. For the apostles are represented as boldly accusing the Sanhedrin: 'The God of our fathers raised Jesus again whom you killed by hanging him on a tree.'[118] Pilate's decisive part in the execution is ignored, thus attesting the success of Mark's transference of responsibility for the Crucifixion from Pilate to the Jewish leaders, a transaction that we have yet to evaluate.[119]

The Gospel of John, although it presents a strikingly different portrait of Jesus and his teaching from those of the other Gospels, constitutes a further stage in the same apologetic theme: it represents Jesus as the victim of Jewish malignity, while heightening his transcendental character.[120] Moreover, consistent also with the concept of the incarnate Logos in the prologue, a definitive repudiation of involvement in contemporary politics is attributed to Jesus. Thus, instead of remaining silent or very reticent before Pilate, as in other Gospels, the Johannine Jesus carefully explains to the Roman governor the spiritual or other-worldly character of his claims: 'My kingship is not of this world; if my kingship were of this world, my servants would fight, that I might not be handed over to the Jews; but my kingship is not from the world.'[121] This is both an amazing and a significant statement. Although it is assumed to be made by Jesus at his trial before Pilate, the Jews are represented as enemies to whom in some unexplained way he had been handed over (*paradothō*). And it is imagined that, if his purpose had lain in this world, Jesus would have enlisted his servants (*huperētai*) to repulse the Jews by arms.[122] These extraordinary statements were made by John, despite his awareness of a credible political aspect to Jesus' career, as we shall see.[123] However, for him the death of Jesus really represented the (temporary) victory of the Devil and his offspring, the Jews.[124] So shocking an interpretation doubtless reflects the increasing antipathy of Christians towards the Jews, which gradually hardened into that hatred which later inspired their persecution as the murderers of Christ.[125]

Our investigation of the Christian situation resulting from the Jewish catastrophe of AD 70 has inevitably been long and intricate; but it now enables us properly to evaluate the only evidence concerning the trial of Jesus that has come down to us. We now see that the Gospel of Mark, which is the fundamental document of our enquiry, was the product of the dangerous and perplexing predicament of the Christian community in Rome about the year 71. Designed to meet that predicament, the Markan Gospel is essentially an apologia.[126] Far from giving an objective account of the career of Jesus, it was composed to assure the Roman Christians that Jesus, though born a Jew, had no essential connection with Judaism, that he had endorsed the Roman rule in Judaea, and that Pilate had recognised his innocence but had been forced by the Jews to crucify him. The fact of the Roman execution of Jesus for sedition was, of course, the basic problem, and to it Mark had to devote particular attention. How he dealt with the evidence at his disposal, to achieve his apologetical purpose, will be our next task of investigation.

Our enquiry into the Christian situation after AD 70 has also helped us to understand how the conception of a pacific Christ was formed, and became the established tradition. This conception was originally both politically and doctrinally necessary. It has remained doctrinally necessary for Christian orthodoxy, since it is impossible to believe that the Divine Saviour of mankind could have become implicated in Jewish-Roman politics in first-century Judaea. But the conception has also great emotive power, especially today. Although there have been periods of Christian history when Christ has been regarded more as the implacable Judge at the Last Judgment,[127] during the present century the tendency has been increasingly to see Jesus as the divine representative of ideals which we treasure but fail to achieve—preeminently, peace and the brotherhood of mankind. Consequently, most of us experience an instinctive reluctance to contemplate the possibility that the historical Jesus may have been other than our idealised portrait of him. But, if we truly seek the historical reality, we must resist that reluctance and consider the evidence with critical objectivity. Hence, it is important that we should have seen how the concept of the pacific Christ grew up during the latter decades of the first century, and found embodiment in the Gospels. And it is important that, as we now come to consider the earliest account we have of the trial of Jesus, we also bear in mind the motives that led Mark to compose it. To discern these motives and appraise them, is not to accuse the Evangelist of conscious deceit. Mark was not writing history as we know it. He wrote from his conviction that Jesus was the Son of God, incarnated to accomplish mankind's salvation. His execution by the Romans must, therefore, have some other explanation than that he was guilty of sedition. Accordingly, Mark's apologia was the fulfilment of a religious obligation. Truth for him was truth about the divine nature and mission of Jesus: in composing his account of the trial of Jesus, he was not writing as a legal historian but as a Christian teacher, concerned to defend the faith and help his fellow-Christians in their danger and perplexity. It is in this light, therefore, that we must sympathetically, but critically, evaluate what he has written about the transaction that resulted in the condemnation of Jesus for sedition.

CHAPTER FOUR

The Scandal of the Roman Cross: Mark's Solution

However ingenious Mark might be in depicting Jesus' loyalty to Rome, the stubborn fact of his execution for sedition against Rome remained. Indeed, by representing Jesus as endorsing the Jewish obligation to pay tribute, Mark actually deepened the problem of Pilate's condemnation. The fact of that condemnation was intractable, and upon its significance critics of Christianity inevitably seized—the sting can be felt in Tacitus' taut phrase: 'by sentence of the procurator Pontius Pilate'.[1]

The Roman cross and its scandal were thus too well known to be ignored, or treated, as Paul had done, as a divinely-planned event that had been unwittingly executed by the daemonic rulers of the planets.[2] The execution of Jesus had happened, as Tacitus reminded his readers, in Judaea a short while before, when Tiberius was emperor. Moreover, the event was graphically recorded in that narrative-tradition about Jesus which formed the 'Gospel' of the Jerusalem Christians, and which was propagated by its emissaries in the Gentile churches. Mark, therefore, in writing his Gospel to cope with the grave situation in which the Christian community of Rome was placed about the year 71, had to find some way of removing the scandal of Pilate's condemnation.

Now, as we have already noted, Mark based his account of the Sanhedrin trial of Jesus on a version designed, by the Jerusalem Christians, to rebut the charge that Jesus had threatened to destroy the Temple.[3] We also saw that the motive behind this version was that of presenting Jesus as the Messiah of Israel, which meant the refutation of any accusation of conduct inconsistent with this Messianic claim. This apologia of the Jerusalem Church was not, however, limited to the Sanhedrin trial; it formed part of an integrated narrative of the events at Jerusalem which resulted in the crucifixion of Jesus.[4] Since this narrative also served as the basis of Mark's version of the tragedy, we must endeavour to distinguish its original form beneath Mark's presentation. For its authority was clearly so well established that Mark was obliged to follow it, although it did in fact lead him into the paradox of describing how Pilate condemned Jesus, when he had, himself, earlier depicted Jesus as so notably loyal to Rome on the question of the tribute.

On analysis, it would seem that the Jerusalem tradition, which Mark followed, was more concerned with the trial of Jesus by the Sanhedrin than with that by Pilate. Thus, the charge brought against Jesus in the former trial, of threatening the Temple, is stated and shown to be 'false witness',[5] and the grounds on which the high priest subsequently condemned Jesus for blasphemy are described at some length.[6] On the other hand, the nature of the charge preferred against Jesus by the Jewish leaders at the Roman tribunal is not mentioned, and nothing explicit is said of the grounds on which Pilate gave the fatal sentence.[7] Moreover, no explanation is given for the fact that the Jewish leaders, having condemned Jesus for blasphemy, hand him over to Pilate who executes him for sedition.[8]

Now, in view of Mark's concern to reduce the scandal of Jesus' condemnation for sedition, it is understandable that he would have been reluctant to reproduce any part of the Jerusalem tradition which made clear that the charge was one of sedition. However, it is important to remember also that the Jerusalem Christians would not have shared such reluctance. Indeed, far to the contrary, the death of Jesus at the hands of the Romans for refusing to accept their sovereignty in the Holy Land of Yahweh, was an honourable death—a martyrdom for Israel.[9] Their concern about his crucifixion had a very different cause. As we have seen, it constituted a grave objection to his being the Messiah of Israel.[10] Consequently, in formulating their account of how Jesus came to be crucified by the Romans, they were motivated by the desire to show that the event did not negate his Messianic role. This meant that their attention was concentrated on such issues as his condemnation by the Sanhedrin, which had significance for Jews. Thus their problem was not Mark's: they had to explain to their fellow-Jews why the death of Jesus did not negate his Messiahship, not that Pilate had sentenced him as a rebel. In fact, the Roman condemnation helped their case, for it enhanced the reputation of Jesus as a martyr for the cause of Israel's freedom.

Behind Mark's narrative, the original Jewish Christian presentation of Jesus as the Messiah of Israel, martyred for Israel by its heathen oppressors and their Jewish collaborators, can be clearly discerned. It commences with his triumphant entry as the Messiah into Jerusalem, riding on an ass according to ancient prophecy,[11] and acclaimed by the people as the one who would restore the long-departed glory of David's kingdom: 'Hosanna! Blessed is he who comes in the name of the Lord! Blessed is the kingdom of our father David that is coming! Hosanna in the highest!'[12]

The next event of signal import is the so-called 'Cleansing of the Temple'. This, beyond doubt, was one of the most crucial actions of Jesus; but, unfortunately, its true significance has been obscured in the Gospel records. As it is presented by Mark, and in turn by the other Evangelists, the deed appears as a symbolic gesture, yet one strangely involving energetic practical action.[13] Jesus is depicted as going, alone, into the Temple, and driving out 'those who sold and bought' and overturning 'the tables of the money-changers and the seats of them who sold pigeons'. In explanation of his action, Jesus is reported by Mark to have declared: 'Is it not written, "My house shall be called a house of prayer for all the nations?" But you have made it a den of robbers.'[14] The impression given by Mark's account is that Jesus thus protested against the dishonest activities of a crowd of petty traders, whose trafficking polluted the sanctity of the Temple. Moreover, it is suggested that Jesus alone cleaned up this disgraceful situation, presumably by the force of his own personality, and that no opposition was offered to this arbitrary interruption of a brisk, if nefarious, trade.

It takes little reflection, however, on the manifest improbabilities of such an account to realise that the actual event must have been very different. Moreover, the account disguises the real nature of the business activities carried on in the Temple, and hence the significance of Jesus' action against them. The Temple at Jerusalem was an immense economic institution as well as the ritual focus of Judaism. Like many other ancient sanctuaries, it served as a treasury, with banking facilities.[15] Further, the maintenance of its cultus involved the provision of a number of ancillary services. Any Jew paying his various ritual dues, had to change his secular coinage into an acceptable Temple currency: hence the need of money-changing facilities. Similarly, for offering an appropriate sacrifice, he needed to be able conveniently to purchase a suitable animal; such service was provided in the Temple.[16] The changing of money and the buying and selling of animals, within the Temple precincts, were, therefore, necessary transactions and were authorised by the sacerdotal authorities. This business was naturally lucrative, and it contributed to the wealth and power of the priestly aristocracy which controlled Jewish affairs under the Romans.[17]

Consequently, it would be naive to suppose that in the so-called 'Cleansing of the Temple' Jesus was merely protesting against the conduct of the money-changers and vendors of sacrificial animals, whose business there was quite legitimate. Indeed, since Jesus, as a devout Jew, took part in the Temple cultus, he must himself have used these services.[18] A clue to the real nature of Jesus' action is given in the verse which concludes Mark's account of the episode: 'And the chief priests and the scribes heard it and sought a way to destroy him; for they feared him, because all the multitude was astonished at his teaching.'[19] The suggestion is that Jesus' action was not against the petty traders of the Temple, but was aimed at the priestly aristocracy who managed the Temple for their own profit and power—men, moreover, who collaborated with the Roman rulers of Israel.[20]

That Jesus' action in the Temple had a political aspect serves to underline the improbability that Jesus acted alone and that he was met by no opposition, according to the Markan report. It is incredible that one man, unsupported, could have interfered with the legitimate and necessary business being transacted in the Temple courts, by overturning the money-changers' tables and driving out the other traders, without violent opposition from all concerned. Moreover, there were Temple police, whose duty it was to maintain peace and order—they would surely have taken prompt action to end such a fracas by arresting him who was responsible for it.[21]

Further, we must ask where were the followers of Jesus on this critical occasion, and also the crowds which on the previous day had welcomed him into the city as the Messiah?[22] Did they not follow Jesus into the Temple, and did they not support him in his action? The inevitable affirmative, which must be returned to these questions, raises in turn that of the real purpose of Jesus' action. A temporary interruption of the business transactions of the Temple would have had little effect on the position of the priestly aristocracy; it would merely have victimised a number of lesser innocent folk, who undoubtedly suffered financial loss in the violent upsetting of their goods and places of business.[23] The possibility must, therefore, be considered that Jesus' action in the Temple was a much graver affair—that it was designed to gain control of the Temple and depose the high-priest, the nominee of Rome, by another chosen according to the Law, as the Zealots did later in the year 66.[24]

Such a design would make sense of what otherwise seems a useless gesture, inflicting loss only on the unfortunate traders who were conducting their lawful business in the Temple courts. It would explain also the determination of the chief priests to destroy Jesus, as well as the main charge, brought against him at the Sanhedrin trial, that he would destroy the Temple. Into the significance of such an attack on the priestly aristocracy, for the purpose of evaluating the career of Jesus, we shall enquire later; for the present we must consider the episode further in the context of the original Jewish Christian apologia.

In relating the course of events which resulted in the death of the Messiah Jesus, such an attempt to purify the high priesthood could be shown as being consistent with the Messianic mission of Jesus, and it would also explain how he incurred the mortal hatred of the chief priests.[25] How far Mark's account of the episode represents the original Jewish Christian version is, however, doubtful. The silence about Jesus' followers and the sense of anti-climax that invests the account may, perhaps, reflect the fact that the attempt proved to be abortive. But, however that may be, it would seem that, though his design had in some way been frustrated, the Jewish leaders were unable to arrest Jesus publicly owing to the popular support which he still enjoyed.[26]

The next turning-point in the drama of the last fateful days in Jerusalem, as related in the original Jerusalem tradition, was doubtless the defection of Judas Iscariot, which explained how the popularly acclaimed Messiah was betrayed into the power of the chief priests, who could not otherwise have taken him.[27] What part the subsequent Gethsemane episode had in the original tradition is difficult to determine.[28] The episode seems to have had three points of concern: that Jesus was faced with an agonising decision on that last night in Gethsemane; that the disciples failed to keep watch as they had been ordered to do; that Jesus was seized there by the retainers of the high priest after some armed resistance, followed by the flight of his disciples. It will be our task, at a later point in our investigation, to try to understand what really did happen in Gethsemane in terms of the purpose and fate of Jesus;[29] but for the present we must continue our reconstruction of the original tradition, and its use by Mark in describing the events that led up to the crucifixion of Jesus.

The arrest in Gethsemane by the retainers of the high priest explains the otherwise curious fact that Jesus was tried by the Sanhedrin before his trial by Pilate. For the narrative goes on to tell how Jesus was taken to the house of the high priest, where the Sanhedrin had assembled.[30] In Mark's account, the subsequent transactions of the Sanhedrin trial are interwoven with the story of Peter's denial of Jesus.[31] Although this interweaving of the two themes is skilfully done and adds greatly to the drama of the occasion, there is much reason, however, for thinking that the Peter story has been added by Mark in pursuance of his policy to denigrate the disciples, which we have already noted.[32] It seems very improbable that the Jerusalem Christians would have composed an account designed to refute the Sanhedrin charge that Jesus had threatened the Temple, but have distracted attention from this vital issue by mixing it up with the tale of Peter's act of denial—an incident quite irrelevant to the trial, and very derogatory to Peter, who was a revered leader of their community.[33]

If the story of Peter's denial is, accordingly, regarded as a Markan addition, an explanation is provided for a curious discrepancy in the account of the Sanhedrin proceedings. This discrepancy occurs between the statements made

in xiv:55 and xv:1, which imply that two separate meetings of the Sanhedrin were held: the first, at night, which concluded with the condemnation
of Jesus to death for blasphemy;[34] the second, early in the morning, which
resulted in delivering him to Pilate on a different, but undisclosed, charge.[35]
By inserting the story of Peter's denial, Mark disguises this discrepancy; but
we may well wonder whether the discrepancy, which a careful reading of the
narrative quickly detects, occurred in the original account of the Jerusalem
Christians. Mark's reluctance to specify the charge on which the Jewish
leaders delivered Jesus to Pilate has probably led him to reshape his source-
material, so that a second Sanhedrin meeting appears quite unrelated to the
first. The hiatus doubtless did not exist in the original account, whose
authors did not share Mark's reticence about the offence of which the Jewish
authorities accused Jesus to Pilate.

It will be well to have before us at this point the account of the Sanhedrin
proceedings, disentangled from the story of Peter's denial; for it will enable
us to see something of the original sequence which Mark's reshaping has
obscured (the dotted lines indicate the 'Peter passages'):

And they led Jesus to the high priest; and all the chief priests and the
elders and the scribes were assembled. . . . Now the chief priests and the
whole council sought testimony against Jesus to put him to death; but they
found none. For many bore false witness against him, saying, 'We heard
him say, "I will destroy this temple that is made with hands, and in three
days I will build another, not made with hands".' Yet not even so did their
testimony agree. And the high priest stood up in the midst, and asked
Jesus, 'Have you no answer to make? What is it that these men testify
against you?' But he was silent and made no answer. Again the high priest
asked him, 'Are you the Christ, the Son of the Blessed?' And Jesus said,
'I am; and you will see the Son of man sitting on the right hand of
Power, and coming with the clouds of heaven.' And the high priest tore
his mantle, and said, 'Why do we still need witnesses? You have heard
his blasphemy. What is your decision?' And they all condemned him as
deserving death. And some began to spit on him, and to cover his face,
and to strike him, saying to him, 'Prophesy!' And the guards received
him with blows. . . . And as soon as it was morning the chief priests, with
the elders and scribes, and the whole council held a consultation; and they
bound Jesus and led him away and delivered him to Pilate. And Pilate
asked him, 'Are you the King of the Jews?' And he answered him, 'You
have said so.' And the chief priests accused him of many things. And Pilate
again asked him, 'Have you no answer to make? See how many charges

they bring against you.' But Jesus made no further answer, so that Pilate wondered.[36]

How far Mark has edited this account is difficult to tell. The chief point for doubt is the ascription to the high priest of words which make him identify the Messiah (Christ) as the Son of God: 'Are you the Christ, the Son of the Blessed?'[37] This point, however, will be best discussed later.[38] For the present we must consider two difficulties about the account which have been raised by certain scholars.

It has been pointed out, in questioning the accuracy of the account, that it would have been unlikely for the Sanhedrin, the supreme Jewish court for dealing with matters relating to the Law, to have met in the high priest's house, seeing that it had its own proper place of assembly.[39] Secondly, that a nocturnal meeting of the Sanhedrin would surely have been irregular.[40] These are valid objections, if the account is to be evaluated as a factual record of what is assumed to be a trial by the Sanhedrin. But to assess the account in that way is to mistake its true nature. As we have already seen, in its original form it was part of a Jewish Christian apologia, designed to show that the execution of Jesus did not negate his claim to be the Messiah. One of the chief objections to that claim was evidently that Jesus had been accused before the Sanhedrin of threatening the Temple. The Jewish Christians were concerned to rebut this charge: their account of the Sanhedrin proceedings does just this by showing that the charge was 'false witness', and that Jesus was condemned by the Sanhedrin not on this charge but for affirming that he was the Messiah.[41]

But now we have to ask the question, implied in those objections which we have just noticed: were the transactions in the high priest's house that night a trial of Jesus by the Sanhedrin? Mark certainly suggests that it was a trial, so that the impression is conveyed to his readers that Jesus was really executed on the sentence of the Sanhedrin for blasphemy—a charge which had none of the dangerous political implications that a Roman sentence for sedition had.[42] But careful analysis of what appears to have been the original account of the Jerusalem Christians indicates a rather different situation.

It must be remembered that the Jewish leaders were a priestly aristocracy, whom the Romans entrusted with the management of Jewish domestic affairs. They had to justify their position by preserving peace among their people and by effective cooperation in maintaining the Roman rule.[43] Jesus, a Messianic figure, backed by considerable popular support, had seriously challenged their control of the Temple, the very source of their wealth and national leadership. Whatever had been his real objective, Jesus had failed to accomplish it in that first attack; but he continued to be powerfully supported, and could only be arrested in a clandestine operation. Once the Jewish leaders had him in their power what was their policy likely to have been? The reported transactions at the high priest's house that night provide some significant clues. First, the unusual place and hour of the proceedings indicate that haste was evidently essential: probably the Jewish leaders could not be certain what the reaction of the people, many of them pilgrims for the Passover, would be when the news of Jesus' arrest became known; success for them lay in presenting the people with some *fait accompli*. The author of John's Gospel represents the high priest, Caiaphas, as expressing his concern also about Roman reaction if Jesus was allowed to continue his activities unchecked.[44] In other words, Jesus had not only challenged the position of the high priest and his party, he also constituted a menace to orderly government, for which Pilate would hold them responsible. We shall see evidence presently that Jesus' activity in Jerusalem coincided with an insurrection there, in which the Romans were directly involved.[45] It was, therefore, the obvious duty of the Jewish leaders to discover the exact nature of Jesus' intentions, which appeared to be subversive of the established order, and, with that evidence, to hand him over to Pilate for judgment and sentence.

Consequently, the fact that the apologia of the Jerusalem Christians depicts the chief issue before the Sanhedrin to have been the question of Jesus' attitude to the Temple is significant. The account suggests that the Jewish leaders had suborned witnesses to give 'false witness' against Jesus, in order to have grounds for condemning him to death.[46] If this were indeed so, then those leaders were curiously punctilious in observing the laws of evidence; for they apparently did not accept such testimony when the witnesses were found to contradict each other.[47] Surely, it must be asked, the Jewish leaders would have arranged things better, if they sought only for a legal pretext for destroying Jesus? And there is another point for consideration here. To foretell the destruction of the Temple was not regarded as an offence meriting death. Thus Josephus records the activities of a peasant, named Jesus, son of Ananias, who began to prophesy, four years before the War, in the Temple during the feast of Tabernacles: 'A voice from the east, a voice from the west, a voice from the four winds; a voice against Jerusalem and the sanctuary, a voice against the bridegroom and the bride, a voice against all the people.' Josephus goes on to relate how this Jesus was punished by the Jewish authorities; but since he did not desist from his ill-omened prophecies they handed him over to the procurator, Albinus. He had him scourged to the bone; but when this did not silence him, the Roman dismissed him as mad. Jesus continued his prophesying for more than seven years, until he was killed by a ballista-stone during the siege of the city.[48]

The case of Jesus ben Ananias, accordingly, affords an instructive parallel to that of Jesus of Nazareth. If the latter had only foretold the coming destruction of the Temple, the Sanhedrin were hardly likely to concentrate on this as providing an adequate cause for a sentence of death. Their concern about Jesus' attitude to the Temple, therefore, clearly had some deeper motive. There can be little doubt what this motive was: to learn what exactly had been Jesus' objective in his so-called 'Cleansing of the Temple'. We have seen reason for concluding that his action in the Temple had been a far more serious affair than it is represented in the Gospels. The followers of Jesus had surely been involved in a struggle that may have anticipated the successful action of the Zealots there in 66.[49] The attack had evidently failed to achieve its objective; but it had constituted a grave threat to the establishment. It was important, therefore, to know the aims of Jesus and who were his leading followers.[50] The conflict of testimony, which the Jewish Christian tradition describes, doubtless reflects a natural confusion of reports about what Jesus had said and done on that occasion. Indeed, a note of puzzlement seems to be sounded in the high priest's question to Jesus: 'Have you no answer to make? What is it that these men testify against thee?'[51] The reported silence of Jesus is significant; he evidently was careful not to supply the high priest with the information he wanted.

The Jewish Christians' apologia, as we have seen, was concerned to repudiate the charge that Jesus threatened the Temple, in the interests of their presentation of him as the Messiah of Israel.[52] Having shown that the charge could not be sustained, the narrative goes on to describe how the high priest, unable to extract any information from Jesus about the Temple affair, asked him directly whether he was the Messiah: 'Are you the Christ, the Son of the Blessed?'[53] That the words 'the Son of the Blessed', or their Aramaic equivalent, were actually said by the high priest is most improbable; for the basic monotheism of Judaism precluded such a relationship even for the Messiah.[54] It would seem most likely that they were added by Mark, in view of his theme of the divinity of Jesus.[55] However that may be, the significance of the passage lies in the fact that the Jerusalem Christians, in their apologia, described Jesus as answering 'yes' to the high priest's question, thus affirming unequivocally that he was the Messiah.[56] The continuation of Jesus' answer expresses succinctly the apocalyptic faith of the Jerusalem Church: 'you will see the Son of man sitting on the right hand of Power, and coming with the clouds of heaven'.[57] The reaction of the high priest and the Sanhedrin is one of outrage, and Jesus is adjudged to have blasphemed and to be deserving of death. Such a decision is difficult to understand; for Josephus does not mention that any other of the many Messianic pretenders, whom he records, was adjudged worthy of death for blasphemy.[58]

This account of the Sanhedrin's decision, we must remember, is part of the apologia of the Jerusalem Christians; it serves their apologetical purpose of showing that Jesus was not guilty of threatening the Temple, but was condemned by the Sanhedrin for affirming that he was the Messiah. Now, if the high priest did ask Jesus whether he was the Messiah, the question must have been put in the context of the high priest's search for evidence of the subversive nature of Jesus' teaching and activity. What he learned certainly did not cause him and the Sanhedrin, despite their alleged sentencing of Jesus to death, to make arrangements for his execution by stoning, which was the customary death for blasphemy.[59] In making this observation, we touch upon a very complicated question: did the Sanhedrin have the power at this time to inflict the death penalty?

That there is a question here is due to two facts. The first is that, despite the Gospel record of the Sanhedrin's condemnation, it was the Roman governor who ordered Jesus' execution and Roman soldiers who carried it out. The second fact is that, according to the Gospel of John, the Jews, in handing Jesus over to Pilate, declared: 'It is not lawful for us to put any man to death.'[60] The impression is given, accordingly, that the Jewish authorities condemned Jesus to death for blasphemy; but, not having the power to carry out the sentence, they were obliged to persuade Pilate to execute him, and to this end they altered the charge from blasphemy to one of sedition. The issue, however, really turns upon the accuracy of John's statement. Without this statement, the problem of why the Sanhedrin did not implement its alleged sentence and put Jesus to death by stoning assumes a different aspect, as we shall see.[61]

A critical examination of John's statement quickly reveals grounds for doubting its accuracy, if it is interpreted as meaning that the Sanhedrin could not execute on a capital charge. These grounds become apparent when the statement is seen in its context:

> Pilate said to them, 'Take him yourselves and judge him by your own law.' The Jews said to him, 'It is not lawful for us to put any man to death.' This was to fulfil the word which Jesus had spoken to show by what death he was to die.[62]

Pilate's order to the Jews logically implies that they had the authority to try Jesus. Their reply, in turn, implies that their own law did not permit the execution of a capital sentence.[63] To interpret the words 'not lawful for us' (*hēmin ouk exestin*), in this context, as referring to the Sanhedrin's legal disability under the Roman government, as is often done, is certainly not necessary either from the point of view of logic or grammar. To interpret them so is to invoke other considerations such as the fact that the Romans executed Jesus, instead of the Jews who had first condemned him to death. However that may be, there is an even more cogent reason for doubting the historical accuracy of John's statement.

The reason is found in the concluding comment in John's statement: 'This was to fulfil the word which Jesus had spoken to show by what death he was to die.' This comment reveals John's real intention in representing the Jewish leaders as declaring that it was not lawful for them to put any man to death. John was concerned to explain how Jesus had come to suffer crucifixion, which was not a Jewish punishment. The logic of his previous narrative led to the expectation that the Jews would kill Jesus: indeed, he had depicted Jesus as calling the Jews murderers because they were intent on killing him[64]—they had even tried to stone him.[65] Consequently, he had to prepare his readers for what did actually happen. To this end, earlier in his Gospel, he had described Jesus as foretelling his death by crucifixion: 'and I, when I am lifted up from the earth, will draw all men to myself'. And to this cryptic utterance he added the explanatory comment: 'He said this to show by what death he was to die.'[66] This preparation was astute, because it enabled him, in his record of the trial, to account for the otherwise unexpected Roman execution of Jesus by referring back to Jesus' prophecy that he would die by crucifixion.

Considered as a historical question, what evidence there is on the subject of the competency of the Sanhedrin to execute on a capital charge seems to indicate that the court had this power, subject to Roman confirmation. Thus the protracted proceedings concerning Paul's fate, as described in the Acts of the Apostles, are only intelligible on the supposition that the Roman authorities might have handed him over to the Jews for judgment, which would certainly have resulted in his execution on a religious charge.[67] In the case of James, the brother of Jesus, as we have seen, the way in which the high priest Ananus had acted illegally, in executing James and his companions, was in convoking the Sanhedrin in the absence of the procurator.[68] The case of Jesus, son of Ananias, which we noticed above, is perhaps the most significant for us. According to Josephus, the Sanhedrin first punished him by beating; when this failed to stop his prophecies, they handed him over to the procurator for more severe treatment.[69] That the procurator had the ultimate decision in the matter of life or death is clearly stated by Josephus.[70] The Sanhedrin administered the Jewish Law for their own people, subject to procuratorial confirmation of capital sentences.[71]

If such, then, was the constitutional position, the fact that the Sanhedrin did not proceed to obtain Pilate's confirmation of its alleged condemnation of Jesus for blasphemy, and that he was not executed by stoning, must mean that the proceedings in the high priest's house were not a formal trial. This conclusion confirms the other evidence we have noted, that the Sanhedrin was concerned that night to investigate Jesus' ideas and actions, in order to prepare a case for handing him over to Pilate. And that case was based upon the political, not the religious, significance of Jesus. Naturally, Judaism being what it then was, political and religious factors were inextricably intertwined, as we have seen in the ideals and aims of the Zealots. However, the Jewish leaders were primarily concerned with Jesus as one who menaced the existing social and political order, and not as a religious heretic.[72] His activities in the last few days, especially his attack on the Temple establishment, convinced them that he was a subversive force, for whose suppression the Romans would hold them responsible.

To return to our attempt to disentangle the original account of the Jerusalem Christians from Mark's recasting of it, we may look again at our earlier suggestion about the discrepancy in the Markan narrative that makes it appear that the Sanhedrin held two separate meetings. It was suggested that Mark, by interposing the story of Peter's denial, sought to disguise the awkward transition from his presentation of the Sanhedrin investigation as a trial, at which Jesus was condemned for blasphemy, to the subsequent trial of Jesus by Pilate for sedition.[73] We noted, also, that the Jerusalem Christians would not have shared Mark's embarrassment about the Roman execution of Jesus—in fact, it would greatly have helped in recommending Jesus to their fellow-Jews to have emphasised his martyrdom at the hands of the hated Romans. Consequently, it is probable that their original account made it clear that, after their interrogation of Jesus, the Jewish leaders formulated their charge of sedition and delivered him to Pilate, for the confirmation and execution of the prescribed penalty. In taking this action, the Jewish leaders, as we have seen, were performing their constitutional duty. The Jerusalem Christians, however, in formulating their apologetic, would have had the advantage of being able to denigrate the action of these unpopular magnates, in handing over Jesus, as pro-Roman, sycophantic and unpatriotic.

Behind Mark's failure to explain why the Jewish leaders, having condemned Jesus for blasphemy, delivered him to Pilate, and behind his reluctance also to say on what grounds these leaders accused Jesus to the procurator, may be discerned his embarrassment about the charge. For the first question Pilate asks of Jesus is: 'Are you the King of the Jews?' Quite clearly Pilate's question must have been formulated in accordance with the information laid by the Jewish priests.[74] Moreover, the fact that Pilate uses the title 'King of the Jews' on three other occasions,[75] that it is also used in derision by the Roman soldiers,[76] and the equivalent 'King of Israel' is tauntingly addressed to the crucified Jesus by the Jewish leaders,[77] indicates that it figured prominently in the original account as being the basis of the Jewish accusation. As a title, its significance is great—in fact, definitive. For, of the many things of which Jesus might have been accused, that of political pretension was thus clearly the charge preferred by the Jewish leaders, accepted by the Romans, and recorded by the Jerusalem Christians. The very attribution of such a title, moreover, implied commitment to leadership of a politically-freed Israel. That it was attributed to Jesus inevitably means that there was that in his teaching and conduct as known to the Jews and Romans which rendered the attribution reasonable and pertinent. And further, the fact that it was recorded, without challenge, in the apologia of the Jerusalem Christians reveals that it was not a title which they repudiated for Jesus.[78]

What was the proper procedure for a Roman governor on the delivery of a prisoner, accused of sedition by the Jewish authorities, is not known from any of our sources.[79] It would seem probable that the governor would normally be disposed to accept the charge without further trial, unless there was strong reason for acting otherwise. He would doubtless ask the accused formally what he had to say to the charge which the accredited authorities of his own people had brought against him. In cases of sedition, it would be likely that the governor would already have some knowledge of the activities of the person charged through his own intelligence sources: this was probably so with Pilate in the case of Jesus. From what Mark has chosen to record of the transactions at Pilate's tribunal, something of the form of procedure sketched there can be made out. After asking Jesus whether he was the 'King of the Jews' and getting a non-committal reply, Pilate again asks, with reference to the accusations of the Jewish leaders: 'Have you no answer to make? See how many charges they bring against you.'[80] Jesus' refusal to answer these charges is reported to have surprised Pilate, who was probably accustomed to accused persons vehemently protesting their innocence.[81]

From this point, our attempt to make out the original Jewish Christian account, underlying Mark's presentation, becomes involved in one of the greatest enigmas of the Roman trial of Jesus. This is the episode concerning the choice which, according to Mark, Pilate caused the Jews to make between Jesus and Barabbas.[82] The episode presents us with a twofold problem:

whether it is founded on historical fact, and how Mark uses the alleged choice in pursuance of his apologetical theme. The latter problem will occupy us at some length presently; for the moment we must consider the question of the historicity of the episode, particularly in relation to the original apologia of the Jerusalem Christians on which Mark's narrative was based.

It will be well to have the relevant passage, as it stands in Mark's Gospel, before us. The passage follows immediately on the statement that Pilate wondered at Jesus' refusal to answer the accusations of the Jewish leaders about his subversive ideas and activities.[83] In the sequence of Mark's narrative the impression is given that Pilate, puzzled at Jesus' silence and not being certain what he should do, suddenly seized the opportunity that the alleged custom offered to him:

> Now at the feast he used to release for them one prisoner whom they asked. And among the rebels in prison, who had committed murder in the insurrection, there was a man called Barabbas. And the crowd came up and began to ask Pilate to do as he was wont to do for them. And he answered them, 'Do you want me to release for you the King of the Jews?' For he perceived that it was out of envy that the chief priests had delivered him up.[84]

On examination, this passage is found to be a veritable catena of problems. But, before we consider them, let us note that, although the sequence of Mark's narrative makes it appear that the episode concerning Barabbas followed immediately on Pilate's wonder or puzzlement about Jesus' silence, an interval of time is implied, during which the crowd gathered and demanded their customary privilege.[85] Such an interval would mean some unexplained interruption in the course of the proceedings in Pilate's tribunal. From what we have been able to deduce from Mark's curiously evasive account of Pilate's interrogation of Jesus, it would seem reasonable to expect that Pilate would have accepted the evidence laid before him by the Jewish authorities and proceeded to order the execution of Jesus. This expectation, moreover, is endorsed by the fact itself that Pilate did duly order the execution and Jesus was put to death for sedition. This being so, the statement that Pilate 'wondered' at the silence of Jesus must surely be taken as an interpretative comment made by Mark; for it implies psychological insight into the mind of Pilate which only an acute eye-witness of the proceedings at the Roman tribunal could have had, and we may legitimately doubt whether Mark's source actually embodied such a report.[86] This note about Pilate's 'wonder' was obviously required by Mark's use of the Barabbas episode, which he was now about to introduce into his narrative, in order to make

Pilate testify to Jesus' innocence. However, although Mark thus sought to bridge the gap between Pilate's interrogation of Jesus and the new episode about Barabbas, that gap is a fact which must be reckoned with in our assessment of Mark's account of the Roman trial.[87]

But now we must turn to the basic problem of the historical credibility of the Barabbas episode. According to Mark's statement, it was the custom in Judaea, at the feast of the Passover, for the Roman governor to release a prisoner chosen by the people—presumably those in Jerusalem at that time. We must begin our enquiry, therefore, by carefully scrutinising what Mark actually says about this alleged custom; then we must consider carefully its implications, if the custom did in fact exist.

Mark's statement: 'at the feast he used to release (apeluen) for them one prisoner whom they asked', means literally that it was Pilate's practice to grant this amnesty.[88] The point is important, as we shall see, because it represents the custom as being the personal creation of Pilate. Matthew, following Mark here, makes the custom appear as one observed by the Roman governors generally: 'Now at the feast the governor was accustomed to release for the crowd any one prisoner whom they wanted.'[89] Next, it is to be noted that Mark does not specify for whom the release was made. He uses the unsupported pronoun 'they' (autois), which suggests that he was so eager to introduce this episode that he forgot to explain the identity of those on whose behalf the alleged custom existed. This use of an unsupported pronoun emphasises the sudden break and switch of attention that occur in Mark's narrative after mentioning Pilate's 'wonder' at the silence of Jesus.

The following verse in the Barabbas episode continues this impression of haste to get on to the new theme, thus attesting its importance to Mark in the development of his apologetic—'and among the rebels in prison, who had committed murder in the insurrection, there was a man called Barabbas'. This statement appears to be quite out of context with the preceding verse and with what follows; indeed, it is not until four verses further on that the information which it gives about Barabbas becomes relevant.[90] That Mark introduces it where he does, so out of context, surely indicates that the name of 'Barabbas' was dominating his mind at this point because of its significance for his theme. The statement itself, however, has the appearance of having been taken from source-material that Mark was using for this part of his narrative. It implies some foregoing narration about an insurrection which accounted for the imprisonment of Barabbas and other rebels. This implication is of the greatest significance; for it means that Mark had at his disposal some account about an insurrection that had taken place, presumably in Jerusalem, about the same time as Jesus' activity there.[91] Further, his premature mentioning of Barabbas, reveals that Mark was very concerned about some connection of which he knew between Barabbas and Jesus.

Having thus unwittingly betrayed his agitation about Barabbas, in the next verse Mark turns back to his introductory statement, to connect up with the subject of the alleged amnesty-custom: 'And the crowd came up, and began to ask Pilate to do as he was wont to do for them.' The suggestion of this verse is that the crowd suddenly arrived at Pilate's residence or tribunal, and reminded him of the custom. They are not described as naming a prisoner for release. If such a custom existed, it would seem to have been an unorganised affair; for the crowd, apparently unled, take the initiative in asking for the annual amnesty. The implication of the next verse is that Pilate quickly responded to the crowd's request; but no indication is given that he suspended the proceedings of the tribunal to attend to the crowd—Mark seems to have forgotten that transaction. Pilate counters the crowd's demand with a question: 'Do you want me to release for you the King of the Jews?' An explanation of this question is immediately added by Mark: 'For he (Pilate) perceived that it was out of envy that the chief priests had delivered him up.'

Mark thus makes his first suggestion that Pontius Pilate, the Roman governor of Judaea, had recognised that Jesus was innocent and that he perceived the motive of the Jewish leaders in accusing him of sedition. The motive named sounds curiously naive. Several more convincing motives could be attributed to the Jewish leaders than 'envy': for example, fear of the danger that Jesus constituted, or hatred for what he had done in the Temple and his critical attitude towards them, or *odium theologicum*.[92] But whatever the motive, Mark's statement raises two related questions: how did Pilate know that the chief priests' accusation was inspired by jealousy, and, therefore, false; and how did Mark know the mind of Pilate about the matter?

It is necessary to consider the implications of the former question more deeply. As we have seen, the evidence points to the fact that, after his attack on the Temple establishment, the Jewish leaders decided that Jesus was politically dangerous, and that their interrogation on the night of his arrest was designed to prepare a case for handing him over to Pilate as a subversive person. Further, the fact that Pilate applied the title 'King of the Jews' to Jesus, including its use in the *titulus* on the cross, together with his ordering the crucifixion of Jesus, all point to Pilate's accepting the case against Jesus presented by the chief priests. Pilate doubtless had little love for the Jewish leaders, or they for him; but it was their mutual duty and interest to cooperate in the efficient government of the country. Mark provides no evidence that Pilate had found fault with the Jewish case presented to him; and it is scarcely likely that he would have omitted to mention the fact, if Pilate had publicly indicated that he was not convinced. Moreover, if Pilate had not been satisfied with the evidence laid by the Jewish leaders, he could have dismissed the case or re-tried it more thoroughly himself.

Mark's claim to know Pilate's mind about the Jewish leaders was doubtless not examined critically by his Christian readers in Rome, and it disposed them to the strange presentation of Pilate that followed. In order that we may savour how strange is that presentation, it is necessary to quote the rest of the Barabbas episode. After suggesting that Pilate offered to release Jesus to the crowd in order to save him, having recognised his innocence and the chief priests' malignity, Mark continues:

> But the chief priests stirred up the crowd to have him release for them Barabbas instead. And Pilate again said to them, 'Then what am I to do with the man whom you call the King of the Jews?' And they cried out again, 'Crucify him'. And Pilate said to them, 'Why, what evil has he done?' But they shouted all the more, 'Crucify him'. So Pilate, wishing to satisfy the crowd, released for them Barabbas; and having scourged Jesus, he delivered him to be crucified.[93]

The drama of the situation is immense, and it is superbly presented by Mark in a vivid dialogue and a moving conclusion. The influence of the scene depicted has been incalculable, and it has imprinted itself indelibly upon the mind of countless generations of Christians. Indeed, so graphic is the description of this fatal transaction that it carries the reader along convinced of its truth; however, when carefully and detachedly examined, it is found to contain some very grave objections to its authenticity as a record of what actually did happen on that fateful occasion in Jerusalem.

To appreciate how extraordinary is this transaction related by Mark, it is necessary that we should first view it as a whole, detached from the overtones of significance that centuries of Christian belief have found in it. We are told that the appointed authorities for Jewish domestic affairs delivered to the Roman governor a member of their own nation charged with subversive ideas and activities. This person, who claimed to be the Messiah and was recognised as such by his followers, had recently attacked the Temple establishment, and was so powerfully supported by the people that he could not be arrested publicly. The Roman governor interrogates the prisoner about the charges, but can elicit no answer from him. After describing the governor's surprise at the prisoner's silence, the account of the proceedings abruptly ends without any mention of a decision. Attention is then switched to a completely different situation. The governor is now faced by a Jewish crowd demanding the release of an unspecified prisoner, in accordance with what is alleged to be the governor's annual practice. The governor, who for some unexplained reason has become convinced of the innocence of the prisoner with whom he is dealing, and the malevolence of the Jewish authorities towards him, offers the crowd the release of this prisoner. But the Jewish authorities are now surprisingly able to persuade the crowd, which they had formerly feared, to ask for the release of another prisoner who had been captured in a recent insurrection, which had caused the death of some of the Roman forces.[94] The governor, who had strangely resorted to the amnesty-custom to save an innocent prisoner instead of releasing him on his own authority, frustrated by the manœuvre of the Jewish authorites, then asks the crowd what he is to do with the innocent prisoner, whose innocence he publicly acknowledges. The crowd replies that he is to be crucified. So the Roman governor obeys, and orders the scourging and crucifixion of a man whom he had declared to be innocent and desired to save.

When viewed thus, objectively, as a reported transaction between a Roman governor, who was supported by a strong military force, and native magistrates and a native mob, the whole account is patently too preposterous and too ludicrous for belief. In the first place, there is the sudden switch from the interrogation of Jesus by Pilate to the completely different situation of the dialogue between Pilate and the crowd about the amnesty.[95] We may legitimately ask how did the interrogation end? If Pilate was baffled at Jesus' refusal to answer the accusations of the Jewish leaders, certain obvious courses of action were open. He could, presumably, have tortured Jesus, if he felt it to be necessary to secure information from the prisoner himself.[96] If, on the other hand, he was already convinced of Jesus' innocence, as Mark seems to suggest, he could have released Jesus, perhaps with an order to conduct himself more discreetly, backed up by a cautionary beating.[97] Pilate had both the authority and the power thus to dismiss the case; but as an able and experienced magistrate, responsible to the Emperor for maintaining peace and good order in Judaea, he would surely have wanted very good reason for dismissing the charges brought by the Jewish leaders.[98] These men were authorised to take such action, and they were fulfilling their duty in delivering Jesus to him, if they had evidence of his seditious conduct. Moreover, the very fact that the chief priests had handed one of their own nationals over to him charged with sedition would surely have constituted a weighty presumption of his guilt. If Pilate had intuitively doubted the truth of the accusations brought by the chief priests, for this is what Mark seems to suggest, he had one very obvious and convenient solution. He could have postponed a decision there in Jerusalem, and called the case for trial at his own headquarters in Caesarea, thus allowing time for further investigation. Somewhat similar action was taken later by Claudius Lysias, the garrison commander in Jerusalem, in the case of Paul: fearing that Paul would not get a fair trial in Jerusalem, he sent him to the governor at Caesarea.[99]

The most reasonable conclusion, therefore, which we can draw from the situation as it is known to us, is that Pilate, unless he had had good cause for acting otherwise, would have accepted the case presented against Jesus by the Jewish authorities and ordered his execution. And the fact that he did indeed execute Jesus as a rebel obviously confirms that conclusion. Only Mark's insertion of the Barabbas episode, in the curious form in which he presents it, contradicts this legitimate and natural conclusion.

But, the Barabbas episode not only interrupts the logical sequence of events from Pilate's interrogation of Jesus to his ordering of his execution, it also presents an incredible situation. For, quite apart from the question of the historicity of the alleged custom, it depicts a most extraordinary and illogical transaction. We are asked to believe that a tough-minded Roman governor bargained with a Jewish mob for the release of a prisoner in his custody, whom he knew to be innocent.[100] This governor, moreover, possessed a strong military force, capable of backing his decision to release the prisoner, if he so chose, or to transfer his case to Caesarea for re-trial. And that is not all: we are told, without explanation, of the chief priests' ability to persuade a crowd, whose support of Jesus a few days before they had so greatly feared, to demand his crucifixion.[101]

We must notice now another aspect of Mark's account. Although he does not explicitly say so, it is evident that he intends to imply that Pilate, in order to save Jesus, presented the crowd with a choice between Barabbas and Jesus.[102] Matthew, following and expanding Mark's narrative, makes this choice quite clear: 'So when they had gathered, Pilate said to them, "Whom do you want me to release for you, Barabbas or Jesus who is called Christ?" For he knew that it was out of envy that they had delivered him up.'[103] Now, when we recall that, according to Mark, Jesus was pro-Roman in his attitude to the tribute question,[104] for Pilate to have sought to save Jesus by causing the crowd to choose between him and Barabbas, makes Pilate a fool beyond belief. On Mark's own showing, Pilate was offering a Jewish crowd the release of either a patriot, who had fought against their hated Roman oppressors, or of one who had declared that it was their duty to pay tribute to heathen Rome. Indeed, if Pilate had wanted to destroy Jesus instead of saving him, he could have devised no surer way—inevitably the crowd would ask for the release of the patriot Barabbas.

But Mark, in his endeavour to represent Pilate as convinced of Jesus' innocence, was not content to leave the matter there. As we have just seen, to achieve this, he makes the Roman governor a fool beyond compare in thus giving the Jewish mob such a choice. However, even if he had acted so foolishly, the mob's choice would only have deprived him of using the amnesty to release Jesus. He still had Jesus in his custody, at his own disposal. Yet, according to Mark, having received the crowd's answer about Barabbas, he goes on to ask them about Jesus' fate: 'Then what am I to do with the man whom you call the King of the Jews?' The implication of the question is that Pilate had not only to accede to the crowd's demand for the release of Barabbas, but he was obliged also to consult them about what he should do with Jesus. The very idea of such a situation is ludicrous in the extreme. Even on Mark's own showing, the Jewish leaders had handed Jesus over to Pilate for judgment, since he was the paramount judicial authority in the state. Now, in the Barabbas episode, not only is Pilate frustrated in his plan to amnesty Jesus, but he is also represented as having to accept the crowd's ruling about Jesus. And so we are treated with the preposterous spectacle of a Roman governor consulting a Jewish mob about a prisoner, whose innocence he acknowledges, and as replying weakly to their demand for his crucifixion: 'Why, what evil has he done?'[105]

Such an absurd presentation can be adequately explained in one way only: it resulted from Mark's concern to remove the scandal of the Roman crucifixion of Jesus. His purpose throughout the Barabbas episode is clearly twofold: to show that Pilate recognised the innocence of Jesus; and to exonerate Pilate from responsibility for the crucifixion of Jesus by representing him as compelled by the Jewish leaders and people to order the execution. Mark appears to invoke the episode, as a kind of desperate expedient, to explain away the intractable fact of the Roman cross after he had done all he could in emphasising the evil intent of the Jewish leaders. That his explanation depicted an impossible situation, which any acute and well-informed reader would have immediately detected, would not have worried Mark. His Roman Christian readers were no more critical or better informed than those of the apologist Tertullian, who, in the second century, had the temerity to assert that evidence existed in the public archives at Rome that, through a report, presumably, of Pontius Pilate, the Emperor Tiberius was convinced of Christ's divinity.[106]

It is thus intelligible that Mark's apologetical purpose led him to interrupt his narration of the Roman trial of Jesus with the Barabbas episode, which he used to explain how Pilate both testified to the innocence of Jesus and was forced to crucify him. But now we must face the question whether the episode was wholly of Mark's invention.

To begin with, we must note that the alleged custom of releasing one prisoner at the Passover, whether it was a privilege granted only by Pilate or observed by other procurators, is not confirmed by any other evidence. Attempts have been made to find examples of similar customs; but the instances are very few and afford no convincing parallels.[107] Moreover, the fact that Josephus mentions no such custom is especially serious; for, though this might be deemed an *argumentum a silentio*, its witness is particularly cogent here. For this Jewish historian was concerned to show his Gentile readers the various privileges which the Jews enjoyed from the Romans, in token of their mutual accord:[108] it would indeed be strange, therefore, that he should have neglected to mention so extraordinary a custom as that described by Mark and the other Evangelists. Next, there is the inherent improbability of such a custom to consider. Since there is no evidence that such a custom was a traditional Jewish practice at the time of the annexation of Judaea to the Roman Empire, if such a custom did exist, it must have been a Roman creation; but on whose authority? The Emperor's or the procurator's? Mark represents it as Pilate's own custom, which would seem unlikely without imperial endorsement. If it had imperial endorsement, we should have to ask why Tiberius should have granted such an extraordinary privilege to the Jews only? However, more serious are the administrative and security objections. Judaea was seething with unrest from the natural Jewish resentment of the Roman yoke and the activities of the Zealots. For the Roman governor to have been obliged, by a self-imposed custom, to release at each Passover a prisoner, chosen by the Jewish crowd, would have been a most grave handicap to the maintenance of peace and good order. If Mark's evidence is to be believed, at this particular Passover, Pilate was obliged to release a dangerous rebel, doubtless a Zealot leader, who had recently been responsible for a serious insurrection.[109]

When all these grave objections are considered to Mark's assertion that such a custom existed, it seems necessary to conclude that he has in some way misrepresented some incident that occurred at the time of Jesus' trial in Jerusalem. This seems to be a sounder conclusion than to dismiss the Barabbas episode as a complete fabrication of Mark's. For certain incidental remarks in his account suggest derivation from a tradition of which he was well informed, but which he was reluctant to disclose fully to his readers. Thus, his reference to 'the insurrection' reveals his knowledge of a well-known event at that time.[110] Then his premature mention of Barabbas, which we noted, indicates his preoccupation with a rebel leader whose fate, as he knew, had been linked with that of Jesus on this fateful occasion. It is significant also that Pilate, when he refers to Jesus during this Barabbas episode, uses the loaded expression 'the

King of the Jews'.[111] Finally, the chief priests are described as prompting the people to ask for the release of Barabbas—he was evidently not the people's spontaneous choice.[112]

The evidence of these various points indicates some incident in Jerusalem at this time which resulted in Pilate's ordering the execution of Jesus, instead of that of a notable rebel named Barabbas.[113] Since Mark's depiction of the matter cannot be accepted as authentic, we must endeavour to relate the bare fact that there was some decisive connection between Jesus and Barabbas to what other evidence we have.

The first, and surely the most significant fact, of which the Barabbas episode informs us, is that an insurrection had recently taken place. How recently and where it had happened is not disclosed by Mark. Luke, however, locates it in Jerusalem,[114] and there is every reason for thinking that it had occurred very recently; for the Passover, which crowded Jerusalem with pilgrims, provided a most opportune occasion for a rising.[115] Now, the coincidence, or very near coincidence, of Jesus' attack in the Temple, with an insurrection also in the city, which Roman forces had quelled with some loss, must surely be regarded as significant. Jerusalem was a small place, and it is difficult to believe that the two commotions would not have been related in some way, if only in the minds of the authorities. That Barabbas was a Zealot is most probable,[116] and of the religious inspiration of the Zealots' opposition to Rome we are now well acquainted. We may, therefore, legitimately infer that this insurrection had been religiously inspired as Jesus' action had been in the Temple. Could the two movements, happening about the same time, have also been linked in both principle and purpose? We are not told where in Jerusalem the action against the Romans, in which Barabbas was involved, had occurred. If it had been directed against one or both of the chief Roman centres in the city, the two obvious locations would be the Antonia fortress on the north-western side of the Temple, and the Herodian palace in the upper city.[117] An attack on the Romans in the Antonia, coincident with Jesus' attack in the Temple, would have constituted an intelligible pattern of insurrectionary action, designed to involve at one time the forces both of the procurator and the high priest.[118] That both operations, though seriously challenging these authorities, had failed, is significant, and further supports the likelihood that they were concerted.

The hypothesis, which we have explored, is reasonable, and it provides an intelligible explanation of the sparse but suggestive evidence of the momentous events which took place in Jerusalem at that Passover feast. It can only remain an hypothesis, since our sources are so baffling in their tendentious narratives. However, the indubitable fact that the fate of Jesus was linked with that of Barabbas, and that Pilate ordered the execution of Jesus for sedition instead of that of Barabbas certainly requires some more convincing explanation than is provided by Mark.

Now, as we have noted, Jesus' action in the Temple would doubtless have been associated in the minds of the authorities with that in which Barabbas was implicated, even if the two actions were not in fact connected.[119] Hence both authorities, Roman and Jewish, would have been predisposed to regard Jesus and Barabbas as being fellow-conspirators. The fact that Mark shows the chief priests as prompting the people to demand the release of Barabbas may well represent his specially angled version of what did actually happen, though in a somewhat different way. It is feasible that the Jewish leaders in presenting their case against Jesus, represented him to be the real leader of the insurrection, instead of Barabbas. That Mark depicts Pilate as using the title 'King of the Jews' for Jesus, would further support this interpretation.[120] Jesus, acclaimed as the Messiah and accorded the royal title, would obviously appear as the more dangerous of the two. Hence Pilate decided to make him the example of the fate that awaited any who aspired to kingship against Caesar. The fact, moreover, that Mark records that Pilate ordered two *lēstai* to be crucified on either side of Jesus significantly confirms this interpretation.[121] For as we have seen, *lēstai* ('brigands') was the customary pejorative for Zealots—to Pilate's mind, it was fitting that the 'King of the Jews' should pay the price of rebellion between two of his accomplices, captured in the recent insurrection which he was believed to have led.[122]

The mocking of Jesus by the Roman soldiers, after his sentencing and scourging, affords cruel but significant evidence of how these men also understood the ambition of Jesus.[123] Mark's vivid description surely derives from the original Jewish Christian portrayal of Jesus as the Messiah-King, martyred for Israel by its heathen oppressors:

> And the soldiers led him away inside the palace (that is, the *praetorium*); and they called together the whole battalion. And they clothed him in a purple cloak, and plaiting a crown of thorns they put it on him. And they began to salute him, 'Hail, King of the Jews!' And they struck his head with a reed, and spat on him, and they knelt in homage to him. And when they had mocked him, they stripped him of the purple cloak, and put his own clothes on him. And they led him out to crucify him.[124]

The intention of this burlesque is obvious: to the Roman troops, Jesus was a rebel who claimed to be a king. But there is reason for thinking that some of their horse-play had a meaning not immediately apparent to us. The 'crown of thorns' certainly seems to be a mock-crown of royalty and a thing of torment.[125] It could, however, have also been intended by the soldiers to have been a mocking surrogate for the radiate crown of the divinised king or emperor.[126] Further, the smiting of the head of Jesus with a reed might be intelligible as an act of comic abuse; but a reed seems a rather ineffective thing to use when more hurting implements would surely have lain at hand in a barrack-room. The reed, however, becomes more appropriate when it is known that its name in Aramaic was *qana*, sounding thus like the word for 'Zealot' (*qannāyā*).[127] Since these Roman troops doubtless had a working knowledge of Aramaic, their seemingly strange action of hitting Jesus with a reed had a grim symbolism—regarding their prisoner as a Zealot leader, they mockingly smote him with a 'zealot', doubtless enjoying their punning joke.[128]

That it was the political aspect of Jesus that inspired the form of the soldiers' horse-play is consistent with the political aspect of his trial, and also with the form of death decreed for him—crucifixion was the usual Roman punishment in Judaea for sedition, and countless Zealots died that way.[129] On Golgotha, where the penalty was enacted, it was the political aspect of Jesus that was publicly announced as the cause of his execution: 'And the inscription of the charge against him read, "The King of the Jews".'[130] Then, if the tradition, which evidently underlies Mark's account of the drama on Golgotha, is to be trusted, Jesus' action in the Temple as well as his political claims were the subjects on which he was derided as he hung dying on the Roman cross.[131] And of especial significance is it that the chief priests are represented as connecting both the Messianic and royal title in their taunt about Jesus' inability to save himself:

> . . . the chief priests mocked him to one and another with the scribes, saying, 'He saved others; he cannot save himself. Let the Christ, the King of Israel, come down now from the cross, that we may see and believe.'[132]

As Josephus records, the *goētes*, or wonder-working Messianic pretenders, offered the people 'signs of deliverance'.[133] Now, in the hour of his agony and defeat, the Jewish leaders mockingly reminded Jesus of his own message of salvation and the kingdom that he would restore to Israel.

As we have already seen, Mark added to the original story of the martyrdom of Jesus the account of the two incidents that so aptly concluded his *apologia ad Christianos Romanos*. The Rending of the Temple Veil at the moment of Jesus' death symbolised the obsolescence of the Temple cultus, which the Roman destruction of the shrine in AD 70 did in fact achieve.[134] And the Roman centurion's recognition of the divinity of the dying Jesus symbolised Gentile sympathy in contrast to Jewish hate.[135]

18   Betrayal of Judas Iscariot

19   The Sanhedrin trial

Sixth-century mosaics in the basilica of Sant' Apollinare Nuovo, Ravenna (see p. 159)

20 Arrest of Christ; Peter's denial; Christ before Annas and Caiaphas; Pilate washing his hands

Ivory lipsanotheca, late fourth century Museo Civico dell' Età Cristiana, Brescia (see p. 158)

21 Judgment of Pilate

22 Christ on the way to Calvary; Simon bears the cross

Sixth-century mosaics in basilica of Sant' Apollinare Nouvo, Ravenna (see p. 159)

The account of the burial of Jesus, which follows,[136] appears to belong to a different cycle of tradition from that concerning the trial and execution of Jesus. Although Pilate and the centurion are both involved in the transaction that led to the burial of Jesus in the tomb prepared by Joseph of Arimathea, the purpose of the account is to explain how Jesus came to be buried in a private sepulchre and not in the common fosse. [137] The story was doubtless designed originally to rebut Jewish objections to the presentation of Jesus as the *Messias redivivus*, who would shortly return on the clouds of the heaven to complete his Messianic role.[138] To show that Jesus had not just disappeared into an anonymous common grave, Joseph of Arimathea's petition to Pilate for the crucified body was cited. From the tomb in which Joseph placed it, it could be argued that God had raised up the body of Jesus, because that tomb, so it was claimed, had subsequently been found empty by the disciples.[139] The claim provoked the counter-claim, recorded in Matthew's Gospel, that the disciples had, themselves, stolen away the body.[140] However, the story of the Empty Tomb, as proof of the Resurrection of Jesus, appertains to a different issue from that of the trial of Jesus with which we are concerned.[141]

Our analysis of Mark's account of the two trials of Jesus, unavoidably complicated as it has been, has revealed the way in which he shaped the original tradition of the Jerusalem Christians to serve his own apologetical purpose. That tradition was primarily concerned to show that Jesus' crucifixion had not negated his claims to be the Messiah. This Jerusalem apologia was accordingly orientated to present Jesus as the martyred Messiah of Israel, killed by the Romans and their Jewish collaborators.[142] Although one of its chief points of concern was to refute the accusation that Jesus had threatened the Temple, this apologia of the Jerusalem Christians was not embarrassed by the fact that the Romans had executed Jesus for sedition—indeed, death on that charge enhanced his reputation as the martyred Messiah of Israel.

Very different was the concern of Mark. For him, and for the Christians of Rome for whom he wrote, the Roman cross was a scandal and offence. The fact that the Romans had crucified Jesus as a rebel was too well known to be ignored; it could only be explained away. How Mark sought to do this in his Gospel we have seen at length. Obliged to follow the apologia of the Jerusalem Christians, he amended it with some skill, so as to make Pilate a witness to the innocence of Jesus, instead of the judge who decreed his death. To counterbalance this exoneration of Pilate from responsibility for the death of Jesus, Mark portrayed the Jewish leaders as planning to destroy Jesus from the very start of his ministry. These leaders, having succeeded in trapping

Jesus and condemning him to death for blasphemy, finally force a reluctant Pilate to crucify him.[143]

Mark's presentation, however, is essentially a *tour de force* that persuades on a cursory reading, but will not stand up to detailed scrutiny. Its weak links and absurdities are quickly discerned, and it is well to enumerate them: the failure to explain why the Jewish leaders, having condemned Jesus for blasphemy, hand him over to Pilate; the failure to specify the charges, obviously political, which the Jewish leaders brought against Jesus at Pilate's tribunal; the sudden switch from relating the outcome of Pilate's enquiry into the case against Jesus to recounting the Barabbas episode; the neglect to explain why Pilate, convinced of Jesus' innocence, did not release him but sought to save him by invoking the alleged custom of the amnesty; the ludicrous situation of Pilate's having to ask the Jewish mob what he should do with Jesus after they had chosen Barabbas; Pilate's idiotic action in giving the Jewish mob a choice between the patriot Barabbas and the pro-Roman Jesus, if he wanted thus to save Jesus; the sudden ability of the Jewish leaders to persuade the mob against Jesus, when they had so thoroughly feared its support of Jesus on the previous day.

The logic of this catalogue of discrepancies is obvious—Mark had to contend with facts too intractable for his apologetical purpose. For Pilate had accepted the evidence laid against Jesus by the Jewish authorities and, in consequence, he had ordered his crucifixion for sedition. Fortunately, in his endeavour to use the Barabbas episode to show why Pilate sentenced Jesus, though recognising his innocence, Mark has unwittingly provided us with valuable evidence about the situation in Jerusalem at that fateful Passover. Thus he reveals the crucial fact that an insurrection had taken place about the same time as Jesus' action in the Temple. And so we may legitimately conclude that the two events were doubtless associated in the minds of the authorities, even if not in fact, and that the Jewish leaders presented Jesus, instead of Barabbas, as the real rebel leader, deserving of exemplary execution.

CHAPTER FIVE

Other Versions of the Trial of Jesus: the Gospels of Matthew, Luke and John

To Mark belongs the unique distinction of publishing the first account of the trial and crucifixion of Jesus, integrated into a biographical narrative of his career. That account, as we have seen, was essentially an apologetical interpretation of a Jerusalemite Christian tradition, which also had an apologetical purpose, though one that significantly differed from that of Mark. For Mark's interpretation was designed to answer the needs of the Christian community in Rome, and it reflects the situation of that community shortly after the Flavian triumph in AD 71. By setting his interpretation of the trial of Jesus in the sequence of Jesus' career, Mark cleverly succeeded in explaining the Roman execution of Jesus as the achievement of the long-determined purpose of the Jewish leaders to destroy him. But Mark also succeeded in doing more than this. He provided his fellow-Christians in Rome with a convincing interpretation, presented in graphic narrative-form, of what was basically a very paradoxical situation. For they had been taught to believe that Jesus, a Jew whom the Romans had executed as a rebel, was the incarnate Son of God and the Saviour of mankind. Of this puzzling and embarrassing involvement of Jesus in Jewish-Roman politics, Mark had given them a welcome solution: Jesus had been the innocent victim of Jewish malice, and his divinity had been first perceived by a non-Jew at the very moment when God had signified his abrogation of the Temple cultus.[1]

Mark had written primarily with the needs of his fellow-believers in Rome in mind; but he had, unwittingly, pioneered an interpretation of the career of Jesus which was destined to form the foundational pattern of all subsequent Christian thought. How quickly, and by what means, his Gospel came to be known to other Christian communities in the Roman Empire we have no certain knowledge. The Christian Church in Rome was obviously one with which other Christian communities, after the disappearance of the Mother Church of Jerusalem, were likely to have communication.[2] Hence, the Gospel of Mark would soon have become known outside the Roman Church, and doubtless copies were quickly made and circulated in other churches.[3] Acquaintance with the new work seems to have had a twofold effect in certain places. The Gospel was evidently very influential; yet its presentation of the life of Jesus was not regarded as sacrosanct. It provoked emulation; but, although attempts were made to improve its record according to current needs, the basic pattern of its presentation was generally followed.[4]

Three attempts, dating from the last decades of the first century, to improve on Mark's Gospel have survived, and they are known to us severally as the Gospels of Matthew, Luke and John.[5] Although each is longer than the Markan Gospel and is distinguished by its use of material peculiar to itself, these later compositions provide evidence of the existence of only one other important source of information about Jesus not used by Mark. This is a collection of sayings of Jesus, known professionally to New Testament scholars as Q (from the German Quelle='source').[6] Among these sayings there seems, however, to have been nothing of significance, relating to the trial and crucifixion of Jesus, which the writers of these other Gospels thought to be worth preserving. Consequently, we have to conclude that, apart from certain minor episodes which we shall discuss, no tradition about the trial and crucifixion of Jesus existed other than that used originally by Mark.[7]

Whether the authors of the Gospels of Matthew, Luke and John had direct access to the tradition of the Jerusalem Christians, which Mark had used for his account of the trial, is unknown. Since Matthew follows Mark's version very closely, in fact almost literally, it would seem that he did not have such access, or, if he had, he preferred to use Mark's version.[8] Luke presents a more difficult problem: he adds an episode not found in the Markan account,[9] and specifies the Jewish charges against Jesus at Pilate's tribunal; yet he omits completely the charge about Jesus' threatening the Temple which, as we have seen, formed the chief concern of the Jerusalemite tradition.[10] John's account of the trial of Jesus is even more puzzling in this connection. He seems to be mindful of Mark's version, which he appears to amend or supplement in places.[11] However, although he gives the impression of having access to special information about the political background of Jesus' arrest, it seems improbable that he was drawing directly on the apologia of the Jerusalem Christians.[12] We may reasonably infer, therefore, that the authors of these three Gospels possessed no important information about the trial of Jesus which enabled them significantly to supplement Mark's account. They wrote, mindful of Mark's account, to present the trial and execution of Jesus according to their own particular viewpoints and their estimate of the needs of those for whom they wrote. On some minor points they doubtless had information which Mark did not have or did not choose to disclose;[13] but generally their accounts reveal more about their own outlook than increase our knowledge about the trial of Jesus. However, since each is an individual evaluation, each account merits separate consideration. Moreover, since these three Gospels were also incorporated into the canon of the New Testament, they were accorded the same sacred authority by Christians as the Gospel of Mark, and in some respects their presentations of the trial have been more influential than that of Mark.[14]

It will be well to commence our study of these other accounts of the trial by examining that in the Gospel of Matthew, and comparing it with Mark's version. For, as we have seen from earlier studies, there is much reason for thinking that Matthew's Gospel was written in Alexandria, and that it reflects the critical situation of the Christian community there after the fall of Jerusalem in AD 70.[15] A convenient starting-point for our enquiry is provided by Matthew's version of the arrest of Jesus in Gethsemane.[16] As we have already seen,[17] Matthew adds to Mark's guarded account the information that it was one of Jesus' disciples who resisted the arrest by drawing his sword and cutting off the ear of the slave of the high priest. Matthew uses the incident to present Jesus as repudiating armed violence to further his cause. The saying which he attributes to Jesus on this occasion must have had a specific reference as we saw, because as a general axiom it is manifestly untrue: 'Put your sword back into its place; for all who take the sword will perish by the sword.' The saying would surely have been understood by Matthew's readers as referring to the Jerusalem Christians, who had joined the revolt against Rome and perished in consequence. This repudiation of armed resistance and revolt characterises Matthew's Gospel, and it inspired, as we saw, his concept of the Pacific Christ.[18] The author's primary concern in developing this theme was undoubtedly similar to that of the leaders of the Jewish community in Alexandria. As Josephus tells us, these leaders, warned by the disaster that had befallen their nation in Judaea, were intent on preventing rebellion by their people in Alexandria and Egypt, among whom survivors of the Sicarii of Judaea were spreading their seditious propaganda.[19] The Jewish Christian community, for which Matthew wrote, would not have been immune from such dangers, especially if, as seems likely, refugees from the Jewish Christians of Judaea, burning with hatred for Rome, had joined it.[20] However, in seeking to damp down such feeling by presenting Jesus as desisting from calling to his aid twelve legions of angels to combat the legions of Rome,[21] Matthew was evidently much preoccupied also with the fate of his nation and the destruction of its holy city.

A significant indication of this preoccupation is to be seen in the parable of the Marriage Feast,[22] and it adumbrates the fateful addition which Matthew makes to Mark's account of the Trial of Jesus, as we shall see. In reproducing this parable, the source of which is obscure,[23] Matthew was intent on making it fit exactly the Jewish tragedy of AD 70. The invited guests are depicted as not only despising the king's invitation to attend the marriage feast of his son; they also ill-treat and kill his servants.[24] Consequently, 'the king was angry, and he sent his troops and destroyed those murderers and burned their city'.[25] Quite clearly, Matthew is here interpreting the catastrophe that had befallen his people. As a Jewish Christian, he instinctively sought its cause in his compatriots' rejection of Jesus. The parable, as a whole, in Matthew's interpretation, is really a philosophy of recent Jewish history as seen by a Jew who was also a Christian. His own people were the rightfully invited guests to the Messianic banquet; they refuse the invitation and persecute God's messenger; divine anger falls upon them; their place at the Messianic banquet is then taken by Gentiles. The final verses of the parable reflect the sad resignation of a Jewish Christian to the resulting entry of the Gentiles into what was rightfully Israel's heritage. The king says to his servants: '"The wedding is ready, but those invited were not worthy. Go therefore to the thoroughfares, and invite to the marriage feast as many as you find." And those servants went out into the streets and gathered all whom they found, both bad and good; so that the wedding hall was filled with guests.'[26] Matthew adds, as a kind of appendix to this parable, the curious little parable of the guest without a wedding garment, which reveals his anxiety about the entry of Gentiles into Israel's heritage without the necessary preparation of the Jewish Law.[27]

Writing thus a decade or so after the composition of Mark's Gospel, and with that Gospel before him, Matthew was moved by its example to compose an account of the career of Jesus, specially designed for his fellow-Christians in Alexandria who were mostly Jews like himself. With this purpose in mind, and preoccupied, as we have seen, by the catastrophe of AD 70, Matthew was duly faced with the task of presenting the trial of Jesus. He evidently accepted Mark's account of it, and he decided to reproduce it in his own Gospel, making just those amendments that he deemed necessary from his own point of view.[28]

Mark's version of the Sanhedrin's proceedings seems to have needed but slight amendment, intended apparently to elucidate its record on the points concerned. Thus Matthew adds the name, omitted by Mark, of the high priest Caiaphas, to whose residence Jesus was taken after his arrest.[29] In his account of the accusation brought against Jesus of threatening the Temple, Matthew is careful to mention that the accusation was made by two witnesses, thus conforming to the requirements of the sacred Law, as his Jewish readers would have understood.[30] In the place of Mark's simple statement that the high priest asked Jesus if he was the Messiah, Matthew represents the high priest as saying: 'I adjure you by the living God, tell us if you are the Christ [Messiah], the Son of God.'[31] What this more dramatic presentation, together with Jesus' less direct answer, was intended to convey beyond Mark's simpler record is not clear.[32] Jesus' reply, according to Matthew, cannot surely have been intended to mean less than Mark's version: 'I am.'[33] The next notable variant occurs in Matthew's account of the early morning meeting of the Sanhedrin. Instead of Mark's obscure statement, which we have noted, that the Jewish leaders and other members of the Sanhedrin, 'having prepared a consultation, and bound Jesus, led him away and delivered him to Pilate', Matthew writes:

> When morning came, all the chief priests and the elders of the people took counsel against Jesus to put him to death (*hōste thanatōsai auton*); and they bound him and led him away and delivered him to Pilate the governor.[34]

Careful comparison with Mark's statement, however, reveals no real elucidation of the reason for this apparent second meeting of the Sanhedrin. Matthew reproduces the pattern of Mark's narrative, namely, the interweaving of the story of Peter's denial with the account of the nocturnal interrogation of Jesus by the high priest and the Sanhedrin.[35] And he also follows Mark in concluding this transaction with the Sanhedrin's decision that Jesus deserved death for blasphemy.[36] Consequently, his addition to Mark's cryptic statement about the morning meeting of the Sanhedrin, that its purpose was to put Jesus to death, does not really give any further information, unless it is interpreted as implementing the decision taken at the end of the Sanhedrin's nocturnal session. Thus, it would be feasible that, if the nocturnal session had really been a trial which ended with a formal verdict of death for blasphemy, the Sanhedrin might have met again in the morning to make arrangements for the execution of their sentence. This would have meant obtaining Pilate's confirmation for the stoning of Jesus to death.[37] However, the fact that Jesus did not die this way, but by Roman crucifixion for sedition, together with the fact that Matthew follows Mark in his account of the Roman trial, precludes this interpretation. What is quite evident is that Matthew followed Mark as closely in his account of a morning meeting of the Sanhedrin as he did in his account of the nocturnal proceedings. His addition, therefore, to Mark's statement, that the Sanhedrin met in the morning 'to put Jesus to death' must be adjudged as being merely a reference back to the verdict at the night session.[38]

But one thing that does emerge clearly from these considerations, and it is of great significance for us, is that Matthew was unable to elucidate Mark's cryptic statement about a second meeting of the Sanhedrin in the morning, following on its meeting during the previous night. However, as our earlier discussion of this matter showed, Mark's account of these Sanhedrin transactions is not to be evaluated primarily as a record of historical fact, but as apologetic.[39] Mark was concerned to show that the Jewish leaders were responsible for the crucifixion of Jesus, and not Pilate. Hence, he represents the Jewish investigation as a Sanhedrin trial of Jesus, ending with his condemnation to death for blasphemy. In the further pursuit of his apologetical theme, he interweaves his narrative of the Sanhedrin proceedings with the story of Peter's denial. Then, having to prepare his readers for the consequent paradox of Jesus' execution by the Romans for sedition after being sentenced by the Sanhedrin for blasphemy, he seeks to bridge the gap by his cryptic account of a morning session of the Sanhedrin, which results in Jesus' being handed over to Pilate on an unspecified charge. That Matthew reproduces this obviously artificial composition cogently confirms what we have inferred on other grounds: that Matthew had at his disposal no information that enabled him significantly to amend Mark's version of the trial of Jesus. And to that conclusion we may add a further observation: if Matthew had had access to the Jerusalemite Christian tradition, which underlay Mark's account, it is unlikely that his own version would show just the same evasiveness as Mark's about the nature of the offence with which the Jewish leaders charged Jesus before Pilate's tribunal.[40]

This conclusion, that Matthew was essentially dependent upon Mark's version of the Sanhedrin proceedings, also holds for all that he says of the trial before Pilate. For, not only does he not specify the charge brought against Jesus by the chief priests and elders, but he similarly depicts Pilate as asking Jesus, apparently at random, 'Are you the King of the Jews?'[41] Further, his whole account of the Roman trial, which was obviously the most crucial episode in the sequence of events which ended with the execution of Jesus, is equally as meagre and cryptic as Mark's. Surely, it must be asked, if Matthew had possessed more information, he would have expanded Mark's inadequate record of the decisive affair that took place before the tribunal of Pilate?

Matthew's treatment of the Barabbas episode provides more positive evidence of his own interpretation of the trial. He gives the impression of seeking to enhance Mark's account of the matter by inserting two otherwise unknown incidents concerning Pilate's conduct during the strange transaction. To facilitate our evaluation of these additions, it will be well to have the relevant part of Matthew's narrative before us:

Now at the feast the governor was accustomed to release for the crowd any one prisoner whom they wanted. And they had then a notorious prisoner [Jesus who was] called Barabbas.[42] So when they had gathered, Pilate said to them, 'Whom do you want me to release for you, [Jesus who is called] Barabbas or Jesus who is called Christ?' For he knew that it was out of envy that they had delivered him up. Besides, while he was sitting on the judgment seat, his wife sent word to him, 'Have nothing to do with that righteous man, for I have suffered much over him today in a dream.' Now the chief priests and elders persuaded the people to ask for Barabbas and destroy Jesus. The governor again said to them, 'Which of the two do you want me to release for you?' And they said, 'Barabbas'. Pilate said to them, 'Then what shall I do with Jesus who is called Christ?' They all said, 'Let him be crucified.' And he said, 'Why, what evil has he done?' But they shouted all the more, 'Let him be crucified.' So when Pilate saw that he was gaining nothing, but rather that a riot was beginning, he took water and washed his hands before the crowd, saying, 'I am innocent of this man's blood; see to it yourselves.' And all the people answered, 'His blood be on us and on our children!' Then he released for them Barabbas, and having scourged Jesus, delivered him to be crucified.[43]

This elaboration of the Barabbas episode by Matthew provides an even more dramatic *montage* than Mark's, and it has impressed itself indelibly on the Christian imagination, with some terrible consequences. On analysis, however, it is seen to be as much dependent on Mark's account as is the preceding narrative. It proves, accordingly, if further proof were needed, that the Barabbas episode, as it has been preserved in Christian tradition, is the invention of Mark from some original incident which we have endeavoured to reconstruct.[44]

Matthew, in editing the Markan version, makes it clear that Pilate offered the crowd a choice between Jesus and Barabbas; he thus interprets the obvious implication of Mark's account, as we have seen.[45] It would appear also that he felt that he could abbreviate Mark's account, probably in the interest of his own material which he intended to introduce, by omitting Mark's description of Barabbas and the crowd's initiative in asking for the amnesty (*Mk.* xv:7-8). The omission, however, is not carefully done, and it results in the awkward unsupported plural participle, 'when they were gathered', in verse 17.[46] The omission, however, does not help him to avoid the discrepancy in Mark's account between the time and place of the Roman trial and where and when the Barabbas episode occurred. As we saw, by breaking off suddenly from his account of the trial before Pilate's tribunal and switching to the Barabbas episode, Mark produces the awkward impression of the chief priests being left standing at the tribunal, owing to Pilate's sudden departure to deal with the crowd's request, and their unexplained appearance, immediately after, in control of the crowd.[47] Matthew's handling of Mark's version actually makes for greater confusion in this respect. He switches as suddenly from the tribunal scene to the Barabbas episode, which appears to be located in some place where a crowd can gather; then, in introducing the incident concerning the dream of Pilate's wife, the scene is back again at the tribunal.[48] After this interlude, the scene is changed to the activity of the Jewish leaders in persuading the crowd to ask for Barabbas.[49]

This rather inept editing of Mark's account was obviously due to Matthew's desire to insert the story of the intervention of Pilate's wife. He uses the story to reinforce Mark's statement, which he reproduces, that Pilate knew that the Jewish leaders had delivered Jesus 'through envy'.[50] Possibly he felt that this statement was insufficient to explain how the Roman governor knew that Jesus was innocent.[51] The story of the intervention of Pilate's wife dramatically attests Jesus' innocence, especially in view of the importance attached to dreams in ancient society.[52] The lady's dream was tantamount to a supernatural revelation of the innocence of Jesus, as well as a warning to Pilate not to involve himself in the murderous intent of the Jewish leaders. What was the source of Matthew's story, or whether it was his own invention, is unknown: it is perhaps significant of the novelty of the story that Pilate's wife is not named, as she is in later Christian legend.[53] Of the essential purpose of the tale in the context of Matthew's presentation of the trial of Jesus there can be no doubt. It was intended both to explain Pilate's recognition of the innocence of Jesus, and to prepare for the symbolic act by which, according to Matthew, Pilate repudiated responsibility for the death of Jesus and the Jews eagerly accepted it. To that act and its significance for Matthew's interpretation of the death of Jesus, and the awful consequences which its record has had for the Jewish people, we must now turn our attention.

Matthew follows Mark's account of the Barabbas episode, apparently oblivious of its manifest improbabilities; indeed, he even heightens those improbabilities by making clearer the choice, implied by Mark, which Pilate offered the crowd between Jesus and Barabbas.[54] He also follows Mark's incredible statement that, after the crowd had chosen Barabbas, Pilate went on to ask them what he should do with Jesus.[55] Matthew then uses the crowd's demand that Jesus be crucified, as recorded by Mark, to introduce his ill-fated account of Pilate's public repudiation of responsibility for the death of Jesus. Accordingly, he represents Pilate as realising that it was hopeless to oppose further the crowd's savage demand, and that to persist in his attempt to save

Jesus would cause a riot.[56] Consequently, he performs the symbolic act of washing his hands. This ritual ablution was a Jewish, not a Roman, custom, and its significance would have been understood by Matthew's Jewish Christian readers.[57] Pilate's accompanying statement is clearly intended to be a formal and definitive repudiation of his responsibility for the death of Jesus: 'I am innocent of this man's blood; see to it yourselves.'[58]

That Matthew could describe such a piece of play-acting as constituting a valid repudiation of responsibility, without some comment on its specious nature, reveals how powerful was the motive which impelled him in so doing. He had thus to exculpate the Roman so absolutely, in order to remove an obvious objection to his own interpretation of the death of Jesus. For he was obviously conscious of the fact that Jesus had, after all, been executed by the Romans for sedition, and from that fact it could be argued that the Jews could not be held as primarily responsible. Accordingly, he anticipates such an objection by a twofold attestation. First, he represents Pilate as disavowing publicly responsibility for his decision; then, he describes the willing acceptance of the Jews of this responsibility—'And all the people answered, "His blood be on us, and on our children!"'[59]

No more unequivocal acceptance of guilt for the death of Jesus could be devised than that which Matthew, himself a Jew, attributes here to his own compatriots. He wrote, however, as a Christian Jew for fellow-believers of his own race, to interpret the death of Jesus in the light of the catastrophe that had befallen his people in AD 70. He saw that terrible disaster as the self-invoked penalty that Israel had incurred through rejecting and killing its Messiah.[60] Wholly exonerating the Romans who had actually executed Jesus as a rebel against their government in Judaea, Matthew chose thus to make those of his own nation who rejected Jesus, exclusively guilty of the awful deed. But he little knew, when he represented them as eagerly shouting: 'His blood be on us, and on our children!', what a terrible legacy he was thus imposing upon subsequent generations of his own people. For those fierce words came to be enshrined in the sacred scriptures of the Christian Church, where they were seen as the self-confession of the Jews to the murder of Christ. In the succeeding centuries, down to this present age, those words have inspired hatred for the Jews and justified their cruellest persecutions.[61] Indeed, it is one of the strange ironies of history that it is in the most Jewish of the four Gospels that the Jews are so dramatically portrayed as the murderers of Christ.[62]

Having thus added this fatal episode to Mark's account of the trial and sentencing of Jesus, Matthew continues to follow Mark's narrative of the mocking of Jesus and his crucifixion and death, with only a few minor deviations of no particular significance.[63] Indeed, evaluated as a whole, Matthew's account of the trial and execution of Jesus is essentially a reproduction of Mark's presentation, supplemented by the incidents concerning Pilate's wife and Pilate's public repudiation of responsibility for the death of Jesus. The effect of these additions is to exonerate the Romans and incriminate the Jews even more thoroughly than is done by Mark. However, Matthew's purpose was different from Mark's. For, whereas Mark was concerned to show the Gentile Christians of Rome that Jesus was loyal to Rome and Pilate was forced by the Jewish leaders to execute him,[64] Matthew was intent on interpreting the Jewish catastrophe of AD 70 to Jewish Christians as divine punishment for the death of Jesus. That Matthew exceeds Mark in his effort to exonerate Pilate was not primarily due to his desire to explain away the scandal of the Roman cross; it was motivated by his need to show that the Jews freely accepted the guilt of killing Jesus, for which they had so terribly paid in AD 70.[65]

The Gospel of Luke, in its account of the trial of Jesus, faces us with a different problem from that which has concerned us in comparing Matthew's version with that of Mark. Matthew follows carefully Mark's pattern of events, except for his addition of the two incidents discussed, which do not disrupt that pattern. Luke, however, while clearly mindful of Mark's version of the trial, makes certain omissions and one remarkable addition to the Markan pattern of events, which suggest that he may have had some supplementary information, even though the differences in his account are only of a minor nature and do not seriously challenge Mark's presentation.

To assess the significance of these differences from the Markan version of the trial, it is necessary to bear in mind certain general features of Luke's Gospel. There is unfortunately no clear indication of the Gospel's place of origin. It would seem probable that it was written at a considerable distance from Alexandria, where the Gospel of Matthew appears to have originated, and that it was intended for a Greek-speaking Gentile church.[66] Further, although it generally follows Mark's narrative framework and draws on Q, Luke's Gospel had access to various other material of somewhat secondary importance.[67] Its author's professed aim, as stated in the preface to his work, was 'to write an orderly account', in apparent contrast to the records of Jesus' life that already existed.[68] As we shall see, his account of the trial seems to be a 'rationalised' version of Mark's presentation, which may well explain some of its omissions from the Markan narrative. We should also note what is surely an indication of Luke's evaluation of the events which resulted in Jesus' condemnation and death. It occurs in a remark which he represents

Jesus as making to those who arrest him, and which is not given by Mark or Matthew: 'But this is your hour, and the power of darkness.'[69] The significance of these words is great. They reveal that, whereas the other two Evangelists were concerned with current problems arising from Jesus' trial and execution, Luke viewed these events from a more detached and theological point of view.[70]

This suggestion, that Luke viewed the trial of Jesus without that personal involvement in the consequences of the Jewish catastrophe in AD 70 which so profoundly influenced Mark and Matthew in their accounts, is supported by other evidence. The Gospel of Luke is the first of a two-volume study of the beginnings of Christianity, the second volume being the Acts of the Apostles.[71] This fact enables us to have a wider view of the outlook and methods of the author of the Gospel, whom we may conveniently call Luke.[72] His treatment of Christian Origins in the Acts of the Apostles, as we have already had cause to see, is a very tendentious one.[73] He was concerned to present an account of the spread of Christianity from Jerusalem to Rome, in which Paul is the great protagonist and the Jews the malevolent enemies of the new faith. In writing this account, Luke was evidently in possession of certain information about the original Jerusalem Church. How he acquired this information, writing as he did about two decades after the disappearance of the Jerusalem Church, is unknown. There is some possibility that he may have got it from the Christian community in Caesarea, with which he seems to have had some connection.[74] This community was probably mainly Gentile in membership; for Caesarea was the headquarters of the Roman government of Judaea, and predominantly a Hellenistic city.[75] However, although he had access of some kind to traditions about the original Christian church in Jerusalem, Luke selected and moulded those traditions to suit his own special interpretation of Christian Origins. Thus he omitted, for example, all mention of so important an event as the attempt of the Emperor Gaius to desecrate the Temple, and he is responsible for that curiously evasive picture of James, the brother of Jesus, which we noted.[76] The witness of such evidence is clear. Luke, despite his possession of some early traditions, was not concerned to write an accurate account of what really happened in those decisive years in Jerusalem. His purpose was to present an idealised picture, in accordance with his own theological and ecclesiastical interest.[77]

These inferences about Luke's outlook and methods, drawn from the Acts of the Apostles, greatly assist our evaluation of his account of the trial of Jesus in his Gospel. The two main points which concern us here are his handling of Mark's version and his introduction of an account of Jesus' trial before Herod, which does not appear in the other three Gospels.

In his account of the Sanhedrin proceedings, Luke diverges from the Markan narrative in two curious ways. He agrees with Mark in recording that Jesus was taken, after his arrest in Gethsemane, to the house of the high priest, and he also follows Mark in locating the story of Peter's denial there.[78] But, instead of interweaving this story with an account of Jesus' interrogation by the Sanhedrin, Luke omits the interrogation completely and gives the impression that the only notable happening in the house of the high priest was Peter's denial. This omission means that Luke says nothing of the charge brought against Jesus of threatening the Temple, which, as we have seen, was the chief issue in the original Jerusalemite apologia about the Sanhedrin 'trial'.[79] However, Luke reveals that he is still mindful of Mark's arrangement of events by recording, at the end of the story of Peter's denial, the ill-treatment of Jesus by the retainers of the high priest.[80] The passage is badly out of context, and contains an unsupported pronoun as its subject;[81] it gives the impression of having been put in as an afterthought, after reference back to Mark's narrative where it appears in a more logical setting.[82] Having thus rounded off the story of Peter's denial and omitting any report of the Sanhedrin's night-session, Luke then represents the Sanhedrin as meeting, for the first time, in the morning: 'When day came, the assembly of the elders of the people gathered together, both the chief priests and scribes; and they led him away to their council, and they said, "If you are the Christ, tell us"'.[83] Luke, accordingly, suppresses Mark's account, which Matthew also reproduces, of an interrogation of Jesus during the night, at which the chief issue was the threat to the Temple, and he expands the morning session of the Sanhedrin, which Mark only mentions briefly, into a more impressive affair at which Jesus is asked a similar question to that put to him at night by the high priest, according to Mark.[84]

Luke's account of the transactions at this morning session is curiously indeterminate. He continues, after recording the question put to Jesus about his Messianic claim, with Jesus' reply, which is a strangely involved one:

> But he said to them, 'If I tell you, you will not believe: and if I ask you, you will not answer. But from now on the Son of man shall be seated at the right hand of the power of God.' And they all said, 'Are you the Son of God, then?' And he said to them, 'You say that I am.' And they said, 'What further testimony do we need? We have heard it ourselves from his own lips.'[85]

But this is all that happens. Luke does not tell whether the Sanhedrin passed any verdict about Jesus, or indeed what it was that they had learned 'from his own lips'. The natural inference to make from the Sanhedrin's question:

'Are you the Son of God?', and Jesus' reply, is that he was deemed to have uttered blasphemy. But this is not made clear, nor is Jesus condemned for blasphemy, as in Mark's account.[86]

The only conclusion, it would seem, that can reasonably be drawn from what Luke records of the Sanhedrin proceedings is that he decided drastically to abbreviate Mark's account. Consequently, after relating that Jesus was brought, a prisoner, to the high priest's house, he tells only of Peter's denial there and the ill-treatment of Jesus; then he ends the episode with a rather careless, inconclusive summary of a Sanhedrin interrogation held in the morning. The impression which Luke creates, by this treatment of Mark's narrative, is that he felt that the only item worth recording for his readers was the story of Peter's denial. This he gives, accordingly, in full detail, and reduces to a kind of minimum setting for it the transactions of the Sanhedrin, which he probably thought to be unimportant and of no particular interest to his Gentile readers.

This impression is confirmed by his treatment of the trial of Jesus by Pilate. In the place of the meagre and evasive account of the Roman trial given by Mark,[87] Luke's is relatively full and informative. Doubtless he regarded this trial as the really decisive transaction, compared with the Sanhedrin proceedings, and he knew that it was also the one that concerned his readers. For our subsequent discussion of it, it will be well to have his version before us; it follows on immediately after his account of the Sanhedrin session:

> Then the whole company of them arose, and brought him before Pilate. They began to accuse him, saying, 'We found this man perverting our nation, and forbidding us to give tribute to Caesar, and saying that he himself is Christ a king.' And Pilate asked him, 'Are you the King of the Jews?' And he answered him, 'You have said so.' And Pilate said to the chief priests and the multitudes, 'I find no crime in this man.' But they were urgent, saying, 'He stirs up the people, teaching throughout all Judaea, from Galilee even to this place.'[88]

In notable contrast to Mark's reticence, Luke's explicit statement of the charges which the Jewish leaders brought against Jesus at Pilate's tribunal, are intelligible and significant. The three charges all concern political subversion: misleading the people; forbidding payment of the Roman tribute; pretension to royal status as the Messiah. The area of Jesus' revolutionary activity is also stated: it is from Galilee to Jerusalem. Apart from the question whether these accusations were justified, it must be recognised that they represent an intelligible pattern of revolutionary activity in Judaea at this time. With the exception of the claim to royal status, the charges could very well have described the activity of Judas of Galilee, who founded the Zealot movement.[89] That Luke formulates these charges so clearly, in striking contradistinction to Mark's evasive reticence, is very significant. It bears out, also, our previous inference that Luke was not so involved in the immediate political embarrassment caused by the Roman execution of Jesus.[90] Although he was as eager as Mark to assert Jesus' innocence, when he wrote it was possible to look more frankly at the actual charges which were brought against Jesus, and on which he was in fact sentenced to death.

The question which now confronts us, as we consider Luke's frank statement about these charges, is that of the source of his information. Mark's reticence about the charges, as we noted, was undoubtedly due not to ignorance but to discretion.[91] We also saw that it was probable that the apologia of the Jerusalem Christians, on which Mark based his account, had clearly recorded that Jesus had been condemned by the Romans for sedition.[92] For martyrdom at the hands of the heathen oppressors of Israel would have redounded to his credit; it helped also in forming his presentation to the Jews as the martyred Messiah, who would soon return to complete his Messianic task. In the light of these considerations, it would seem feasible, therefore, that Luke, who drew on traditions of the Jerusalem Church in the Acts of the Apostles, had access also to information from that source concerning the trial of Jesus—indeed, perhaps the same apologia from which Mark so discreetly drew.[93] This conclusion would, in turn, explain the otherwise curious fact that Luke, while being so full and explicit about the charges preferred against Jesus, is so uninformative about Pilate's rejection of these charges. For he merely states that Pilate, after hearing Jesus' enigmatic answer to his question about his being the King of the Jews, told the Jews: 'I find no crime in this man.'[94] If Luke was in fact using the Jerusalem apologia about the trial, he would have found no refutation therein of the accusation that Jesus had opposed the Roman rule in the Holy Land. Instead, he would have had a full description of the charges which attested Jesus' patriotism. Consequently, he would have been left to his own devices in seeking to show that Jesus was innocent of them. This is exactly the pattern of things reflected in Luke's account of the Roman trial: having convincingly described the charges, he can only, very unconvincingly, aver that Pilate recognised that Jesus was not guilty of them.

Luke next introduces the episode which does not appear in the accounts of the other three Gospels. He cleverly prepares for it by recording that the Jews had mentioned Galilee among the places in which Jesus had been guilty of seditious action:[95]

When Pilate heard this, he asked whether the man was a Galilaean. And when he learned that he belonged to Herod's jurisdiction, he sent him over to Herod, who was himself in Jerusalem at that time. When Herod saw Jesus, he was very glad, for he had long desired to see him, because he had heard about him, and he was hoping to see some sign done by him. So he questioned him at some length; but he made no answer. The chief priests and the scribes stood by, vehemently accusing him. And Herod with his soldiers treated him with contempt and mocked him; then, arraying him in gorgeous apparel, he sent him back to Pilate. And Herod and Pilate became friends with each other that very day, for before this they had been at enmity with each other.[96]

The episode is a strange one, and it contributes nothing of importance to the sequence of events which Luke is professedly tracing out, as leading to the crucifixion of Jesus. Taken as a whole, there is nothing obviously impossible about this interlude, although there are some serious difficulties which we shall notice. It is conceivably possible that Pilate might have consulted Herod (Antipas), the tetrarch of Galilee, about a Galilaean accused of sedition, if he had required more information about him.[97] However, according to Luke, this was not what Pilate did; he implies, instead, that Pilate handed the case over to Herod, which seems to be very improbable in view of the fact that Jesus was accused of seditious action also within Pilate's area of jurisdiction.[98] Further, after unsuccessfully questioning Jesus, Herod is not described as having reached any decision, neither did he apparently send any report back to Pilate when he returned the prisoner to him.[99] The Jewish leaders are mentioned as attending this 'trial', and making accusations; but no notice seems to have been taken of them.[100] Finally, no explanation is given why Herod should have sent Jesus back, arrayed 'in gorgeous apparel'. Doubtless some form of mockery is implied, but it is certainly not explicit.[101] The note about the consequent reconciliation of Pilate and Herod is interesting; it suggests knowledge of the contemporary political background, but it could also be Luke's own comment, rounding off the story with a touch of authenticity.[102]

Of the source of Luke's story we can only speculate. Certain references in the Gospel and the Acts of the Apostles can be interpreted as indicating that he might have had access to information from Herod's household.[103] But, if such a notable incident had happened, why is it not mentioned in any of the other Gospels? This question is especially pertinent so far as Mark is concerned, because he shows a distinct interest in denigrating Herod—surely he would have taken this opportunity of doing so, if he had known of such an encounter?[104]

In view of these considerations against the authenticity of the incident, we must ask what was Luke's purpose in inserting the story of it in his account of the trial of Jesus? The only obvious answer is that he wished to add Herod's testimony to Jesus' innocence to the testimony of Pilate—indeed he subsequently represents Pilate as informing the Jews that Herod also had not found Jesus guilty of anything deserving death.[105] It is, however, worth noting that in a prayer which he attributes to the Jerusalem Christians in the Acts of the Apostles, Luke associates Herod with Pilate as having been enemies of Jesus, and not as witnesses to his innocence.[106] It is possible that this association was invoked as a fulfilment of a prophecy that was interpreted as applying to the sufferings of Jesus: 'The kings of the earth set themselves in array, and the rulers were gathered together, against the Lord and against his Anointed.'[107] But such a contradiction in the evaluation of Pilate and Herod is puzzling; it certainly warns us that Luke was more concerned with effect than with historical truth in his writing. Thus, in the Gospel, he was concerned to present Pilate and Herod as witnesses to the innocence of Jesus against the accusations of the Jewish leaders. But, in the Acts of the Apostles, his purpose was different; hence the pair appear as the enemies of Christ in accordance with a divine prophecy.

After the interruption of this episode, Luke represents Pilate as resuming his trial of Jesus, if such it can properly be called. The situation implied is equally as ludicrous as that described by Mark, although the circumstances are somewhat different. According to Luke, Pilate had found Jesus to be guiltless; but, since Galilee had also been mentioned in the accusation, he had sent him to Herod. The tetrarch having also deemed him to be guiltless and sent him back, it should surely have been for Pilate to have released Jesus. And he had both the authority and power to have done so. However, Luke describes him as going to the trouble of calling together not only the Jewish leaders, but also the people.[108] Why the people (*laos*) should be summoned, and where such a mass was accommodated, are pertinent and practical questions which Luke does not trouble to answer. The basic assumption of his account is that the Jewish leaders and people were intent on having Jesus condemned for sedition against Rome, and that the Roman governor did not want to agree to this and take the consequent action. In other words, the transaction which Luke describes, like that described by Mark and Matthew, is not really a trial of Jesus by Pilate; it is a contest over the fate of Jesus waged by Pilate on one side, and the Jewish leaders and people on the other. Luke makes this contest apparent before mentioning the Barabbas episode, in which the contest finds expression in the other accounts:

Pilate then called together the chief priests and the rulers and the people, and said to them, 'You brought me this man as one who was perverting the people; and after examining him before you, behold, I did not find this man guilty of any of your charges against him; neither did Herod, for he sent him back to us. Behold, nothing deserving of death has been done by him. I will therefore chastise him and release him.'[109]

Luke, accordingly, represents Pilate as trying to strike a bargain with the Jewish leaders and people. Although Jesus had been found to be guiltless, Pilate was willing to satisfy the Jews by flogging him before release.[110] Thus Luke subtly changes his picture of a Roman governor's dealings with a subject people, who had presented one of their own nation as guilty of sedition against Rome. In the place of that picture, he now depicts the governor as endeavouring to placate the accusers of an innocent man by substituting a flagellation for death. This change prepares the way for the worrying paradox, which Luke had next to record, of a Roman governor's sentencing to death one whom he had publicly proclaimed to be guiltless. That paradox could, however, be accounted for in terms of the implacable hatred of the Jews towards Jesus, as the sequel shows when Pilate makes his offer:

> But they all cried out together, 'Away with this man, and release to us Barabbas'—a man who had been thrown into prison for an insurrection started in the city, and for murder. Pilate addressed them once more, desiring to release Jesus; but they shouted out, 'Crucify him, crucify him!' A third time he said to them, 'Why, what evil has he done? I have found in him no crime deserving death; I will therefore chastise him and release him.' But they were urgent, demanding with loud cries that he should be crucified. And their voices prevailed. So Pilate gave sentence that their demand should be granted. He released the man who had been thrown into prison for insurrection and murder, whom they asked for; but Jesus he delivered up to their will.[111]

Presented thus, Jesus is the victim whose death the Jews implacably demanded of Pilate. In this Luke follows Mark's lead; but he exceeds Mark's tacit avoidance of admitting that Pilate had sentenced Jesus to death by representing Pilate as only surrendering Jesus to the Jews—'but Jesus he delivered up to their will (*paredōken tō thelēmati autōn*)'.[112] His use of the Barabbas episode is also instructive. He seems to invoke it as a kind of afterthought. He says nothing about the alleged annual custom of the amnesty, with the notice of which Mark introduces the episode.[113] Representing the crowd as suddenly demanding the release of Barabbas, Luke has to give a brief explanation about

Barabbas' case in parenthesis—but he omits to explain why the crowd should have made such a sudden and extraordinary demand for the release of this prisoner. In other words, he merely uses the Barabbas episode, which Mark adapted to exonerate Pilate from responsibility for the execution of Jesus, as a minor theme in his presentation of Jewish guilt.

Another divergence of Luke's account from that of Mark has need to be noted. He omits the scourging of Jesus on Pilate's order, and also the mocking of Jesus by the Roman soldiers.[114] The only apparent reason for the latter omission is that Luke had already described a somewhat similar mocking by Herod and his soldiers.[115] The introduction of the 'trial' before Herod into his narrative doubtless provided Luke with a more convenient setting for this act of mocking. For it was obviously more consistent with his thesis of Jesus as the victim of Jewish hatred, to record that he was so shamefully derided by troops of a Jewish ruler rather than by those of the Roman governor.

Thus Luke presents his account of the happenings that resulted in the crucifixion of Jesus. His emendation of Mark's account of the Sanhedrin proceedings concentrates attention on the trial of Jesus by Pilate. In describing this, Luke frankly records the political nature of the charges which the Jewish leaders brought against Jesus at Pilate's tribunal. However, he was no more concerned than Mark or Matthew to provide an intelligible account of that trial, which resulted in Pilate's sentencing Jesus to death for sedition. Instead, he transforms the trial into a contest between Pilate and the Jews over the fate of Jesus. He also adds Herod to Pilate as a witness of Jesus' innocence, and he depicts Pilate as thrice testifying to his innocence. Correspondingly, he emphasises the Jewish demand for Jesus' death by crucifixion, and he carefully points out that the Jews preferred to release a murderer.[116] He ends by suggesting that the crucifixion of Jesus, which followed, was essentially the will of the Jewish leaders and people.

As a tendentious presentation, designed to convince Gentile readers that the crucifixion of Jesus was a Jewish crime which Pilate had striven hard to prevent, Luke's narrative was doubtless successful. But it will no more stand up to critical analysis than those of Mark and Matthew, which we have similarly examined. Although Luke's version of the Roman trial has the merit of clearly stating the Jewish charges against Jesus, as a record of that trial it is basically as ludicrous and irrational. For, like the other two accounts, it starts by portraying Pilate as the supreme juridical authority to whom the Jewish leaders deliver Jesus, accused of sedition. But suddenly this intelligible situation is transformed into an unintelligible one. Instead of being the judge with full executive power, Pilate becomes a powerless magistrate, trying to bargain with a subject people for the life of an innocent prisoner in his custody.

Instead of releasing the prisoner, whose innocence he has publicly recognised, and implementing that decision with the military power at his disposal, he is depicted as actually asking the Jewish mob what he should do with the prisoner. And Luke unwittingly makes this incredible situation even more incredible by emphasising that Pilate released a man who was both a rebel and a murderer at the insistence of the Jews.[117]

Luke's subsequent account of the crucifixion of Jesus contains no significant differences from the accounts of Mark and Matthew.[118] He does, however, add an incident, as occurring on the way to Golgotha, which identifies the destruction of Jerusalem in AD 70 as punishment for the Crucifixion. Jesus warns the women of Jerusalem to mourn for themselves and their children instead of him:

> 'For behold, the days are coming when they will say, "Blessed are the barren, and the wombs that never bore, and the breasts that never gave suck!"'[119]

Since the development of the critical study of the New Testament, scholars have regarded the Gospel of John as constituting a different and later type of Gospel from those of Mark, Matthew and Luke, which they group under the title of 'Synoptic Gospels'.[120] John's Gospel, although it purports to be a narrative account of the public career of Jesus, ascribes to Jesus long discourses of a highly mystical character. This portrayal of Jesus contrasts notably with that found in the Synoptic Gospels. Another notable difference is that John indicates that the public career of Jesus lasted for three years, whereas the Synoptic writers allow one year only.[121] This chronological difference involves another, and for us a particularly important, issue. In John's Gospel the 'Cleansing of the Temple' comes at the beginning of Jesus' public career, instead of preluding the fatal climax as in the Synoptic versions.[122] It is difficult to accept John's dating of this event as correct. Such an action then would obviously have constituted a definitive crisis in Jesus' relations with the Jewish leaders at the very start of his career. The placing of the incident in the last week at Jerusalem by the Synoptic writers is both more logical and convincing.

Despite such general differences, John's Gospel presents an account of the trial of Jesus that compares favourably, as a historical record, with the Synoptic accounts on many points. In particular, it reveals a significant awareness of the political factors involved in Jesus' career, and it gives the impression of knowing about incidents not mentioned in the other Gospels.[123] Most notably it appears to be aware that the kingly aspect of Jesus' Messiahship had been a decisive, perhaps the most decisive, factor that ultimately resulted in his execution by the Romans. Thus John mentions that, after the miraculous feeding of the five thousand in the wilderness of Galilee, the people were so impressed by the power of Jesus that 'they were about to come and take him by force to make him king'.[124] John naturally represents Jesus as withdrawing himself, to avoid being put in so compromising a position.[125] However, rather illogically, he depicts Jesus on the next day as again teaching the crowd, with no reference made to the momentous happening of the previous day. Yet, in the long discourse that follows concerning the mystical 'bread of life', a parallel is significantly cited between Jesus' miracle of providing bread in the wilderness and the provision of manna when the ancestors of Israel wandered in the wilderness after the Exodus.[126] Although this discourse is replete with the mystical imagery that characterises so much of John's Gospel, the parallel is an interesting one, especially because of its close connection with the crowd's attempt to make Jesus king. It recalls the 'signs of salvation', which Josephus ascribes to the many Messianic pretenders (*goëtes*) during the troubled years in Judaea preceding the revolt in 66.[127] These 'signs of salvation', which won these would-be Messiahs popular support, were often patterned upon the miraculous events of Israel's deliverance from Egypt and its sojourn in the desert, which was the prophetic 'golden age' of the past.[128]

The next reference to the kingship theme occurs, significantly, in John's description of Jesus' triumphal entry into Jerusalem. The royal aspect of the incident is brought out more vividly by John than by any of the other Evangelists:

> The next day a great crowd who had come to the feast heard that Jesus was coming to Jerusalem. So they took branches of palm trees and went out to meet him, crying, 'Hosanna! Blessed is he who comes in the name of the Lord, even the King of Israel!' And Jesus found a young ass and sat upon it; as it is written,
>
> > 'Fear not, daughter of Zion;
> > behold, your king is coming,
> > sitting on an ass's colt!'[129]

John remarks that the disciples of Jesus did not understand the significance of this, until after 'Jesus was glorified'.[130] However, more realistically, he records that the Pharisees certainly understood what it meant, and lamented their inability to oppose Jesus. He represents them as saying to each other: 'You see that you can do nothing; look, the world has gone after him.'[131]

The concern which the Pharisees then expressed had already been felt by them after another miracle by Jesus. Thus John describes how perturbed the

Pharisees had been when Jesus had raised Lazarus from the dead, and how they had apparently reported the matter back to Jerusalem:

> So the chief priests and the Pharisees gathered the council, and said, 'What are we to do? For this man performs many signs. If we let him go on thus, everyone will believe in him, and the Romans will come and destroy both our holy place and our nation.'[132]

The significance of this statement is very great, even though the phraseology is perhaps a little odd.[133] It means that John was aware of the fact that the activity of Jesus was regarded by the Jewish leaders primarily as constituting a political threat: no mention is made of the religious aspect of what Jesus taught and did. The form of the threat is also notable. The Jewish leaders fear that Jesus' activity will provoke the intervention of the Romans on such a scale that 'they will destroy both our holy place and our nation'. In other words, a national revolt is feared, and its suppression by Rome was calculated to involve both the Temple and the whole nation in destruction.[134] The idea of a revolt of such proportions, having such consequences, for which Jesus might be responsible, is amazing. It is natural to think that the author of John's Gospel, knowing of the devastation caused by the Jewish revolt of 66–70, allowed his imagination to attribute the fear of such a catastrophe to the Jewish leaders when faced by the activity of Jesus some forty years earlier. However that may be, what is important for us is that John did believe that the Jewish leaders were primarily moved by the very serious political threat which Jesus constituted.

What follows this statement in John's record is equally significant. Continuing his account of this meeting of the Sanhedrin, John relates how:

> one of them, Caiaphas, who was high priest that year, said to them, 'You know nothing at all; you do not understand that it is expedient for you that one man should die for the people, and that the whole nation should not perish.' He did not say this of his own accord, but being high priest that year he prophesied that Jesus should die for the nation, and not for the nation only, but to gather into one the children of God who are scattered abroad. So from that day they took counsel how to put him to death.[135]

After due allowance is made for John's theological comment here, a most remarkable explanation of what led to the death of Jesus remains. According to John, the Sanhedrin had eventually become profoundly alarmed about the seriousness of the political danger that Jesus constituted. The high priest Caiaphas ended their perplexity by counselling them to take action to destroy Jesus. He argued that drastic action was necessary to save the nation from the disasters that Jesus would inevitably bring upon it, if allowed to continue his subversive activity. In this ruthless thesis of Caiaphas, that it was expedient that 'one man should die for the people', John characteristically saw a divine prophecy of the universal efficacy of the death of Jesus.[136] But the practical implications which lie behind that thesis, if historical, are immense. As Caiaphas saw it, the precarious balance of Jewish relations with the Roman occupying power was imperilled by Jesus. Consequently, although he was one of their own nation, his suppression in the interests of preserving that balance was imperative.[137]

In consequence of the Sanhedrin's decision to destroy Jesus, and in preparation for the part that Judas was to play, John represents the Jewish leaders as giving orders that, 'if any one knew where he (Jesus) was, he should let them know, so that they might arrest him'.[138] The statement obviously means that the Jewish leaders sought to know any secret rendezvous of Jesus; for, as the sequel shows, Jesus entered Jerusalem very much in public, and was not arrested. Indeed, the demonstration of popular support accorded to him then drew forth the Pharisees' complaint, which was quoted above, that they could do nothing—'the world has gone after him'.[139]

John's account of the arrest of Jesus and his subsequent interrogation before being brought to Pilate, contains some curious divergences from the Synoptic accounts. In the first place, although he omits to tell of Judas' arrangement with the Jewish leaders to betray Jesus, John depicts Judas as initiating the arrest: 'So Judas, procuring a band of soldiers and some officers from the chief priests and the Pharisees, went there (i.e. Gethsemane) with lanterns and torches and weapons.'[140] In the resistance which was offered to the arrest, Peter is named as injuring the high priest's slave, whose name is given as Malchus.[141] The next cause for puzzlement comes in John's statement that Jesus, after his arrest, was first led to 'Annas; for he was the father-in-law of Caiaphas, who was high priest that year. It was Caiaphas who had given counsel to the Jews that it was expedient that one man should die for the people.'[142] The fact, unexplained, that Jesus should have been taken to Annas is surprising, and the reference back to the earlier mention of Caiaphas seems somewhat awkward.[143] These difficulties become greater in the sequel. For John proceeds to tell of Peter's denial, which takes place in 'the court of the high priest'.[144] This high priest is not named; but he was certainly not Caiaphas, as we shall see, and we can only conclude that reference is being made back to Annas, who had been high priest.[145] If this is so, then the high priest who questions Jesus is not Caiaphas, the reigning high priest, but Annas. After the interrogation, Annas is described as sending Jesus, bound, to Caiaphas.[146] Nothing is recorded to have happened while Jesus is with Caiaphas,

23 Trial before Pilate

Illumination from the sixth-century Rossano Gospels (see p. 159)

24 Christ before Pilate: medieval representation

Detail from the choir screen, Naumberg Cathedral, c. 1250

and the next move mentioned is that 'they led Jesus from the house of Caiaphas to the praetorium'.[147]

This strange involvement of two high priests with the fate of Jesus has naturally caused much discussion among scholars. Some have interpreted it as proof that the author of John's Gospel was in possession of reliable information about what had actually happened.[148] Thus it can be argued that the manifest objection to there being two high priests involved precludes invention, especially in view of the fact that the earlier Synoptic accounts, which John evidently knew, refer only to one high priest.[149] It can further be maintained that Annas, as an ex-high priest of distinction and closely related to Caiaphas, might have initiated and handled the unpleasant business of dealing with Jesus. But such an interpretation has the effect of reducing Caiaphas to a nonentity in the fateful transaction. And it would also not explain why it is recorded that Jesus was sent to the house of Caiaphas when nothing seems to have happened there.[150] These same difficulties, on the other hand, have caused other scholars to doubt whether the name of the high priest, who dealt with Jesus, had ever been preserved in the original tradition of the trial. The names of Caiaphas and Annas are explained as later insertions, drawn from Jewish records to give the Gospel accounts the semblance of historical records.[151] Such a solution necessarily involves excising certain passages, as unauthentic, from well-established texts, where there is no manuscript authority for so doing.[152]

No obvious solution offers itself for these problems. The fact that they exist must be duly noted as further evidence of the vague and tenuous nature of primitive Christian tradition about the last days of Jesus. It means, moreover, that even by the end of the first century no definitive version of the trial of Jesus had emerged and been accepted as such. But John's divergences from the Synoptic Gospels are not limited to the question of the identity of the high priest who dealt with Jesus. For he presents the Jewish interrogation in a very different form from that which it has in the accounts of Mark and Matthew, and also from the variant version given by Luke.[153] The proceedings have no semblance of being a trial by the Sanhedrin: there is no mention of the charge of threatening the Temple, nor is the high priest recorded to have asked Jesus whether he was the Messiah, and nothing is said about blasphemy.

In fact, from the arrest onwards the whole of the Jewish proceedings, except for the interweaving of the narrative with the story of Peter's denial,[154] is invested with a quite different character from that apparent in the Synoptic records. Most notably, the terminology used by John for the soldiers who arrest Jesus suggests that they were Roman troops.[155] It would indeed be surprising, if they had been Roman; for the operation is clearly represented by Mark and Matthew as being organised by the Jewish authorities, who had a police force sufficient for such an undertaking as depicted by the Synoptic writers.[156] However, the implications of John's suggestion must be carefully considered. For, if the troops were indeed Roman, the arrest of Jesus must have been a combined operation, planned by Pilate in conjunction with the Jewish leaders, whose officers assisted.[157] The significance of such a conclusion would be great: it would mean that Jesus was so strongly supported that the Jewish leaders felt incapable of undertaking his arrest, even though clandestinely, with their own forces. It would follow, also, that Pilate was acquainted with the danger that Jesus constituted, and that he had agreed to supply Roman troops to ensure the success of the operation. In other words, if John's indication that the arrest of Jesus was effected by the Romans were to be accepted as authentic, then the political aspect of Jesus and his movement takes on even more serious proportions than is implied in the Synoptic Gospels.[158] For, instead of his arrest being a police operation undertaken by the Jewish authorities after Jesus' action in the Temple, we should be obliged to see it as a Roman military measure against one considered to be a dangerous rebel leader.

With this interpretation of John's version of the arrest his account of the high priest's enquiry agrees in a remarkable manner. As we noted above, the transaction described by John is in no wise a Sanhedrin trial for blasphemy, as it is portrayed in the Synoptic Gospels. It is essentially a fact-finding enquiry. John's account of it has the appearance of being an objective report:

> The high priest then questioned Jesus about his disciples and his teaching. Jesus answered him, 'I have spoken openly to the world; I have always taught in synagogues and in the temple, where all Jews come together; I have said nothing in secret. Why do you ask me? Ask those who have heard me, what I said to them; they know what I said.'[159]

From this passage and the account of the arrest, it is possible to construct an intelligible picture of what had happened up to this point. If the arrest of Jesus had been a combined operation between Pilate and the Jewish leaders, it would be feasible that Jesus might have been taken first to a Jewish leader of repute and long experience as Annas was, in order that he might be interrogated by an expert on Jewish affairs. This might have been deemed a more convenient plan than involving Caiaphas, the reigning high priest, at this stage. The purpose of Annas' interrogation of Jesus is also clear: it was necessary to have more exact knowledge about Jesus' movement, particularly his aims and the identity of his chief followers. The reported reply of Jesus, which forms a striking contrast to his silence or very laconic answers in the Synoptic versions, contains nothing manifestly unauthentic. It could well represent the reply of a prisoner in such circumstances: rather than incriminate himself, he suggests that his interrogator gathers the information required for himself.[160]

Such an enquiry would certainly have been needed, if a report had to be prepared for Pilate. If it were thought that Jesus claimed to be the Messiah-King, Pilate would probably have decided that it would assist his own evaluation of the matter, if he were informed about the prisoner's ideas and aims by a Jewish expert. Hence, an intelligible sequence of events emerges. Jesus is first interrogated by Annas, who, having drawn his conclusions and embodied them in specific charges, sends him to Caiaphas, as the official head of the Jewish state, appointed to deal in such matters with the Roman governor.[161]

This interpretation which makes sense of John's otherwise strange account, is not, however, borne out by the sequel as given in the extant text of the Gospel. To appreciate the problems which the succeeding narrative poses, it will be well to have the first episode before us:

> Then they led Jesus from the house of Caiaphas to the praetorium. It was early. They themselves did not enter the praetorium, so that they might not be defiled, but might eat the passover. So Pilate went out to them and said, 'What accusation do you bring against this man?' They answered him, 'If this man were not an evildoer, we would not have handed him over.' Pilate said to them, 'Take him yourselves and judge him by your own law.' The Jews said to him, 'It is not lawful for us to put any man to death.' This was to fulfil the word which Jesus had spoken to show by what death he was to die.[162]

At first sight, some features of the passage suggest that it is based upon an authentic tradition. Thus the refusal of the Jews to enter the *praetorium* seems to be a factual detail, unrecorded in the Synoptic Gospels, that derives from memory of the actual event.[163] The reason given for this refusal, namely, the imminence of the passover, raises a problem. It contradicts the chronology of the Synoptic versions, which place the passover on the previous evening; but arguments can be produced to show that John is the better informed here.[164] However, apart from such touches, there are serious grounds for doubting whether the passage does reflect an authentic tradition. First, we must notice the discrepancy between its presentation of the relevant situation and what had gone before. The passage represents Pilate as having no previous knowledge of Jesus.[165] Now, if, as we have seen good reason for believing, John implies that Jesus had been arrested by Roman troops, Pilate must have taken such action in concert with the Jewish leaders.[166] Consequently, there is a contradiction of statement here by John: for, if he is right in representing the arrest as being made by the Romans, then Pilate could not have been ignorant of Jesus when the Jewish authorities delivered him at the *praetorium*. Conversely, if Jesus' case was indeed unknown to Pilate, then John cannot be right about the Roman arrest.

The next difficulty lies in the alleged reply of the Jews to Pilate's question about the nature of the charge preferred against Jesus. If Pilate knew nothing of Jesus, his question was obvious and necessary. But the answer of the Jews, as given by John, is not only impertinent, it is also absurd: 'If this man were not an evildoer, we would not have handed him over.'[167] It makes nonsense of the very situation it is supposed to be describing. The Jewish leaders had handed Jesus over to Pilate as an offender; but how could Pilate deal with him, if no charge was specified? The impression, which John's lack of logic makes here, is that he was more concerned with preparing for the piece of mystical exegesis that was to follow than with factual sense. This becomes even more apparent in the statement attributed to Pilate in reply to the churlish answer of the Jewish leaders: 'Take him yourselves and judge him by your own law.'[168] According to John, this was actually the instruction given by a Roman magistrate to the representatives of a subject people who had delivered a prisoner to him charged with an offence which they refused to specify.[169] However, the absurdity of the statement was doubtless unavoidable, in order to bring the dialogue between Pilate and the Jewish leaders to the point where John could give his explanation of why Jesus died by the Roman punishment of crucifixion. As we have already seen, the consequent statement of the Jews, that it was not lawful for them to inflict capital punishment, requires very careful qualification before it can be accepted as a statement about historical fact.[170] But John's real concern in making it was to explain that thus was fulfilled 'the word which Jesus had spoken to show by what death he was to die'. In this laboured manner he refers back to a strange saying, earlier attributed to Jesus as a prophecy of his crucifixion.[171]

The tedious nature of the analysis and criticism here is regretted; but it has been unavoidable. It should, at least, serve to show how difficult is the task of evaluating John's account of the trial of Jesus. We have seen enough so far to realise how complex is its interwoven pattern of apparent fact, theological interpretation, and mystical imagery. At one point it seemed to promise a more authentic presentation of the proceedings than is given by the Synoptic Gospels; but then it followed with statements that strain credulity, or others that forcibly remind one that the theme is theology, not history. This impression continues to be given in the remaining narrative of the trial. As drama it is superb; its emphasis on the motif of Jesus' kingship commands attention; yet it contains a similar abundance of problems as the preceding passage. In view of its intricate nature, we must examine successively the distinctive episodes into which the narrative divides. Our next quotation follows on immediately after the section we have been considering:

> Pilate entered the praetorium again and called Jesus, and said to him, 'Are you the King of the Jews?' Jesus answered, 'Do you say this of yourself, or did others say it to you about me?' Pilate answered, 'Am I a Jew? Your own nation and the chief priests have handed you over to me; what have you done?' Jesus answered, 'My kingship is not of this world; if my kingship were of this world, my servants would fight, that I might not be handed over to the Jews; but my kingship is not from the world.' Pilate said to him, 'So you are a king?' Jesus answered, 'You say that I am a king. For this I was born, and for this I have come into the world, to bear witness to the truth. Every one who is of the truth hears my voice.' Pilate said to him, 'What is truth?'[172]

Again we are confronted with a narrative that gives, in places, the impression of verisimilitude, while in others it is manifestly inconsequential or elusive. To deal with it *seriatim*, we may begin by remarking that Pilate's first question to Jesus closely parallels Mark's version at this point: there is the same lack of information about the charge which the Jewish leaders brought against Jesus, as well as Pilate's leading question which presupposes that Jesus had been accused of claiming to be the King of the Jews.[173] John's account, however, has an inconsistency here which does not occur with Mark. For, whereas Mark records the Jewish leaders as making a number of unspecified charges against Jesus, John previously describes them as refusing to specify what their accusation was.[174] However that may be, the dialogue that follows is exceedingly interesting in that it centres on the kingship of Jesus. Jesus' reply to Pilate's leading question has important implications, besides having an air of verisimilitude. To reply by asking a question could be a piece of clever dialectic: 'Do you say this of yourself, or did others say it about me?'[175] If it were authentic, it could mean that Jesus sought to elicit from Pilate how much knowledge he had of himself and how far he understood his claims. However, we can safely evaluate the question only in the context of John's version of the trial. In this setting, it would seem to indicate that John knew, despite his contrary statement, that the Jewish leaders had specifically accused Jesus of claiming kingship, and had probably explained the Messianic connotation of such a claim.[176]

Pilate's reply, 'Am I a Jew?', appears to confirm that John, in composing this dialogue, was aware that a Roman would have been impatient of Jewish nuances of meaning concerning Messianic kingship.[177] The rest of Pilate's answer is revealing: 'Your own nation and chief priests have handed you over to me; what have you done?'[178] It indicates, by its association of the Jewish nation with the chief priests, that John sought to implicate the whole Jewish people in the action that led to the death of Jesus. This intention, as we next see, has become a fundamental thesis of John's. Jesus is represented as explaining carefully to Pilate that his kingship, despite what Pilate might naturally infer, was 'not of this world'. We may note, incidentally, that Jesus' statement here is an admission of the significant fact that he did claim kingship.[179] After explaining the transcendental nature of his kingship, Jesus is then represented as adding in further explanation: 'If my kingship were of this world, my servants would fight, that I might not be handed over to the Jews; but my kingship is not from the world.'[180] The significance of this statement for our evaluation of John's presentation of the trial of Jesus is very great. John, in attributing these words to Jesus, seems to forget that, according to his own narrative, Jesus had been handed by the Jewish leaders and people over to Pilate for judgment.[181] Instead, he now envisages a quite different situation, in which Jesus is in danger of being handed over (*paradouthō*) to the Jews, by some power unspecified. This extraordinary interpretation of the situation of Jesus at his trial is clarified by a subsequent statement which concludes the account of the Roman trial. John records there: 'Then he (Pilate) handed him (Jesus) to them (the Jews) to be crucified.'[182] In other words, John actually represents the crucifixion of Jesus as being determined and carried out by the Jews. We shall see presently the discrepancies which this view involves in the narrative of the Crucifixion.[183] For the moment, we must contemplate the significance of the view for our evaluation of John's version of the trial. The idea of the Roman trial as resulting in the delivery of Jesus to the Jews, who crucify him, is not an isolated concept. The trial and Crucifixion, in fact, constitute the culminating act in the dualistic drama with which John's Gospel is really concerned. The life of Jesus, as the incarnated 'Word (*Logos*) of God', is seen as a contest between Jesus and the Devil, who is the 'Prince of this world'.[184] In this signal struggle, the Jews are portrayed as the enemies of Jesus and children of the Devil.[185] This shocking dualism, which is reminiscent of that between the 'Sons of Light' and the 'Sons of Darkness' in the Dead Sea Scrolls,[186] forms the basic theme of John's Gospel, and it clearly inspires his interpretation of the trial of Jesus. Hence, despite occasional passages that appear to stem from a credible historical tradition, John's narrative is essentially designed to present this dualistic theme.

Continuing our examination of the passage, we have next to note that to Pilate's confirmatory question, 'So you are a king?', Jesus answers by affirming that this was his destiny from birth, and also the purpose of his incarnation.[187] Jesus' references to 'the truth' cause Pilate (who would surely have been justifiably baffled, if he had indeed listened to such an esoteric statement) to ask his famous question: 'What is truth?'[188]

According to John, Pilate did not wait for an answer to his question:

> After he had said this, he went out to the Jews again, and told them, 'I find no crime in him. But you have a custom that I should release one man for you at the Passover; will you have me release for you the King of the Jews?' They cried out again, 'Not this man, but Barabbas!' Now Barabbas was a robber (lēstēs).[189]

This passage has all the appearance of being a kind of *précis* of Mark's account of the Barabbas episode. The statement that the Jews 'cried out again (*palin*)' is clearly derived from *Mk.* xv:13; for John had mentioned no previous offer by Pilate, in connection with the custom, to release Jesus.[190]

After this brief incorporation of the Barabbas episode into his narrative, John launches out again into his own peculiar account of the matter in which Jesus was so fatally involved with Pilate. What he next relates seems to be a dramatic conflation of Mark's story of the mocking of Jesus with an alternating dialogue between Pilate and the Jews and Pilate and Jesus, designed to show the Roman governor's growing realisation of the numinous character of Jesus, and his vain attempt to save him from the Jews. The description of the scourging and mocking of Jesus does not need quotation; for it differs from the Markan record only by omitting the smiting with the reed.[191] What follows is vividly presented, and it has inspired many Christian artists to portray the dramatic moment designated: *Ecce homo!*[192]

> Pilate went out again, and said to them, 'Behold, I am bringing him out to you, that you may know that I find no crime in him.' So Jesus came out, wearing the crown of thorns and the purple robe. Pilate said to them, 'Here is the man!' When the chief priests and officers saw him, they cried out, 'Crucify him, crucify him!' Pilate said to them, 'Take him yourselves and crucify him, for I find no crime in him.' The Jews answered him, 'We have a law, and by that law he ought to die, because he has made himself the Son of God.' When Pilate heard these words, he was the more afraid; he entered the praetorium again and said to Jesus, 'Where are you from?' But Jesus gave no answer. Pilate therefore said to

him, 'You will not speak to me? Do you not know that I have power to release you, and power to crucify you?' Jesus answered him, 'You would have no power over me unless it had been given you from above; therefore he who delivered me to you has the greater sin.' Upon this Pilate sought to release him, but the Jews cried out, 'If you release this man, you are not Caesar's friend; for every one who makes himself a king sets himself against Caesar.' When Pilate heard these words, he brought Jesus out and sat down on the judgment seat at a place called The Pavement, and in Hebrew, Gabbatha. Now it was the day of the Preparation of the Passover; it was about the sixth hour. He said to the Jews, 'Here is your King!' They cried out, 'Away with him, away with him, crucify him!' Pilate said to them, 'Shall I crucify your King?' The chief priests answered, 'We have no king but Caesar.' Then he handed him over to them to be crucified.

So they took Jesus, and he went out, bearing his own cross, to the place of a skull, which is called in Hebrew Golgotha. There they crucified him, and with him two others, one on either side, and Jesus between them. Pilate also wrote a title and put it on the cross; it read 'Jesus of Nazareth, the King of the Jews'. Many of the Jews read this title, for the place where Jesus was crucified was near the city; and it was written in Hebrew, in Latin, and in Greek. The chief priests of the Jews then said to Pilate, 'Do not write, "The King of the Jews", but, "This man said, 'I am the King of the Jews'". Pilate answered, 'What I have written I have written.'[193]

Concerned, as we are, to investigate the earliest extant evidence about the trial of Jesus, what are we to make of this dramatic presentation composed by John some seventy years after the event? As theatre, the *montage* is superb, and it has profoundly affected subsequent generations of Christians. But what is its value as historical evidence? Can we really believe that a tough and experienced Roman governor, with military power at his disposal, would have moved to and fro between a prisoner and his accusers, questioning the former and haggling with the latter for his release? John himself, unwittingly, gives the lie to his own presentation by causing Pilate to remind Jesus: 'Do you not know that I have power to release you, and power to crucify you?'[194] For, having thus recognised that Pilate had such plenary power, John seems curiously oblivious of the logic of the fact. He goes on inconsistently, as do the other Evangelists, to represent Pilate as seeking in vain to release Jesus, whose innocence he has publicly recognised. And this is not all. Pilate is also described as having to haggle with the Jewish leaders and people, as though the power of release lay with them, and not with himself. The only explanation which John seems to suggest for this paradox is that the Jews opposed Pilate's intention with the threat: 'If you release this man, you are not Caesar's friend; for every one who makes himself a king sets himself against Caesar.'[195] If this statement is intended to be an explanation, the implication is that the Jews would have reported the matter to the Emperor, and that this would have had serious consequences for Pilate. If this is indeed John's argument, it is naive in the extreme. It ignores the practical difficulties that such an action, by a subject people against their accredited governor, would encounter; and it assumes that the Emperor would have accepted the Jewish report against that of his own Roman officer, whose ten years' tenure of office attests the trust that was placed in him.[196] Further, it also overlooks the fact that Pilate would have been in far greater danger when the Emperor learned that he had released Barabbas, a rebel leader recently involved in a serious insurrection—that is, if such an incident did in fact ever occur.[197] And there is one further aspect for comment. Like the authors of the Synoptic Gospels, John also presents the situation as one in which Pilate had to give an immediate decision. But, as we have already noted, Pilate would have had other ways open to him, if he had found the case too involved with the passions of the moment: he could, for example, have postponed a decision and called the case to Caesarea for further investigation.[198]

But however the matter may be as to the details, when we consider John's account as a whole, we see that we cannot evaluate it as a record of a trial; for it is essentially the presentation of a contest between Pilate and the Jews over the fate of Jesus. Thus, without explaining how he reached such a conclusion, Pilate is depicted as convinced of the innocence of Jesus.[199] The Jewish leaders, from formally laying a case of sedition against Jesus, are suddenly transformed into enemies who vehemently demand Pilate to crucify him.[200] All semblance of judicial proceedings vanishes, and in its place a dramatic struggle is presented. The protagonist is the representative of Rome, who testifies to the innocence of Jesus and seeks to save him. The antagonists are the Jewish leaders and people, who represent the Devil, and seek to destroy the Son of God, who is also the Messiah-King of Israel.[201] The historical realities of the situation are forgotten in portraying this dualistic drama, namely, that Pilate is the Roman governor, with supreme authority and the force to back it; that the Jewish high priest is appointed by him and responsible to him for native affairs. The motif, which inspires this presentation, is obvious: the crucifixion of Jesus must be seen as a Jewish, and not as a Roman act, which in fact it was. This pretence is maintained to the end— Pilate is represented, without expressing any verdict, as delivering Jesus to the Jews, who proceed to crucify him.[202]

Although this presentation cannot thus be taken as historical reality, there are, however, certain aspects of it that seem to reflect a real situation. We have already noticed that John seems to be aware that it was the political significance of Jesus' activities that concerned the Jewish leaders.[203] It is interesting, therefore, that the kingship of Jesus is depicted as the sole issue at his 'trial'. Jesus is represented as carefully explaining to Pilate that his 'kingship is not of this world'; he does not, significantly, repudiate the attribution of kingship as a popular misconception, nor as a calumny of his enemies. What Pilate might have made of a kingship 'not of this world' can only be a matter for curious speculation. However, it is significant that John represents the Jews as arguing that 'every one who makes himself a king sets himself against Caesar'. The logic of this argument was, indeed, obvious. For any claim to kingship, even if 'not of this world', ran a grave risk of being misunderstood as a seditious act against Roman suzerainty. John's preoccupation with this kingship theme does, in fact, give the impression that he was uncomfortably aware that this had been the decisive issue at the Roman trial of Jesus. And this impression is strengthened by the assertion which he attributes to the chief priests of the Jews: 'We have no king but Caesar.'[204] The attribution of such an assertion to the official representatives of the Jews, by anyone cognisant with Jewish-Roman relations during this period, must surely be ironic. For denial of the kingship of Caesar was the fundamental principle of Zealotism, and Josephus tells how the Romans tortured the Sicarii to make them acknowledge 'Caesar as lord'.[205] Jesus, as the Messiah-King, did in effect repudiate the kingship of Caesar as definitively as any Zealot.

John's presentation of the crucifixion of Jesus as being performed by the Jews inevitably involved him in self-contradiction, and it further underlines the fact that he was primarily concerned with theology, and not with history. Thus, although he represents the Jews as actually crucifying Jesus, he records that Pilate had placed a *titulus* on the cross of Jesus, which was designed to indicate the crime for which the penalty was exacted.[206] The placing of the *titulus* was in fact a proclamation of the Roman sentence of death. And the subsequent description of the attendant happenings at the Crucifixion refers to the involvement of soldiers who appear to be Roman, even though no mention is made of the centurion and his attestation to Jesus' divinity which Mark and Matthew record.[207] That Pilate was responsible for the Crucifixion, and not the Jews, is also implied by the fact that he is described as giving the body of Jesus to Joseph of Arimathea for burial.[208] The fact is also confirmed by the reported request of the Jews themselves to Pilate that the legs of the three crucified should be broken, to hasten their deaths.[209] John would doubtless have justified his representation of the crucifixion of Jesus by the Jews as signifying their ultimate responsibility for the deed. But, however that may be, his designedly elusive narrative has the effect of avoiding the depiction of Roman soldiers as the actual executioners. And so, although Pilate did in fact order the execution and his soldiers carried it out, John conveys the impression that Pilate only surrendered Jesus to the Jews, and that too under duress. And the actual Crucifixion, according to him, was the work of the Jews, who did the will of their father, the Devil.[210]

And so we conclude our survey of the accounts of the trial of Jesus as given in the Gospels of Matthew, Luke and John. None of them substantially differs from the major theme of Mark's presentation. For, like him, they seek to show that the Jews were responsible for the crucifixion of Jesus and that Pilate witnessed to his innocence. With the exception of Luke, they show a similar reluctance to disclose the nature of the charges which the Jews brought against Jesus, and on which Pilate condemned him. Their accounts are no more careful records of a trial than is Mark's; for they follow him in describing what is really a contest between Pilate and the Jews over the fate of Jesus. Similarly, the contradictions, absurdities, reticence and elusiveness manifest in these accounts are all found to stem from the embarrassing fact of the Roman execution of Jesus for sedition. Although in certain ways their motives differed from that which produced Mark's apologetical version of the trial, Matthew, Luke and John shared his concern to explain away the scandal of the Roman cross. Hence their common endeavour to make Pilate a witness to the innocence of Jesus, and the Jews solely responsible for his death.

CHAPTER SIX

The Historical Reality: what did happen?

Our foregoing investigation of the Gospel accounts of the trial of Jesus has led us to one certain conclusion. It is, admittedly, of a somewhat negative character; but it is pregnant with suggestion concerning the real situation. This conclusion is that all four Evangelists were deeply embarrassed by the scandal of the Roman cross. The fact that Jesus had been executed for sedition on the order of Pontius Pilate was too well known for them to deny; it could only be explained away.

But this embarrassment, it is important to note, was one felt exclusively by Gentile Christians; it did not trouble the original Jewish followers of Jesus. These latter had, in effect, emphasised the Roman cross, because it enhanced the reputation of Jesus as the martyred Messiah of Israel.[1] They had looked to the speedy return of Jesus, with supernatural power, to 'restore the kingdom to Israel', which meant the overthrow of the Roman rule in the Holy Land of Yahweh.[2] The chief concern of these original disciples, resident in Jerusalem, was to rebut the charge that Jesus had threatened to destroy the Temple. Hence, the record which they had composed of the last fatal days of Jesus' career was conditioned by this concern. It refuted the accusation about the Temple, brought during the Sanhedrin enquiry, as being 'false-witness', and it described how the unpopular Jewish leaders had cooperated with Pilate in crucifying Jesus as a rebel against the Roman government of Judaea.[3]

It was Mark, writing for the Christians of Rome, embarrassed and endangered by the Flavian triumph there in AD 71 over rebel Judaea, who initiated a different version of the trial of Jesus. Presenting Jesus as endorsing the Jewish obligation to pay tribute to Rome, he went on to show that the Jewish leaders condemned Jesus for blasphemy and forced Pilate to crucify him. He set the pattern, elaborated by the later Evangelists, of representing the Roman trial as a contest between Pilate, who recognised the innocence of Jesus and sought to save him, and the Jews, who were intent on his destruction.

Mark's account of the trial of Jesus is thus essentially apologetic, not history. But it was successful; for, despite its discrepancies so obvious to the modern historian, it gave Christians of that time what they wanted. The scandal of the Roman cross was explained. The Jews were shown to be criminally responsible for its infliction on Jesus—those Jews, whom the Roman world hated for their fanaticism and rebellion, and on whom condign punishment had fallen in AD 70.[4] This anti-Jewish pattern, with its concomitant attestation by Pilate of Jesus' innocence, once it was formulated, inspired the writers of the other Gospels to develop the portrait of the Pacific Christ. The conception had the dual virtue of compatibility with the divinisation of Jesus, and of assuring the Roman government that Christianity was not politically subversive.[5]

Though theologically necessary and politically convenient, these versions of the trial of Jesus were essentially misrepresentations of what had actually happened. They have, consequently, had the effect of obscuring or transforming the real historical Jesus and the true reason for his tragic death. In their nature and effect, the Gospel accounts of Jesus are hybrid compositions. For they assume his divinity and the saving efficacy of his death; but, unlike Paul, they are unable to cut loose from the setting of the historical Crucifixion and present it as a transcendental event, accomplished by the daemonic powers that rule the lower universe.[6] That they were thus unable to follow Paul completely, and that they remained preoccupied with the historical situation, is certainly fortunate. For, although they misrepresent that situation, the Gospels, in their accounts of the trial of Jesus, have preserved the only detailed evidence we have of it. Consequently, they present the modern historian with both an opportunity and a challenge. An opportunity, in that they provide him with the earliest extant traditions of the trial of Jesus; a challenge, in that they prompt him to try to understand, from such tendentious material, what really did happen.

That challenge we shall now accept, and endeavour to discern behind the Gospel presentations some more probable semblance of historical reality. But such an undertaking can only construct an interpretation out of the material provided by the Gospels. Our reconstruction will thus be an interpretation based on other interpretations, for that is what the Gospel accounts essentially are. But we can at least claim that its aim is to achieve something like historical probability, and not theological apologetic. And we may perhaps hope that from the attempt a more credible portrait of Jesus of Nazareth will emerge—credible, that is, in terms of the contemporary situation in first-century Judaea.

Our attempt at reconstruction will best begin from the one fact of which we can be certain, namely, the Roman execution of Jesus for sedition. The

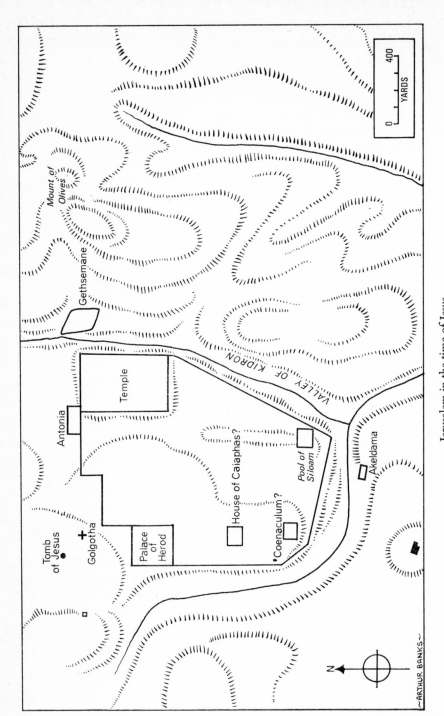

Jerusalem in the time of Jesus

In the reign of Herod Agrippa (40–44), about ten years after the Crucifixion, a city wall was built on the northern side, enclosing the area of Golgotha and the tomb of Jesus. Recent excavation

natural inference to draw from this fact is that Pontius Pilate, as the Roman governor of Judaea, was convinced that Jesus was guilty of sedition, and so ordered his crucifixion as other rebels were similarly sentenced. How Pilate became convinced of the seditious activity of Jesus is the problem which we have to investigate. The Gospel writers deny that Jesus was thus guilty; but we have found their accounts to be so unconvincing on this point that we have to conclude that Pilate did verily believe that Jesus was guilty, and the brute fact of the Roman cross inevitably requires this conclusion. The conclusion does not necessarily mean that Jesus was guilty; for it is conceivable, though not probable, that Pilate could have been mistaken or misled about the evidence, or even induced to execute an innocent man.[7] The *prima facie* case, to be drawn from the fact that he did order the crucifixion of Jesus, is that Pilate was convinced of his guilt. Our task now will be to see whether, from what evidence can be gleaned from the Gospel accounts of the activity of Jesus, that *prima facie* case is corroborated or not.

The Gospels trace the public career of Jesus from his baptism by John the Baptist, with whom he appears to have been in some way associated for a time.[8] Considerable obscurity invests the character and activity of John and his relations with Jesus. He certainly seems to have been in the line of Jewish prophetic and apocalyptic tradition.[9] According to the Gospel writers, John's purpose was to prepare an elect community, by repentance of sins and baptism, for the coming of the Messianic Kingdom.[10] He incurred the wrath of Herod Antipas and Herodias by denouncing their illegal marriage, and Mark gives a colourful account of the occasion of his execution.[11] Josephus, however, attributes the execution to the tetrarch's fear that John's preaching would cause a rebellion.[12] The fact is significant, and it does not necessarily contradict the cause of John's death as given by Mark.[13] In other words, Jesus was connected at the beginning of his career with an apocalyptic movement which the Jewish ruler of Galilee regarded as politically dangerous. It is to be noted also, in this connection, that, according to Luke, Herod Antipas sought to suppress Jesus, whom he recognised as the successor of John.[14]

That Jesus did in fact continue the theme of John's apocalyptic message is attested by Mark, who records: 'Now after John was arrested, Jesus came into Galilee, preaching the gospel of God, and saying, "The time is fulfilled, and the kingdom of God is at hand; repent, and believe in the gospel."'[15] What was meant by the 'kingdom of God' is not defined; but there can be little doubt that, in terms of current Jewish apocalyptic belief, it denoted the establishment of Yahweh's sovereignty, and that it signified in turn the overthrow of the existing political and social order.[16] That Jesus was to be the chief agent in this apocalyptic revolution is evident from the fact that he was regarded as 'the mightier one', whose advent John had foretold.[17] Such a rôle was in fact that of the Messiah, and all the evidence points both to Jesus' claim to be the Messiah and to his popular acceptance as such.[18]

But how did Jesus conceive of the way in which he was to fulfil his Messianic rôle and establish the kingdom of God? So far as an answer can be inferred from the disparate evidence of the Gospels, it would seem that at first it was by continuing John's programme. This was the preparation of a holy people, qualified to inherit the divine kingdom. The basic idea was that Israel would be delivered, by God, from its bondage, so soon as its members repented and kept the sacred Law.[19] Hence the ethical aspect of Jesus' teaching, which is a characteristic feature of the Gospel tradition.[20] However, in the Palestine of those days, as indeed in other human situations, an ethical teaching alone, however eloquently preached, was not calculated to effect a revolution. More immediate and dynamic aims were needed, and these were supplied by contemporary Messianic expectation and the plight in which the Jews, as Yahweh's chosen people, found themselves in their Holy Land. The Jews were looking for a saviour who would deliver them from the oppression of the Romans and the tyranny of Herod.[21]

Jesus first proclaimed his message in Galilee, the home of Judas, the founder of Zealotism, where there was a strong tradition of religious patriotism.[22] Those who heard and responded to that message were not placid country-folk, of quiet-going ways, content to wait patiently on God for better times, practising in simple piety a code of good-neighbourly conduct.[23] They were people who had been nourished on the Maccabean tradition of holy war against the oppressors of Israel; Zealotism, with its gospel of violent resistance and readiness for martyrdom, was their natural response.[24]

It was from among such men that Jesus drew his apostles. One, Simon, was actually a professed Zealot;[25] Peter, an impetuous character, bore the suspicious sobriquet of *Barjona* ('Terrorist'),[26] while James and John were called *Boanerges*, which Mark euphemistically interprets as 'Sons of Thunder'.[27] The fact that one of Jesus' apostles was known specifically as 'the Zealot' has an ambivalent significance. On the one hand, it implies that the rest of the apostles were not professed Zealots, for the title 'the Zealot' was surely meant to distinguish Simon by this means from the rest. On the other hand, the fact that Jesus chose a Zealot for an apostle means that he saw nothing incompatible between the profession of Zealotism and his own movement.[28] From what we know of the principles of both movements this is not surprising. Judas of Galilee maintained the absolute sovereignty of God, and exhorted his followers to call no man 'lord'.[29] Jesus of Nazareth, being also a Galilaean, similarly maintained God's absolute sovereignty, and forbade

25 Mocking of Christ in the presence of Pilate, by Giotto

Fresco in the Arena Chapel, Padua c. 1305–12

26 Christ bearing his cross to Calvary, by Hieronymus Bosch, *c.* 1505
This picture is notable for its antisemitism

Musée des Beaux-Arts, Ghent

the giving of the things of God to Caesar, just as Judas had done.[30] Like the Zealots, the disciples of Jesus went about armed,[31] and Jesus was prepared for them to use their arms.[32]

It is understandable, therefore, that in proclaiming the imminence of the kingdom of God and being regarded as the Messiah, Jesus encouraged a movement that had dangerous political possibilities. Moreover, like the *goētes*, whom Josephus describes, Jesus performed 'signs of salvation', thus attesting his Messiahship.[33] One of his more notable miracles seems to have led to the brink of rebellion. The 'Feeding of the Five Thousand', assembled significantly in the desert, resulted in an attempt to make him king.[34] The true nature of the incident has been discreetly concealed in the Gospel records; but enough is revealed to make intelligible the *titulus* of his condemnation, placed on the cross on which he was crucified, 'The King of the Jews'.[35]

The fact that Jesus began his movement in Galilee meant that he did not come immediately into contact with the realities of Roman rule. That Herod Antipas, the Roman-appointed tetrarch of Galilee, tried to destroy him, as we have already noted, is significant. However, his chief opponents were the Jewish religious leaders. They repudiated his claims to spiritual authority, even going to the extent of ascribing his miraculous powers to daemonic possession.[36] Thus, in his eyes, they became the main enemy; for, by their high status and influence, they were preventing the conversion of Israel to that state of spiritual preparedness requisite for the coming of the kingdom of God. Until their power was broken, Israel would never achieve the state of grace that would merit its salvation. Hence, they had to be attacked in the very citadel of their power, namely, the Temple.

What was Jesus' attitude to Roman power during the Galilaean period of his activity is unknown. Although obvious evidence of that power did not appear in Galilee, Jesus must have been well acquainted with its brutal reality on his visits to Jerusalem for the festivals.[37] As we have seen, he was very familiar with the Zealot attitude to the cause of Israel's freedom, with which he surely sympathised, though not identifying himself with it.[38] He must have known of the affair of the standards and shields, described severally by Josephus and Philo; but of his reaction we know nothing.[39] In deciding to attack the priestly aristocracy in the Temple, he doubtless realised that he was in effect challenging the Roman government, which appointed the high priest and upon whose power the position of the priestly aristocracy depended. But a Roman-appointed high priest was surely as obnoxious to him as to the Zealots. If Israel were to be spiritually regenerated, the hierarchy would have to be purged of such time-serving collaborators with the heathen oppressors of Israel. Thus Jesus was faced with the same problem as that which the

Zealots sought to solve in the year 66, when they deposed the Roman appointee and replaced him by a high priest chosen by lot, according to the sacred Law.[40]

At what stage in his career came Jesus' first pronouncement on the burning issue of the Roman tribute is not clearly indicated in the Gospels. The famous episode of the Tribute Money is located in Jerusalem during his last fatal visit there;[41] but Luke's report of the accusation of the Jewish leaders suggests that Jesus' denunciation of the tribute was a general feature of his teaching.[42] The location of the Tribute Money episode in Jerusalem at the end of Jesus' career is intelligible; for the Roman tribute would not have been an immediate issue in Galilee. On the other hand, an issue of such basic importance would surely have faced Jesus while in Galilee. For he is scarcely likely to have discriminated carefully in this matter between Herod's area of jurisdiction and that controlled by the Romans—to him, as to all Jews, Judaea and Galilee were indivisible parts of the Holy Land of Yahweh, and the tribute levied on Judaea concerned every patriotic Jew. Of Jesus' attitude towards this Roman tribute there can be no doubt, as we have already seen from our extended study of the question. His ruling:'Render unto Caesar the things that are Caesar's, and unto God the things that are God's' was a definitive condemnation of the giving of the resources of the Holy Land in tribute to the heathen Emperor of Rome.[43]

The Synoptic Gospels agree in representing Jesus as finally deciding to go to Jerusalem for some undefined, but obviously fateful, purpose. Matthew and Luke follow Mark in anticipating the outcome of this visit by depicting Jesus as prophesying:

> 'Behold, we are going up to Jerusalem; and the Son of man will be delivered to the chief priests and the scribes, and they will condemn him to death, and deliver him to the Gentiles; and they will mock him, and spit upon him, and scourge him, and kill him; and after three days he will rise again.'[44]

This carefully articulated prophecy, exactly foretelling the pattern of events which were later to be described, is clearly a literary composition.[45] However, it may well reflect the sense of crisis felt by Jesus and his disciples when he decided to go to Jerusalem at the Passover, perhaps in the year 30.[46] This was to be no ordinary pilgrim-visit, but the occasion for some decisive action. What the plan was we can only infer from what subsequently happened. It was to be a Messianic *coup d'état*, aimed primarily at the sacerdotal aristocracy, whose policy and opposition were deemed obstacles to the conversion of Israel and the establishment of God's kingdom.[47] Jesus must, however, have foreseen that such an attack was likely to involve him with the Romans, and we may well ask whether it was on this occasion that he uttered that saying, nuanced by Zealot martyrdom: 'If any man would come after me, let him deny himself and take up his cross and follow me.'[48] The anticipation of the Roman penalty of crucifixion for rebellion in this saying, is very remarkable; if the saying is authentic, it is surely of the greatest significance that Jesus foresaw that he might suffer the death of a rebel at the hands of the Romans.[49]

That Jesus planned his entry into Jerusalem as a Messianic demonstration is clearly implied in Mark's account of the event.[50] In so doing, he must have realised the political seriousness of his action. To enter Jerusalem, riding on the Messianic animal, acclaimed by his followers and the crowd as the 'King of Israel', was virtually a proclamation of rebellion, and a direct public challenge to the authorities, both Jewish and Roman.[51] Matthew records that the whole city was 'shaken' (*eseisthē*) by the demonstration.[52] But more drastic action was to follow. Either on that day, directly following on his triumphal entry into the city, or on the next day, Jesus attacked the establishment of the Temple.[53] As we have already seen, this action was far more serious than the Gospel records represent it, and it was probably an attempt, made in force, to seize the Temple and reform its hierarchy as was done by the Zealots in 66.[54]

These actions, it must be appreciated, were planned and initiated by Jesus himself, and supported by his followers and the people, who believed him to be the Messiah, the Son of David, and the divinely designated King of Israel. It was dynamic political action of a revolutionary kind, and it constituted a direct challenge to the Roman government of Judaea, and to the Jewish authorites responsible for domestic affairs. In undertaking such action, Jesus must have reckoned with its consequences: that it meant armed revolt and that it would provoke armed reaction to suppress it.[55] The fact that it was undertaken about the same time as the insurrection led by Barabbas, and perhaps coincided with it, is also very significant.[56] For, it would be passing strange, if two such disturbances in Jerusalem at this time were wholly unconnected with each other. The fact, which we have noted, that Jesus' fate became involved with that of Barabbas, and that Pilate ordered two *lēstai* (Zealots) to be crucified with Jesus, suggests that, in the minds of the authorities, the two operations were regarded as connected.[57]

That a concerted attack on the Temple and the Roman positions in the Upper City or the Antonia would be a good tactical move is obvious.[58] That Jesus should have cooperated with the Zealots in such an operation is not, as we can now see, surprising. Their joint aim would doubtless have been that so movingly proclaimed on the Zealot coins issued during the revolt of AD

66–70—the 'Deliverance of Zion'.[59] But both attacks failed. The Romans were evidently successful in suppressing the Zealot assault and capturing its leader, Barabbas, though at the cost of casualties to themselves.[60] The operations in the Temple appear to have been less decisive. Jesus and his followers failed to seize the Temple; but they were too strong to be routed and captured.[61]

The events of the next few days are obscure. Jesus was apparently able to enter the city, and even the Temple, during the day-time, being too strongly supported by the crowd to be arrested openly.[62] But the impetus of the movement had obviously been lost, and Jesus was perplexed as to his future action. He seems to have stayed on until the day of the Passover, probably having arranged a secret rendezvous with his intimate disciples for eating the Passover meal within the Holy City.[63] After the meal, they withdrew in the darkness from Jerusalem, across the Kedron valley, to Gethsemane.[64] There Jesus seems to have been sorely tried in coming to a decision about the future of his movement.[65] He evidently realised by now that he had failed in his original intention, and that, if he stayed in Jerusalem, his enemies would eventually seize and punish him. Mark attributes to Jesus that night the statement: 'I will go before you to Galilee', which he interprets as referring to his subsequent post-Resurrection appearance there.[66] The statement could, however, very reasonably indicate his actual intention then. From the dangers that now threatened him in Jerusalem he would withdraw, probably alone to avoid detection, to the comparative safety of Galilee, where his followers were to rejoin him. One fact, in this connection, which is quite evident, is that Jesus did not intend to surrender himself to his enemies. Luke reveals that he had specially checked, to see that his disciples were armed, before going to Gethsemane.[67] This precaution can have only one meaning: Jesus intended to resist clandestine arrest.

But, during these last days of disillusionment and perplexity, the enemies of Jesus had also been making their plans. Unable to seize him openly, because of the attitude of the people, the Jewish leaders were suddenly given the chance of making a clandestine arrest by the defection of one of Jesus' disciples.[68] The act of betrayal then made by Judas Iscariot has earned him undying infamy, and his motive has long perplexed scholars, unconvinced by the Gospel record that he did it for thirty pieces of silver.[69] Many have sought a clue in his name 'Iscariot'. In its extant form it is meaningless; but there is reason for thinking that it is a corruption of the original form, and much ingenuity has been expended in trying to reconstruct this. Among the more suggestive reconstructions is that which derives 'Iscariot' from *sicarius*, the name given to the Zealot extremists who, armed with a concealed *sica* or curved dagger, secretly assassinated Jewish collaborators with the Roman government.[70] There are, however, several objections to this interpretation, which, though not insurmountable, would make it unwise to conclude that this disciple was a *sicarius*.[71] If he were, the fact would, of course, be of the highest significance, both because of Jesus' choice of such a political terrorist for an apostle and his betrayal of Jesus. As it is, we can only speculate why one of Jesus' apostles did so betray him to his enemies. Greed seems an inadequate motive for such a crime. From our reconstruction of the last fatal days in Jerusalem several more intelligible motives suggest themselves: disillusionment at the failure of Jesus to effect the expected Messianic *coup d'état*; fear of coming retribution for all involved in his attempt; even, perhaps, to force Jesus to use the supernatural power attributed to him by placing him in a desperate position.[72]

Whatever the motives of Judas Iscariot, he gave the Jewish authorities the opportunity they needed. For he revealed the secret rendezvous of Jesus in Gethsemane, where he might be seized, with his chief lieutenants, without the interference of the crowd. It is evident from the Gospel accounts that the Jewish leaders took no chances in arresting Jesus. They sent a strong, well-armed party to Gethsemane;[73] if the record of John is to be trusted, it was a combined Roman-Jewish operation.[74] The function of Judas was to identify Jesus among the shadowy figures of his followers in the garden.[75] The arrest met with armed resistance; but the force sent by the authorities was too strong. They succeeded in seizing Jesus; but in the darkness and confused fighting they failed to arrest the disciples, who made good their escape.[76]

Having at last secured the person of this dangerous revolutionary, for such Jesus surely was in their eyes, the Jewish leaders evidently felt that they had to act swiftly that night. Doubtless they still feared the temper of the people when the arrest of Jesus became known, and so deemed it advisable to deliver him to Pilate for execution early the next morning.[77] Their task that night, therefore, was to discover the full dimensions of the attempted *coup*, particularly the identities of the chief followers of Jesus, who had escaped them.[78] Hence the interrogation by either the ex-high priest Annas, or the Sanhedrin, about the assault in the Temple and Jesus' Messianic claims.[79] Enough was learned from these enquiries, and probably from other sources, to enable an indictment to be drawn up, ready for the handing over of the prisoner to Pilate in the morning. From our investigation of the Gospel accounts, it would seem that the main charge was that of the assumption of royal power as the 'King of the Jews', with subsidiary charges of inciting the people to revolt and not to pay the Roman tribute.[80] Further, Jesus was presented as the real leader of the insurrection, and not Barabbas.[81]

These charges, relating to matters about which Pilate would doubtless already have had some acquaintance, were accepted by him after he had formally questioned Jesus on them.[82] The execution of the consequent sentence for seditious action was ordered forthwith. After the customary scourging, Jesus was crucified, with the *titulus* of his condemnation placed on his cross: the King of the Jews.[83] To complete this warning against rebellion, Pilate also ordered two Zealots, taken during the insurrection, to be crucified on either side of Jesus.[84] Thus was Jesus executed as the leader of the revolt which occurred in Jerusalem, at that historic Passover of the year 30.

In the context of Jewish-Roman relations in Judaea, during the first six decades of the first century, the activity and execution of Jesus of Nazareth constituted one of a number of similar incidents. Josephus describes many Messianic claimants, reputedly endowed with miraculous power, who promised 'signs of deliverance', but whom the Romans promptly suppressed.[85] Their deaths ended their Messianic reputations, even though they were regarded as martyrs for the cause of Israel's freedom. Why, then, should Jesus, who shared a like fate, have become the founder, or rather the deity, of a new religion? To answer this question would require another volume, larger than this. Some indications of the main form of that answer have already been given, incidentally, in the course of our study here. Suffice it to say that the disciples' subsequent conviction, that Jesus had been raised from the dead, caused them to believe that he would shortly return, with supernatural power, to complete his Messianic role. This original form of Christianity was essentially a Messianic movement, intelligible only within the terms of contemporary Judaism. According to the insight of its members, it had continued faithful to the teaching and purpose of Jesus. But it was virtually wiped out when the Jerusalem Church perished in the Jewish catastrophe of AD 70.[86] That Christianity did not disappear then, but survived to become a universal salvation-religion, was due to the transforming genius of Paul. Though defeated in his own lifetime, Paul's interpretation of the death of Christ as a divinely planned event, transcending time and place, was rehabilitated after AD 70 and became the foundational doctrine of Catholic Christianity. Hence, as we have seen, the later Gospel writers were not really describing the trial of the historical Jesus of Nazareth, despite the apparent historical setting of their accounts. They were explaining away an embarrassing involvement of the incarnate Son of God with the Roman procurator Pontius Pilate.

CHAPTER SEVEN

The Trial of Jesus in Early Christian Tradition and Art

Having now completed our study of the Christian evidence for the trial of Jesus, there remains an obvious question, which doubtless has occurred to many readers of this book: were any records of the trial made, during the first century, by persons other than Christians? And, if there were, what happened to them?

To answer this question we have to consider two complicated, but very intriguing, problems. The first concerns the Jewish historian Josephus, who lived during this period and whose writings are our chief source of information about contemporary Jewish-Roman affairs.[1] He, of all possible writers at this time, is the most obvious from whom we might expect an account of Jesus, uninfluenced by those considerations that affected the Gospel writers. In the extant Greek text of the eighteenth book of his *Jewish Antiquities* there is, in fact, a passage about Jesus; but, if Josephus had written it as it stands, he must have been a Christian himself.[2] Since all our other evidence concerning him negates such a conclusion, the general opinion among scholars is that the passage is either wholly or partly a later Christian fabrication.[3] The question is a very complex one, which the present writer has discussed at length elsewhere, and it will suffice here to deal with just those points which concern our understanding of the trial of Jesus.[4]

The present form of the passage can be traced back to the fourth century, when it is first attested by Eusebius, bishop of Caesarea.[5] Since other evidence indicates that Josephus had written about Jesus in a manner distasteful to Christians, there is reason for thinking that about the time of Eusebius the offending text of the Jewish historian had been amended to its present form.[6] The following is a translation of the passage, in which the more obvious amendments are placed in square brackets:

About this time arose Jesus, a wise man (*sophos anēr*), [if indeed it is proper to call him a man]; for he was a doer of marvellous works, a teacher of men who received the truth with pleasure, and he led after him many Jews, and many also of the Greek population. [This was the Christ.] And when Pilate had inflicted on him the punishment of the cross, on the indictment (*endeixei*) of our chief men, those who first loved him did not desist; [for he appeared to them on the third day, being alive again, the divine prophets having told of these and innumerable other wonders concerning him]. And up till now the race (*phylon*) of the Christians, being named after him, has not died out.[7]

That Josephus should have recognised Jesus as the Christ (i.e. Messiah) is incredible, for he held that the world-ruler, prophesied to come out of Judaea, was the Roman Emperor Vespasian, who was elected Emperor while campaigning in that land in AD 69.[8] Josephus also thought that one of the causes of the Jews' fatal resistance to Rome was their belief in an 'ambiguous oracle' about this future world-ruler; for this is how he politically explained the Messianic expectation of his people to Gentile readers.[9] Hence, as we have seen, he describes Messianic pretenders pejoratively as wonder-working charlatans (*goētes*), who misled the people.[10] Such, doubtless, would have been his evaluation of Jesus. Another significant point is that Josephus designates certain Zealot leaders as *sophistes*, so that there is much reason for thinking that the description of Jesus, in the above-quoted passage, as *sophos anēr* may well be a Christian emendation of the original epithet *sophistēs*.[11]

However that may be, what concerns us especially in the passage is the statement about the execution of Jesus. Its terseness has the ring of authenticity. If it preserves, therefore, what Josephus originally wrote, it constitutes important evidence for us. That Pilate 'inflicted on him (Jesus) the punishment of the cross, on the indictment of our chief men' succinctly summarises our own conclusions. For the word 'indictment' (*endeixis*), in this context, is a straightforward legal term denoting the laying of information against a person, or a writ of indictment.[12] Josephus' statement, accordingly, describes what his readers would have understood as a normal form of juridical procedure: the Jewish leaders had presented a case against Jesus which Pilate accepted as proven, and the penalty he decreed indicates that the offence was political.

The fact that Christian scribes amended the text of Josephus, to make him appear as a contemporary Jewish witness to the Messiahship and resurrection of Jesus, is significant for us also in another connection.[13] For, in enquiring whether any non-Christian record of the trial of Jesus was made, the possibility of an official Roman account must be considered. That such accounts were made of judicial transactions by provincial governors, and, where important cases were concerned, reports duly transmitted to the Imperial chancery, is certain.[14] Moreover, the fact that the Christian apologists Justin Martyr and Tertullian asserted, in the second century, that the truth of their claims about Jesus could be proved from the official archives is significant.[15] For, although the extravagant nature of their claims is such as to make it wholly incredible that confirmation of them would be found in the public records of a pagan government, the assumption that Pilate would have reported the case of Jesus must have been deemed reasonable from current official practice.

This presumption of the existence of such a record is strangely confirmed by the action of the Emperor Maximin in 311. As part of his policy of persecuting Christians, according to Eusebius, Maximin caused 'Memoirs of Pilate' (Pilatou hypomnēmata) to be forged and circulated. Copies were even sent to schools for children to study and memorise, so that they had 'every day on their lips the names of Jesus and Pilate and the Memoirs forged to insult us'.[16] Eusebius was a Christian bishop, and he was naturally intent on denigrating the memory of the persecutor Maximin, who had eventually been overthrown by Constantine, the first Christian Emperor of Rome.[17] But the fact that Maximin should have thought of discrediting Christianity by publishing 'Memoirs of Pilate' is both significant and tantalising. It is tantalising because no examples of these 'Memoirs' have survived—when Christianity came to power, they were evidently rounded up and destroyed.[18] Eusebius describes the documents as forgeries; but in the absence of any example of them, we have only his word that this was so. The fact, moreover, that these Acta Pilati were suppressed and that no detailed attempt was apparently made to expose them as forgeries, causes some legitimate suspicion. For it would surely have been a better defence, if no such record of the trial of Jesus had existed in the official archives, to have insisted on the fact that no report had ever been received and preserved there. And from that inference we may fairly go on to observe that, if a report by Pilate favourable to Jesus had existed, without doubt it would have been triumphantly published by Christians once they had acquired power and influence in the Roman state. Consequently, we have to conclude that, in view of the evidence indicating that Pilate had reported officially on the case of Jesus, the fact that both the original report and Maximin's edition did not survive, can only mean that the report also was considered obnoxious and destroyed after the triumph of the Church in the fourth century.[19] In what way it would have been obnoxious we can only surmise; but, since such a report would have concerned the trial of Jesus and his condemnation for sedition, it would seem reasonable to suppose that Pilate reported him to have been guilty of this offence.

The consternation caused by Maximin's publication of the *Acta Pilati* seems to have prompted the creation of a Christian version, designed to supply a more detailed account of the trial of Jesus, in accordance with the tastes of Christian piety.[20] The work is clearly compiled from the Gospel accounts, supplemented by pious, but curious imaginings.[21] It takes a narrative form, and, according to the prologue, it purports to be the work of one Ananias, who claims that he 'sought out the memorials that were made at that season in the time of our master Jesus Christ, which the Jews deposited with Pontius Pilate, and found the memorials in Hebrew (letters), and by the good pleasure of God I translated them into Greek (letters) for the informing of all them that call upon the name of our Lord Jesus Christ'. This editorial work was supposed to have been done in the 18th year of the Emperor Theodosius, i.e. AD 425.[22]

The account is long and meandering, but the following points are worth noticing. Jesus, who is described as the son of Joseph the carpenter, begotten of Mary, is accused by the Jewish leaders of being a sorcerer and claiming to be the Son of God and a king.[23] Pilate is depicted as treating him with great consideration. When Jesus enters the *praetorium*, the images on the Roman standards bow in reverence to him.[24] Long, tortuous dialogues are recorded between Pilate and the Jewish leaders, and Pilate and Jesus. The accusation about destroying the Temple is mentioned and also the Barabbas episode, but clearly without insight into their original significance. Pilate is described as consulting Jesus as to what he should do with him. Jesus replies, obviously exonerating Pilate, that he must 'Do as it hath been given thee', which evidently means that Pilate has to carry out what the prophets had foretold should happen to Jesus.[25] Pilate tries to persuade the Jews to deal with Jesus according to their own law, which, they inform him, decrees death by stoning for blasphemy. But, inexplicably, they insist on his crucifixion.[26] The narrative drags on, often repetitiously, making much of Jesus' miracles. Pilate denounces the Jews for being always seditious; but eventually he washes his hands 'before the sun', declaring his innocence, to which the Jews reply, 'His blood be on us and on our children!', according to Matthew's account.[27] Pilate is then represented as sentencing Jesus:

> 'Thy nation hath convicted thee (accused thee) as being a king: therefore have I decreed that thou shouldest first be scourged according to the law of the pious emperors, and thereafter hanged upon the cross in the garden wherein thou wast taken: and let Dysmas and Gestas the two malefactors be crucified with thee.'[28]

The narrative goes on to tell how the centurion, having witnessed the death of Jesus and the attendant omens, reported to Pilate and his wife what had happened. They are greatly affected by the news, and abstain from food that day.[29] The account continues with a long and involved description of the resurrection of Jesus and its effect on the Jewish leaders.[30]

The tendency of this writing is clearly to elaborate the Gospel thesis that the Jews were responsible for the death of Jesus, thereby exonerating Pilate. This tendency is still further developed in another Greek text, which takes the form of a report by Pilate to the Emperor Tiberius about the crucifixion of Jesus and his resurrection.[31] Pilate puts the blame on the Jews, and on Herod, Archelaus, Philip, Annas and Caiaphas—obviously a list of Jewish magnates, culled carelessly from the Gospels of Matthew and Luke.[32] On receiving the letter, the Emperor is enraged with Pilate and orders his arrest and transport to Rome, and the Jews are enslaved for their wickedness. Pilate is beheaded; but he dies piously, his martyr's death being attested by the voice of Christ from heaven:

'All the generations and the families of the Gentiles shall call thee blessed, because in thy days were fulfilled all these things which were spoken by the prophets concerning me; and thou also shalt appear as my witness (or martyr) at my second coming, when I shall judge the twelve tribes of Israel and them that have not confessed my name.'

An angel of the Lord receives Pilate's head, at the sight of which his pious wife Procla is filled with joy and so expires.[33]

Before this achievement of sanctity by Pilate, the way had been prepared by earlier Christian writers. Justin Martyr (c. 100–165) had cited the 'Acts of Pontius Pilate' as attesting the miracles of Jesus.[34] According to Tertullian (c. 160–220), the Jews had 'extorted it from Pilate that Jesus should be handed over to them to be crucified', and Pilate ('himself in his secret heart already a Christian')[35] reported the whole matter in such a way to Tiberius that the Emperor was convinced of Jesus' divinity and sought to persuade the Roman Senate of it.[36] Origen (c. 185–254) held Caiaphas to be wholly responsible for the Crucifixion, and Herod partly so;[37] but Pilate he completely exonerated, regarding him as a witness to the royalty and Messiahship of Jesus.[38] The second-century Gospel of Peter depicts the Jews and Herod as refusing to wash their hands, in contrast to Pilate, and it curiously represents Herod as being in command of the Crucifixion and Pilate as begging the body of Jesus from him.[39]

Although Procla, the wife of Pilate, was canonised as a saint in the Eastern Church, and Pilate achieved this distinction among the Ethiopian Christians,[40] the tide of Christian opinion seems later to have turned against the procurator.

The reason for this is not certain; but it may have resulted from the fact that, once Christianity had become the established religion of the Roman Empire, the need ceased for presenting Pilate as a witness to the innocence of Jesus of the charge of sedition against Rome.[41] Eusebius marks this change of attitude by relating that Pilate, overwhelmed by misfortune, committed suicide, during the reign of Gaius, 'for the penalty of God, as it seems, followed hard after him'.[42] A later legend, in Latin, provides a fanciful account of how Pilate anticipated his execution by suicide. Tiberius had his corpse, with a millstone attached, flung into the Tiber. Its presence there attracted crowds of demons and caused such consternation that it was transported to Vienne, on the Rhone. After subsequent burial in the territory of Lausanne and conse-quent demonic disturbances, it was deposited in a well or lake surrounded by mountains, where its awful presence continued to provoke diabolical activities.[43]

The presentation of the trial of Jesus in early Christian art is both interesting and instructive. In view of the dominance of the Passion and Crucifixion of Jesus as subjects of Western medieval and Renaissance art,[44] the absence of these subjects in the paintings found in the catacombs of Rome, which provide the earliest examples of Christian art, is surprising.[45] The subjects depicted in these catacombs, where Christians buried their dead and wor-shipped during the period of persecution, seem to be a curious selection from the many dramatic scenes so vividly presented in the Gospels.[46] The chief topics treated are the baptism of Jesus, the curing of the paralytic man, and the raising of Lazarus.[47] That preference should have been given to such subjects, which is paralleled by a similar seemingly curious selection of Old Testament topics, is significant of the outlook and concern of Christians during the second and third centuries.[48] The Old and New Testament sub-jects, chosen for depiction in the catacombs, form a pattern of events symbol-ising salvation and new life. These were the themes that inspired them as they faced persecution and death for their faith. The example of the suffering Christ was probably appreciated by them more as the divine embodiment of the martyr-ideal, in that 'before Pontius Pilate (Jesus had) witnessed a good confession', than as a demonstration of the price paid by the Son of God to redeem mankind according to later theology.[49] The early Christians in-stinctively looked beyond the suffering and death, which were ever-present realities for them, to the new and triumphant life that lay beyond.[50] Moreover, as a scurrilous pagan drawing of a Christian worshipping a crucified human figure with an ass's head significantly shows,[51] the crucifixion of Jesus was not a subject which they chose to emphasise by depicting it in their places of worship and burial. Hence no representation of the Crucifixion has yet been found in the catacombs, and of other scenes of the Passion of Jesus only a problematic depiction of the Crowning with Thorns occurs in the third-century Catacomb of Praetextatus at Rome.[52]

With the ending of persecution and the triumph of Christianity under the Emperor Constantine (c. 288–337), Christian art found more adequate modes and places of expression than in painting on catacomb walls. From the fourth century the custom began of providing stone sarcophagi for the dead, adorned with carvings of a rich variety of subjects of theological significance.[53] One of the earliest of these sarcophagi, known as the Sarcophagus of the Two Brothers, provides our first example of the plastic representation of the trial of Jesus.[54] The scene is placed next to one of Abraham's sacrifice of Isaac, doubtless implying thereby a theological relationship.[55] The scene itself depicts the hand-washing of Pilate, and it is characterised by its restraint in indicating the significance of the act. It would, accordingly, seem necessary to infer that the incident and its meaning were both well known and regarded as constituting the most important aspect of the Trial.[56]

The same incident is represented on the Sarcophagus of Junius Bassus, which fortunately can be exactly dated for the year 359.[57] Jesus, portrayed as a beardless youth, accompanied by two guards, stands before Pilate, who looks away from the accused while a servant prepares to pour water for his act of ablution.[58] In the middle of the series of scenes in the lower register on the sarcophagus is another scene also related to the Passion history, namely, Christ's triumphal entry into Jerusalem.[59] The other episodes depicted, in haphazard juxtaposition but clearly interrelated in theme, deal with sacrifice (Abraham and Isaac), martyrdom (Daniel and Peter), and the Fall of Man (Adam and Eve).[60] Another fourth-century sarcophagus, now in the Lateran Museum, Rome (no. 174), also shows Christ before Pilate, who is depicted in the act of washing his hands.[61]

Evidence of a more concentrated interest in the historical aspect of the Passion of Jesus is provided by a sarcophagus of the same period, now also in the Lateran Museum.[62] Four incidents are depicted, which are separated from each other by interposed columns.[63] The centre of the sculptured panel is evidently intended to interpret and proclaim the theological significance of the scenes. It shows a cross, surmounted with the famous Chi Rho monogram denoting Christ, encircled by a laurel wreath of triumph; beneath the Cross, two sleeping Roman soldiers symbolise the Resurrection of Christ.[64] This note of victory is repeated in various ways in the four scenes. The two scenes to the left of the central motif, represent a single incident, namely, the trial before Pilate. Jesus, shown as a beardless youth in Roman costume, guarded by an armed soldier, is portrayed as addressing Pilate, who turns away in doubt or embarrassment, while a servant prepares vessels for the washing of his hands. Above Pilate hangs a laurel wreath, which, together with the magisterial stance of Christ, denotes his triumph over his Roman judge.[65] The scenes on the other side depict Simon of Cyrene carrying the Cross of Christ, which is surmounted by a victorious laurel wreath, and Christ as being crowned by a wreath of laurel, and not of thorns. The message of this sculptured composition is plain: in the Trial and the Mockery, and on the Way to Calvary, Christ is the victor who triumphs.

The fact that of Christ's Trial only his encounter with Pilate is depicted in the scenes carved on these sarcophagi is interesting; but its meaning is capable of several interpretations. It could denote that in the mind of Christians at this time the Roman trial was regarded as more notable than that before the Jewish Sanhedrin, which the Gospels also record.[66] The fact that Pilate's hand-washing is indicated suggests, however, that Christians were particularly interested in this symbolic act of repudiation of responsibility. But how exactly this interest is to be assessed is not clear. The fact that Pilate is represented as averting his gaze from Jesus suggests that he is embarrassed by his act of condemnation, despite the symbolic washing.[67]

An ivory *lipsanotheca*, or reliquary casket, now in the Museo dellE'tà Cristiana at Brescia, which dates from about the latter end of the fourth century, provides our earliest extant example of an attempt to depict in sequence, the chief incidents of the arrest and trial of Jesus.[68] In the carved panel concerned, the top register shows the agony in Gethsemane, the arrest, and the denial of Peter. The bottom register, from left to right, represents Jesus before Annas and Caiaphas, who wear Roman costume, and his trial by Pilate, who turns away from him to wash his hands.[69]

What seems to be the earliest connected pictorial record of the chief incidents of the Passion, Crucifixion and Resurrection of Jesus is contained on the carved sides of an ivory pyxis, which was probably made in southern Gaul in the early fifth century, and which is now in the British Museum, London.[70] One panel shows, in miniature, a composite scene in which Pilate, engaged in washing his hands, watches Christ bearing his cross, while Peter's denial is denoted by the crowing cock. Another scene depicts the crucified Christ, attended by the Virgin Mary and John, and with the centurion making his gesture of recognition; to the left, the repentant Judas hangs from a tree.[71] The Resurrection of Christ is represented, on another panel, by the Empty Tomb, about which are grouped the sleeping soldiers and the devout women. The realistic depiction of the Crucifixion on this pyxis, together with a carved representation on the wooden doors of the church of Santa Sabina, Rome, dating from about 432, constitute the earliest extant portrayals of the event, which was later to dominate Western Christian art.[72]

We may conveniently conclude our survey of the depiction of the trial of Jesus in early Christian art by noting two remarkable examples of the sixth century. Among a series of mosaics, illustrating the ministry of Christ, which adorn the basilica of Sant'Apollinare Nuovo, Ravenna, are four graphically presented scenes of the arrest in Gethsemane, the Sanhedrin trial, the trial before Pilate, and the passage to Calvary.[73] In all the scenes Christ is represented as the dominant figure, somewhat taller than the rest; he is bearded and his head is encircled with a cross-imposed nimbus—in fact, what was to become the traditional Christ-figure is already achieved here.[74] It would seem that the artist encountered much difficulty in portraying the Sanhedrin: three figures, seated together, before whom Christ stands in an admonishing attitude, serve to represent the members of the supreme Jewish court.[75] The depiction of the Roman trial is particularly interesting for the artist's attempt to show the Jewish leaders as accusing Jesus to Pilate, who washes his hands. Although these scenes appear to be genuine attempts to portray actual historical events, their depiction is invested with a hieratic spirit which reflects the fully developed Christology now current in the Church.[76]

The other notable sixth-century example occurs in the *Rossano Gospels* (*Codex Purpureus*), now in the Museo Diocesano, Rossano (Calabria).[77] It constitutes the most elaborate attempt so far known to represent the trial before Pilate. The procurator occupies the centre of the scene. Before his seated figure is a table, on which writing equipment is laid, and behind his 'seat of judgment' stand two officers holding what are doubtless intended to be Roman military standards. On either side of Pilate, two groups of gesticulating figures represent the Jews vehemently accusing Jesus; two scrolls lying on the ground probably indicate the records of their charges. Pilate is depicted as an elderly magistrate, grave and dignified, whose calm gesture strikingly contrasts with the violent gestures of the malevolently-intentioned Jews.[78] In the foreground, the majestic figure of Christ, his head nimbus-encircled, contrasts with the contorted figure of the manacled Barabbas. The artist has evidently sensed the drama of the choice which, according to the Gospels, Pilate offered to the Jews, between Christ and Barabbas. With considerable ability, he has vividly presented this contrast by emphasising the divine majesty of Christ and the squalid criminality of Barabbas.

We need not pursue our enquiry beyond the sixth century, for by that time Christians could contemplate the Trial of Jesus in terms of a well-established soteriology, which explained the purpose of God from the Creation to the Last Judgment.[79] Moreover, the Gospel presentation of the Trial had lost its original apologetic significance; for the scandal of the Roman cross ceased to be a problem once the Church became the established religion of the Roman Empire. The Trial, accordingly, took its place as an incident in the sacred history of mankind's salvation by the incarnate Son of God. In itself, the Trial had no theological significance, and it naturally tended to be overshadowed by the Crucifixion and Resurrection, which were of fundamental significance in the theology of salvation. However, the human interest in the Trial was guaranteed by the vivid Gospel narrative, with which all Christians became familiar through its reading in liturgical worship. So far as linear and plastic art were concerned, transactions of the Trial made a rather difficult subject for portrayal. Consequently, incidents of the Passion story of more immediate emotional impact, such as the Scourging of Christ and the Crucifixion, naturally tended to be the chief subjects for representation in medieval and later Christian art.[80] The Trial lent itself better to presentation in the theatre, and Pilate and Caiaphas became well-established characters in the medieval mystery plays, often as examples of worldly pomp and arrogance.[81]

Interest in the Trial of Jesus as an historical event had to await the emergence of that acute historical sense which has characterised modern Western thought from the nineteenth century onwards.[82] Bacon's 'jesting Pilate' ceased now to be a type-figure[83] and became a Roman magistrate, whose actions and motives historians sought to evaluate in the light of what was known of Roman history and jurisprudence. Novelists even took a hand, and Anatole France cynically suggested the insignificance of the Trial of Jesus in Pilate's career, when he depicted the aged procurator, in retirement at Baiae, as replying to a question about Jesus: 'Jésus de Nazareth? Je ne me rappelle pas.'[84] But much of this new historical interest in the Trial of Jesus was inspired by a desire to defend the authenticity of the Gospel accounts; for the conviction, stemming from Mark's original apologetic, generally prevailed that Jesus could not have been guilty of seditious action against Rome. However, as the foregoing study has attempted to show, new evidence of Palestinian Judaism in the first century and new approaches in the evaluation of the original evidence have required a radical re-assessment of the traditional presentation.

Earliest Extant Records
of the Trial of Jesus

Gospel of Mark
(Rome, c. 71 AD)
Chap. 14:26 ff.

26 And when they had sung a hymn, they went out to the Mount of Olives. ²⁷And Jesus said to them, 'You will all fall away; for it is written, "I will strike the shepherd, and the sheep will be scattered." ²⁸ But after I am raised up, I will go before you to Galilee.' ²⁹ Peter said to him, 'Even though they all fall away, I will not.' ³⁰And Jesus said to him, 'Truly, I say to you, this very night, before the cock crows twice, you will deny me three times.' ³¹ But he said vehemently, 'If I must die with you, I will not deny you.' And they all said the same.

32 And they went to a place which was called Gethsem'ane; and he said to his disciples, 'Sit here, while I pray.' ³³ And he took with him Peter and James and John, and began to be greatly distressed and troubled. ³⁴ And he said to them, 'My soul is very sorrowful, even to death; remain here, and watch.'ᵈ ³⁵And going a little farther, he fell on the ground and prayed that, if it were possible, the hour might pass from him. ³⁶And he said, 'Abba, Father, all things are possible to thee; remove this cup from me; yet not what I will, but what thou wilt.' ³⁷And he came and found them sleeping, and he said to Peter, 'Simon, are you asleep? Could you not watchᵈ one hour? ³⁸ Watchᵈ and pray that you may not enter into temptation; the spirit indeed is willing, but the flesh is weak.' ³⁹And again he went away and prayed, saying the same words. ⁴⁰And again he came and found them sleeping, for their eyes were very heavy; and they did not know what to answer him. ⁴¹And he came the third time, and said to them, 'Are you still sleeping and taking your rest? It is enough; the hour has come; the Son of man is betrayed into the hands of sinners. ⁴² Rise, let us be going; see, my betrayer is at hand.'

43 And immediately, while he was still speaking, Judas came, one of the twelve, and with him a crowd with swords and clubs, from the chief priests and the scribes and the elders. ⁴⁴ Now the betrayer had given them a sign, saying, 'The one I shall kiss is the man; seize him and lead him away safely.' ⁴⁵And when he came, he went up to him at once, and said, 'Master!' And he kissed him. ⁴⁶And they laid hands on him and seized

Gospel of Matthew
(Alexandria, c. 80 AD)
Chap. 26:30 ff.

30 And when they had sung a hymn, they went out to the Mount of Olives. ³¹ Then Jesus said to them, 'You will all fall away because of me this night; for it is written, "I will strike the shepherd, and the sheep of the flock will be scattered." ³² But after I am raised up, I will go before you to Galilee.' ³³ Peter declared to him, 'Though they all fall away because of you, I will never fall away.' ³⁴ Jesus said to him, 'Truly, I say to you, this very night, before the cock crows, you will deny me three times.' ³⁵ Peter said to him, 'Even if I must die with you, I will not deny you.' And so said all the disciples.

36 Then Jesus went with them to a place called Gethsem'ane, and he said to his disciples, 'Sit here, while I go yonder and pray.' ³⁷And taking with him Peter and the two sons of Zeb'edee, he began to be sorrowful and troubled. ³⁸ Then he said to them, 'My soul is very sorrowful, even to death; remain here, and watchʰ with me.' ³⁹And going a little farther he fell on his face and prayed, 'My Father, if it be possible, let this cup pass from me; nevertheless, not as I will, but as thou wilt.' ⁴⁰And he came to the disciples and found them sleeping; and he said to Peter, 'So, could you not watchʰ with me one hour? ⁴¹ Watchʰ and pray that you may not enter into temptation; the spirit indeed is willing, but the flesh is weak.' ⁴²Again, for the second time, he went away and prayed, 'My Father, if this cannot pass unless I drink it, thy will be done.' ⁴³And again he came and found them sleeping, for their eyes were heavy. ⁴⁴ So, leaving them again, he went away and prayed for the third time, saying the same words.⁴⁵ Then he came to the disciples and said to them, 'Are you still sleeping and taking your rest? Behold, the hour is at hand, and the Son of man is betrayed into the hands of sinners. ⁴⁶ Rise, let us be going; see, my betrayer is at hand.'

47 While he was still speaking, Judas came, one of the twelve, and with him a great crowd with swords and clubs, from the chief priests and the elders of the people. ⁴⁸ Now the betrayer had given them a sign, saying, 'The one I shall kiss is the man;

Gospel of Luke
(*Greece or Syria, c. 85* AD)
Chap. 22:39 ff.

Gospel of John
(*Asia Minor, c. 100* AD)
Chap. 18:1 ff.

---

39 And he came out, and went, as was his custom, to the Mount of Olives; and the disciples followed him. ⁴⁰And when he came to the place he said to them, 'Pray that you may not enter into temptation.' ⁴¹And he withdrew from them about a stone's throw, and knelt down and prayed, ⁴² 'Father, if thou art willing, remove this cup from me; nevertheless not my will, but thine, be done.' ⁴³And there appeared to him an angel from heaven, strengthening him. ⁴⁴And being in an agony he prayed more earnestly; and his sweat became like great drops of blood falling down upon the ground.¹ ⁴⁵And when he rose from prayer, he came to the disciples and found them sleeping for sorrow, ⁴⁶ and he said to them, 'Why do you sleep? Rise and pray that you may not enter into temptation.'

47 While he was still speaking, there came a crowd, and the man called Judas, one of the twelve, was leading them. He drew near to Jesus to kiss him; ⁴⁸ but Jesus said to him, 'Judas, would you betray the Son of man with a kiss?' ⁴⁹And when those who were about him saw what would follow, they said,'Lord, shall we strike with the sword?' ⁵⁰And one of them struck the slave of the high priest and cut off his right ear. ⁵¹ But Jesus said, 'No more of this!' And he touched his ear and healed him. ⁵² Then Jesus said to the chief priests and captains of the temple and elders, who had come out against him, 'Have you come out as against a robber, with swords and clubs? ⁵³ When I was with you day after day in the temple, you did not lay hands on me. But this is your hour, and the power of darkness.'

54 Then they seized him and led him away, bringing him into the high priest's house. Peter followed at a distance; ⁵⁵ and when they had kindled a fire in the middle of the courtyard and sat down together, Peter sat among them. ⁵⁶ Then a maid, seeing him as he sat in the light and gazing at him, said, 'This man also was with him.' ⁵⁷ But he denied it, saying, 'Woman, I do not know him.' ⁵⁸And a little later some one else saw him and said, 'You also are one of them.' But Peter said, 'Man, I am not.' ⁵⁹And after an interval of about an hour still

18 When Jesus had spoken these words, he went forth with his disciples across the Kidron valley, where there was a garden, which he and his disciples entered. ² Now Judas, who betrayed him, also knew the place; for Jesus often met there with his disciples. ³ So Judas, procuring a band of soldiers and some officers from the chief priests and the Pharisees, went there with lanterns and torches and weapons. ⁴ Then Jesus, knowing all that was to befall him, came forward and said to them, 'Whom do you seek?' ⁵ They answered him, 'Jesus of Nazareth.' Jesus said to them, 'I am he.' Judas, who betrayed him, was standing with them. ⁶ When he said to them, 'I am he,' they drew back and fell to the ground. ⁷Again he asked them, 'Whom do you seek?' And they said, 'Jesus of Nazareth.' ⁸ Jesus answered, 'I told you that I am he; if you seek me, let these men go.' ⁹ This was to fulfil the word which he had spoken, 'Of those whom thou gavest me I lost not one.' ¹⁰ Then Simon Peter, having a sword, drew it and struck the high priest's slave and cut off his right ear. The slave's name was Malchus. ¹¹ Jesus said to Peter, 'Put your sword into its sheath; shall I not drink the cup which the Father has given me?'

12 So the band of soldiers and their captain and the officers of the Jews seized Jesus and bound him. ¹³ First they led him to Annas; for he was the father-in-law of Ca'iaphas, who was high priest that year. ¹⁴ It was Ca'iaphas who had given counsel to the Jews that it was expedient that one man should die for the people.

15 Simon Peter followed Jesus, and so did another disciple. As this disciple was known to the high priest, he entered the court of the high priest along with Jesus, ¹⁶ while Peter stood outside at the door. So the other disciple, who was known to the high priest, went out and spoke to the maid who kept the door, and brought Peter in. ¹⁷ The maid who kept the door said to Peter, 'Are not you also one of this man's disciples?' He said, 'I am not.' ¹⁸ Now the servants¹ and officers had made a charcoal fire, because it was cold, and they were standing and warming themselves; Peter

him. [47] But one of those who stood by drew his sword, and struck the slave of the high priest and cut off his ear. [48]And Jesus said to them, 'Have you come out as against a robber, with swords and clubs to capture me? [49] Day after day I was with you in the temple teaching, and you did not seize me. But let the scriptures be fulfilled.' [50]And they all forsook him, and fled.

[51] And a young man followed him, with nothing but a linen cloth about his body; and they seized him, [52] but he left the linen cloth and ran away naked.

[53] And they led Jesus to the high priest; and all the chief priests and the elders and the scribes were assembled. [54]And Peter had followed him at a distance, right into the courtyard of the high priest; and he was sitting with the guards, and warming himself at the fire. [55] Now the chief priests and the whole council sought testimony against Jesus to put him to death; but they found none. [56] For many bore false witness against him, and their witness did not agree. [57]And some stood up and bore false witness against him, saying, [58] 'We heard him say, "I will destroy this temple that is made with hands, and in three days I will build another, not made with hands." ' [59] Yet not even so did their testimony agree. [60]And the high priest stood up in the midst, and asked Jesus, 'Have you no answer to make? What is it that these men testify against you?' [61] But he was silent and made no answer. Again the high priest asked him, 'Are you the Christ, the Son of the Blessed?' [62]And Jesus said, 'I am; and you will see the Son of man sitting at the right hand of Power, and coming with the clouds of heaven.' [63]And the high priest tore his mantle, and said, 'Why do we still need witnesses? [64] You have heard his blasphemy. What is your decision?' And they all condemned him as deserving death. [65]And some began to spit on him, and to cover his face, and to strike him, saying to him, 'Prophesy!' And the guards received him with blows.

[66] And as Peter was below in the courtyard, one of the maids of the high priest came; [67] and seeing Peter warming himself, she looked at him, and said, 'You also were with the Nazarene, Jesus.' [68] But he denied it, saying, 'I neither know nor understand what you mean.' And he went out into the gateway.[j] [69]And the maid saw him, and began again to say to the bystanders, 'This

seize him.' [49]And he came up to Jesus at once and said, 'Hail, Master!'[i] And he kissed him. [50] Jesus said to him, 'Friend, why are you here?'[j] Then they came up and laid hands on Jesus and seized him. [51]And behold, one of those who were with Jesus stretched out his hand and drew his sword, and struck the slave of the high priest, and cut off his ear. [52] Then Jesus said to him, 'Put your sword back into its place; for all who take the sword will perish by the sword. [53] Do you think that I cannot appeal to my Father, and he will at once send me more than twelve legions of angels? [54] But how then should the scriptures be fulfilled, that it must be so?' [55]At that hour Jesus said to the crowds, 'Have you come out as against a robber, with swords and clubs to capture me? Day after day I sat in the temple teaching, and you did not seize me. [56] But all this has taken place, that the scriptures of the prophets might be fulfilled.' Then all the disciples forsook him and fled.

[57] Then those who had seized Jesus led him to Ca'iaphas the high priest, where the scribes and the elders had gathered. [58] But Peter followed him at a distance, as far as the courtyard of the high priest, and going inside he sat with the guards to see the end. [59] Now the chief priests and the whole council sought false testimony against Jesus that they might put him to death, [60] but they found none, though many false witnesses came forward. At last two came forward [61] and said, 'This fellow said, "I am able to destroy the temple of God, and to build it in three days." ' [62]And the high priest stood up and said, 'Have you no answer to make? What is it that these men testify against you?' [63] But Jesus was silent. And the high priest said to him, 'I adjure you by the living God, tell us if you are the Christ, the Son of God.' [64] Jesus said to him, 'You have said so. But I tell you, hereafter you will see the Son of man seated at the right hand of Power, and coming on the clouds of heaven.' [65] Then the high priest tore his robes, and said, 'He has uttered blasphemy. Why do we still need witnesses? You have now heard his blasphemy. [66] What is your judgment?' They answered, 'He deserves death.' [67] Then they spat in his face, and struck him; and some slapped him, [68] saying, 'Prophesy to us, you Christ! Who is it that struck you?'

[69] Now Peter was sitting outside in the

another insisted, saying, 'Certainly this man also was with him; for he is a Galilean.' ⁶⁰ But Peter said, 'Man, I do not know what you are saying.' And immediately, while he was still speaking, the cock crowed. ⁶¹And the Lord turned and looked at Peter. And Peter remembered the word of the Lord, how he had said to him 'Before the cock crows today, you will deny me three times.' ⁶²And he went out and wept bitterly.

63 Now the men who were holding Jesus mocked him and beat him; ⁶⁴ they also blindfolded him and asked him, 'Prophesy! Who is it that struck you?' ⁶⁵And they spoke many other words against him, reviling him.

66 When day came, the assembly of the elders of the people gathered together, both chief priests and scribes; and they led him away to their council, and they said, ⁶⁷ 'If you are the Christ, tell us.' But he said to them, 'If I tell you, you will not believe; ⁶⁸ and if I ask you, you will not answer. ⁶⁹ But from now on the Son of man shall be seated at the right hand of the power of God.' ⁷⁰And they all said, 'Are you the Son of God, then?' And he said to them, 'You say that I am.' ⁷¹And they said, 'What further testimony do we need? We have heard it ourselves from his own lips.'

23 Then the whole company of them arose, and brought him before Pilate. ²And they began to accuse him, saying, 'We found this man perverting our nation, and forbidding us to give tribute to Caesar, and saying that he himself is Christ a king.' ³And Pilate asked him, 'Are you the King of the Jews?' And he answered him, 'You have said so.' ⁴And Pilate said to the chief priests and the multitudes, 'I find no crime in this man.' ⁵ But they were urgent, saying, 'He stirs up the people, teaching throughout all Judea, from Galilee even to this place.'

6 When Pilate heard this, he asked whether the man was a Galilean. ⁷And when he learned that he belonged to Herod's jurisdiction, he sent him over to Herod, who was himself in Jerusalem at that time. ⁸ When Herod saw Jesus, he was very glad, for he had long desired to see him, because he had heard about him, and he was hoping to see some sign done by him. ⁹ So he questioned him at some length; but he made no answer. ¹⁰ The chief priests and the scribes stood by, vehemently accusing him. ¹¹And Herod with his soldiers treated him with contempt and mocked him; then, arraying him in gor-

also was with them, standing and warming himself.

19 The high priest then questioned Jesus about his disciples and his teaching. ²⁰ Jesus answered him, 'I have spoken openly to the world; I have always taught in synagogues and in the temple, where all Jews come together; I have said nothing secretly. ²¹ Why do you ask me? Ask those who have heard me, what I said to them; they know what I said.' ²² When he had said this, one of the officers standing by struck Jesus with his hand, saying, 'Is that how you answer the high priest?' ²³ Jesus answered him, 'If I have spoken wrongly, bear witness to the wrong; but if I have spoken rightly, why do you strike me?' ²⁴Annas then sent him bound to Ca'iaphas the high priest.

25 Now Simon Peter was standing and warming himself. They said to him, 'Are not you also one of his disciples?' He denied it and said, 'I am not.' ²⁶ One of the servants¹ of the high priest, a kinsman of the man whose ear Peter had cut off asked, 'Did I not see you in the garden with him?' ²⁷ Peter again denied it; and at once the cock crowed.

28 Then they led Jesus from the house of Ca'iaphas to the praetorium. It was early. They themselves did not enter the praetorium, so that they might not be defiled, but might eat the passover. ²⁹ So Pilate went out to them and said, 'What accusation do you bring against this man?' ³⁰ They answered him, 'If this man were not an evildoer, we would not have handed him over.' ³¹ Pilate said to them, 'Take him yourselves and judge him by your own law.' The Jews said to him, 'It is not lawful for us to put any man to death.' ³² This was to fulfil the word which Jesus had spoken to show by what death he was to die.

33 Pilate entered the praetorium again and called Jesus, and said to him, 'Are you the King of the Jews?' ³⁴ Jesus answered, 'Do you say this of your own accord, or did others say it to you about me?' ³⁵ Pilate answered, 'Am I a Jew? Your own nation and the chief priests have handed you over to me; what have you done?' ³⁶ Jesus answered, 'My kingship is not of this world; if my kingship were of this world, my servants would fight, that I might not be handed over to the Jews; but my kingship is not from the world.' ³⁷ Pilate said to him, 'So you are a king?' Jesus answered, 'You say that I am a king. For this I was

man is one of them.' ⁷⁰ But again he denied it. And after a little while again the bystanders said to Peter, 'Certainly you are one of them; for you are a Galilean.' ⁷¹ But he began to invoke a curse on himself and to swear, 'I do not know this man of whom you speak.' ⁷²And immediately the cock crowed a second time. And Peter remembered how Jesus had said to him, 'Before the cock crows twice, you will deny me three times.' And he broke down and wept.

15 And as soon as it was morning the chief priests, with the elders and scribes, and the whole council held a consultation; and they bound Jesus and led him away and delivered him to Pilate. ²And Pilate asked him, 'Are you the King of the Jews?' And he answered him, 'You have said so.' ³And the chief priests accused him of many things. ⁴And Pilate again asked him, 'Have you no answer to make? See how many charges they bring against you.' ⁵ But Jesus made no further answer, so that Pilate wondered.

6 Now at the feast he used to release for them one prisoner whom they asked. ⁷And among the rebels in prison, who had committed murder in the insurrection, there was a man called Barab'bas. ⁸And the crowd came up and began to ask Pilate to do as he was wont to do for them. ⁹And he answered them, 'Do you want me to release for you the King of the Jews?' ¹⁰ For he perceived that it was out of envy that the chief priests had delivered him up. ¹¹ But the chief priests stirred up the crowd to have him release for them Barab'bas instead. ¹²And Pilate again said to them, 'Then what shall I do with the man whom you call the King of the Jews?' ¹³And they cried out again, 'Crucify him.' ¹⁴And Pilate said to them, 'Why, what evil has he done?' But they shouted all the more, 'Crucify him.' ¹⁵ So Pilate, wishing to satisfy the crowd, released for them Barab'bas; and having scourged Jesus, he delivered him to be crucified.

16 And the soldiers led him away inside the palace (that is, the praetorium); and they called together the whole battalion. ¹⁷And they clothed him in a purple cloak, and plaiting a crown of thorns they put it on him. ¹⁸And they began to salute him, 'Hail, King of the Jews!' ¹⁹And they struck his head with a reed, and spat upon him, and they knelt down in homage to him. ²⁰And when they had mocked him, they stripped him of the purple cloak, and put his own

courtyard. And a maid came up to him, and said, 'You also were with Jesus the Galilean.' ⁷⁰ But he denied it before them all, saying, 'I do not know what you mean.' ⁷¹And when he went out to the porch, another maid saw him, and she said to the bystanders, 'This man was with Jesus of Nazareth.' ⁷²And again he denied it with an oath, 'I do not know the man.' ⁷³After a little while the bystanders came up and said to Peter, 'Certainly you are also one of them, for your accent betrays you.' ⁷⁴ Then he began to invoke a curse on himself and to swear, 'I do not know the man.' And immediately the cock crowed. ⁷⁵And Peter remembered the saying of Jesus, 'Before the cock crows, you will deny me three times.' And he went out and wept bitterly.

27 When morning came, all the chief priests and the elders of the people took counsel against Jesus to put him to death; ² and they bound him and led him away and delivered him to Pilate the governor.

3 When Judas, his betrayer, saw that he was condemned, he repented and brought back the thirty pieces of silver to the chief priests and the elders, ⁴ saying, 'I have sinned in betraying innocent blood.' They said, 'What is that to us? See to it yourself.' ⁵And throwing down the pieces of silver in the temple, he departed; and he went and hanged himself. ⁶ But the chief priests, taking the pieces of silver, said, 'It is not lawful to put them into the treasury, since they are blood money.' ⁷ So they took counsel, and bought with them the potter's field, to bury strangers in. ⁸ Therefore that field has been called the Field of Blood to this day. ⁹ Then was fulfilled what had been spoken by the prophet Jeremiah, saying, 'And they took the thirty pieces of silver, the price of him on whom a price had been set by some of the sons of Israel, ¹⁰ and they gave them for the potter's field, as the Lord directed me.'

11 Now Jesus stood before the governor; and the governor asked him, 'Are you the King of the Jews?' Jesus said to him, 'You have said so.' ¹² But when he was accused by the chief priests and elders, he made no answer. ¹³ Then Pilate said to him. 'Do you not hear how many things they testify against you?' ¹⁴ But he gave him no answer, not even to a single charge; so that the governor wondered greatly.

15 Now at the feast the governor was

geous apparel, he sent him back to Pilate. ¹²And Herod and Pilate became friends with each other that very day, for before this they had been at enmity with each other.

13 Pilate then called together the chief priests and the rulers and the people, ¹⁴ and said to them, 'You brought me this man as one who was perverting the people; and after examining him before you, behold, I did not find this man guilty of any of your charges against him; ¹⁵ neither did Herod, for he sent him back to us. Behold, nothing deserving death has been done by him; ¹⁶ I will therefore chastise him and release him.'ᵐ

18 But they all cried out together, 'Away with this man, and release to us Barab'bas'—¹⁹ a man who had been thrown into prison for an insurrection started in the city, and for murder. ²⁰ Pilate addressed them once more, desiring to release Jesus; ²¹ but they shouted out, 'Crucify, crucify him!' ²²A third time he said to them, 'Why, what evil has he done? I have found in him no crime deserving death; I will therefore chastise him and release him.' ²³ But they were urgent, demanding with loud cries that he should be crucified. And their voices prevailed. ²⁴ So Pilate gave sentence that their demand should be granted. ²⁵ He released the man who had been thrown into prison for insurrection and murder, whom they asked for; but Jesus he delivered up to their will.

26 And as they led him away, they seized one Simon of Cyre'ne, who was coming in from the country, and laid on him the cross, to carry it behind Jesus. ²⁷And there followed him a great multitude of the people, and of women who bewailed and lamented him. ²⁸ But Jesus turning to them said, 'Daughters of Jerusalem, do not weep for me, but weep for yourselves and for your children. ²⁹ For behold, the days are coming when they will say, "Blessed are the barren, and the wombs that never bore, and the breasts that never gave suck!" ³⁰ Then they will begin to say to the mountains, "Fall on us"; and to the hills, "Cover us." ³¹ For if they do this when the wood is green, what will happen when it is dry?'

32 Two others also, who were criminals, were led away to be put to death with him. ³³And when they came to the place which is called The Skull, there they crucified him, and the criminals, one on the right and one

born, and for this I have come into the world, to bear witness to the truth. Every one who is of the truth hears my voice.' ³⁸Pilate said to him, 'What is truth?'

After he had said this, he went out to the Jews again, and told them, 'I find no crime in him. ³⁹ But you have a custom that I should release one man for you at the Passover; will you have me release for you the King of the Jews?' ⁴⁰ They cried out again, 'Not this man, but Barab'bas!' Now Barab'bas was a robber.

19 Then Pilate took Jesus and scourged him. ²And the soldiers plaited a crown of thorns, and put it on his head, and arrayed him in a purple robe; ³ they came up to him, saying, 'Hail, King of the Jews!' and struck him with their hands. ⁴ Pilate went out again, and said to them, 'Behold, I am bringing him out to you, that you may know that I find no crime in him.' ⁵ So Jesus came out, wearing the crown of thorns and the purple robe. Pilate said to them, 'Here is the man!' ⁶ When the chief priests and the officers saw him, they cried out, 'Crucify him, crucify him!' Pilate said to them, 'Take him yourselves and crucify him, for I find no crime in him.' ⁷ The Jews answered him, 'We have a law, and by that law he ought to die, because he has made himself the Son of God.' ⁸ When Pilate heard these words, he was the more afraid; ⁹ he entered the praetorium again and said to Jesus, 'Where are you from?' But Jesus gave no answer. ¹⁰ Pilate therefore said to him, 'You will not speak to me? Do you not know that I have power to release you, and power to crucify you?' ¹¹ Jesus answered him, 'You would have no power over me unless it had been given you from above; therefore he who delivered me to you has the greater sin.'

12 Upon this Pilate sought to release him, but the Jews cried out, 'If you release this man, you are not Caesar's friend; every one who makes himself a king sets himself against Caesar.' ¹³ When Pilate heard these words, he brought Jesus out and sat down on the judgment seat at a place called The Pavement, and in Hebrew, Gab'batha. ¹⁴ Now it was the day of Preparation of the Passover; it was about the sixth hour. He said to the Jews, 'Here is your King!' ¹⁵ They cried out, 'Away with him, away with him, crucify him!' Pilate said to them, 'Shall I crucify your King?' The chief

clothes on him. And they led him out to crucify him.

21 And they compelled a passer-by, Simon of Cyre'ne, who was coming in from the country, the father of Alexander and Rufus, to carry his cross. 22And they brought him to the place called Gol'gotha (which means the place of a skull). 23And they offered him wine mingled with myrrh; but he did not take it. 24And they crucified him, and divided his garments among them, casting lots for them, to decide what each should take. 25And it was the third hour, when they crucified him. 26And the inscription of the charge against him read, 'The King of the Jews.' 27And with him they crucified two robbers, one on his right and one on his left.ᵍ 29And those who passed by derided him, wagging their heads, and saying, 'Aha! You who would destroy the temple and build it in three days, 30 save yourself, and come down from the cross!' 31 So also the chief priests mocked him to one another with the scribes, saying, 'He saved others; he cannot save himself. 32 Let the Christ, the King of Israel, come down now from the cross, that we may see and believe.' Those who were crucified with him also reviled him.

33 And when the sixth hour had come, there was darkness over the whole landʰ until the ninth hour. 34And at the ninth hour Jesus cried with a loud voice, 'E'lo-i, E'lo-i, la'ma sabach-tha'ni?' which means, 'My God, my God, why hast thou forsaken me?' 35And some of the bystanders hearing it said, 'Behold, he is calling Eli'jah.' 36And one ran and, filling a sponge full of vinegar, put it on a reed and gave it to him to drink, saying, 'Wait, let us see whether Eli'jah will come to take him down.' 37And Jesus uttered a loud cry, and breathed his last. 38And the curtain of the temple was torn in two, from top to bottom. 39And when the centurion, who stood facing him, saw that he thusⁱ breathed his last, he said, 'Truly this man was the Sonᶻ of God!'

40 There were also women looking on from afar, among whom were Mary Mag'dalene, and Mary the mother of James the younger and of Joses, and Salo'me, 41 who, when he was in Galilee, followed him, and ministered to him; and also many other women who came up with him to Jerusalem.

42 And when evening had come, since it

accustomed to release for the crowd any one prisoner whom they wanted. 16And they had then a notorious prisoner, called Barab'-bas.ᵏ 17 So when they had gathered, Pilate said to them, 'Whom do you want me to release for you, Barab'basᵏ or Jesus who is called Christ?' 18 For he knew that it was out of envy that they had delivered him up. 19 Besides, while he was sitting on the judgment seat, his wife sent word to him, 'Have nothing to do with that righteous man, for I have suffered much over him today in a dream.' 20 Now the chief priests and the elders persuaded the people to ask for Barab'bas and destroy Jesus. 21 The governor again said to them, 'Which of the two do you want me to release for you?' And they said, 'Barab'bas.' 22 Pilate said to them, 'Then what shall I do with Jesus who is called Christ?' They all said, 'Let him be crucified.' 23And he said, 'Why, what evil has he done?' But they shouted all the more, 'Let him be crucified.'

24 So when Pilate saw that he was gaining nothing, but rather that a riot was beginning, he took water and washed his hands before the crowd, saying, 'I am innocent of this man's blood;ˡ see to it yourselves.' 25And all the people answered, 'His blood be on us and on our children!' 26 Then he released for them Barab'bas, and having scourged Jesus, delivered him to be crucified.

27 Then the soldiers of the governor took Jesus into the praetorium, and they gathered the whole battalion before him. 28And they stripped him and put a scarlet robe upon him, 29 and plaiting a crown of thorns they put it on his head, and put a reed in his right hand. And kneeling before him they mocked him, saying, 'Hail, King of the Jews!' 30And they spat upon him, and took the reed and struck him on the head. 31And when they had mocked him, they stripped him of the robe, and put his own clothes on him, and led him away to crucify him.

32 As they were marching out, they came upon a man of Cyre'ne, Simon by name; this man they compelled to carry his cross. 33And when they came to a place called Gol'gotha (which means the place of a skull), 34 they offered him wine to drink, mingled with gall; but when he tasted it, he would not drink it. 35And when they had crucified him, they divided his garments among them by casting lots; 36 then they sat down and kept watch over him there. 37And over his

on the left. [34]And Jesus said, 'Father, forgive them; for they know not what they do.'[n] And they cast lots to divide his garments. [35]And the people stood by, watching; but the rulers scoffed at him, saying, 'He saved others; let him save himself, if he is the Christ of God, his Chosen One!' [36] The soldiers also mocked him, coming up and offering him vinegar, [37] and saying, 'If you are the King of the Jews, save yourself!' [38] There was also an inscription over him, 'This is the King of the Jews.'

[39] One of the criminals who were hanged railed at him, saying, 'Are you not the Christ? Save yourself and us!' [40] But the other rebuked him, saying, 'Do you not fear God, since you are under the same sentence of condemnation? [41]And we indeed justly; for we are receiving the due reward of our deeds; but this man has done nothing wrong.' [42]And he said, 'Jesus, remember me when you come in your kingly power.'[p] [43]And he said to him, 'Truly, I say to you, today you will be with me in Paradise.'

[44] It was now about the sixth hour, and there was darkness over the whole land[q] until the ninth hour, [45] while the sun's light failed;[r] and the curtain of the temple was torn in two. [46] Then Jesus, crying with a loud voice, said, 'Father, into thy hands I commit my spirit!' And having said this he breathed his last. [47] Now when the centurion saw what had taken place, he praised God, and said, 'Certainly this man was innocent!' [48]And all the multitudes who assembled to see the sight, when they saw what had taken place, returned home beating their breasts. [49]And all his acquaintances and the women who had followed him from Galilee stood at a distance and saw these things.

[50] Now there was a man named Joseph from the Jewish town of Arimathe'a. He was a member of the council, a good and righteous man, [51] who had not consented to their purpose and deed, and he was looking for the kingdom of God. [52] This man went to Pilate and asked for the body of Jesus. [53] Then he took it down and wrapped it in a linen shroud, and laid him in a rock-hewn tomb, where no one had ever yet been laid. [54] It was the day of Preparation, and the sabbath was beginning.[s] [55] The women who had come with him from Galilee followed, and saw the tomb, and how his body was

priests answered, 'We have no king but Caesar.' [16] Then he handed him over to them to be crucified.

[17] So they took Jesus, and he went out, bearing his own cross, to the place called the place of a skull, which is called in Hebrew Gol'gotha. [18] There they crucified him, and with him two others, one on either side, and Jesus between them. [19] Pilate also wrote a title and put it on the cross; it read, 'Jesus of Nazareth, the King of the Jews.' [20] Many of the Jews read this title, for the place where Jesus was crucified was near the city; and it was written in Hebrew, in Latin, and in Greek. [21] The chief priests of the Jews then said to Pilate, 'Do not write, "The King of the Jews," but, "This man said, I am King of the Jews." ' [22] Pilate answered, 'What I have written I have written.'

[23] When the soldiers had crucified Jesus they took his garments and made four parts, one for each soldier; also his tunic. But the tunic was without seam, woven from top to bottom; [24] so they said to one another, 'Let us not tear it, but cast lots for it to see whose it shall be.' This was to fulfil the scripture,

'They parted my garments among them,
and for my clothing they cast lots.'

[25] So the soldiers did this. But standing by the cross of Jesus were his mother, and his mother's sister, Mary the wife of Clopas, and Mary Mag'dalene. [26] When Jesus saw his mother, and the disciple whom he loved standing near, he said to his mother, 'Woman, behold, your son!' [27] Then he said to the disciple, 'Behold, your mother!' And from that hour the disciple took her to his own home.

[28] After this Jesus, knowing that all was now finished, said (to fulfil the scripture), 'I thirst.' [29]A bowl full of vinegar stood there; so they put a sponge full of the vinegar on hyssop and held it to his mouth. [30] When Jesus had received the vinegar, he said, 'It is finished'; and he bowed his head and gave up his spirit.

[31] Since it was the day of Preparation, in order to prevent the bodies from remaining on the cross on the sabbath (for that sabbath was a high day), the Jews asked Pilate that their legs might be broken, and that they might be taken away. [32] So the soldiers came and broke the legs of the first, and of the other who had been crucified with him; [33] but when they came to Jesus and saw that

was the day of Preparation, that is, the day before the sabbath, 43 Joseph of Arimathe'a, a respected member of the council ,who was also himself looking for the kingdom of God, took courage and went to Pilate, and asked for the body of Jesus. 44And Pilate wondered if he were already dead; and summoning the centurion, he asked him whether he was already dead.*J* 45And when he learned from the centurion that he was dead, he granted the body to Joseph. 46And he bought a linen shroud, and taking him down, wrapped him in the linen shroud, and laid him in a tomb which had been hewn out of the rock; and he rolled a stone against the door of the tomb. 47 Mary Mag'dalene and Mary the mother of Joses saw where he was laid.

head they put the charge against him, which read, 'This is Jesus the King of the Jews.' 38 Then two robbers were crucified with him, one on the right and one on the left. 39And those who passed by derided him, wagging their heads 40 and saying, 'You who would destroy the temple and build it in three days, save yourself! If you are the Son of God, come down from the cross.' 41 So also the chief priests, with the scribes and elders, mocked him, saying, 42 'He saved others; he cannot save himself. He is the King of Israel; let him come down now from the cross, and we will believe in him. 43 He trusts in God; let God deliver him now, if he desires him; for he said, "I am the Son of God." ' 44And the robbers who were crucified with him also reviled him in the same way.

45 Now from the sixth hour there was darkness over all the land*m* until the ninth hour. 46And about the ninth hour Jesus cried with a loud voice, 'Eli, Eli, la'ma sabach-tha'ni?' that is 'My God, my God, why hast thou forsaken me?' 47And some of the by-standers hearing it said, 'This man is calling Eli'jah.' 48And one of them at once ran and took a sponge, filled it with vinegar, and put it on a reed, and gave it to him to drink. 49 But the others said, 'Wait, let us see whether Eli'jah will come to save him.'*n* 50And Jesus cried again with a loud voice and yielded up his spirit.

51 And behold, the curtain of the temple was torn in two, from top to bottom; and the earth shook, and the rocks were split; 52 the tombs also were opened, and many bodies of the saints who had fallen asleep were raised, 53 and coming out of the tombs after his resurrection they went into the holy city and appeared to many. 54 When the centurion and those who were with him, keeping watch over Jesus, saw the earth-quake and what took place, they were filled with awe, and said, 'Truly this was the Son*x* of God!'

55 There were also many women there, looking on from afar, who had followed Jesus from Galilee, ministering to him; 56 among whom were Mary Mag'dalene, and Mary the mother of James and Joseph, and the mother of the sons of Zeb'edee.

57 When it was evening, there came a rich man from Arimathe'a, named Joseph, who also was a disciple of Jesus. 58 He went to Pilate and asked for the body of Jesus. Then Pilate ordered it to be given to him.

laid; ⁵⁶ then they returned, and prepared spices and ointments.

On the sabbath they rested according to the commandment.

Matthew: continued from previous column

⁵⁹And Joseph took the body, and wrapped it in a clean linen shroud, ⁶⁰ and laid it in his own new tomb, which he had hewn in the rock; and he rolled a great stone to the door of the tomb, and departed. ⁶¹ Mary Mag'dalene and the other Mary were there, sitting opposite the sepulchre.

⁶² Next day, that is, after the day of Preparation, the chief priests and the Pharisees gathered before Pilate ⁶³ and said, 'Sir, we remember how that impostor said, while he was still alive, "After three days I will rise again." ⁶⁴ Therefore order the sepulchre to be made secure until the third day, lest his disciples go and steal him away, and tell the people, "He has risen from the dead," and the last fraud will be worse than the first.' ⁶⁵ Pilate said to them, 'You have a guard^o of soldiers; go, make it as secure as you can.'^p ⁶⁶ So they went and made the sepulchre secure by sealing the stone and setting a guard.

he was already dead, they did not break his legs. ³⁴ But one of the soldiers pierced his side with a spear, and at once there came out blood and water. ³⁵ He who saw it has borne witness—his testimony is true, and he knows that he tells the truth—that you also may believe. ³⁶ For these things took place that the scripture might be fulfilled, 'Not a bone of him shall be broken.' ³⁷And again another scripture says, 'They shall look on him whom they have pierced.'

³⁸ After this Joseph of Arimathe'a, who was a disciple of Jesus, but secretly, for fear of the Jews, asked Pilate that he might take away the body of Jesus, and Pilate gave him leave. So he came and took away his body. ³⁹ Nicode'mus also, who had at first come to him by night, came bringing a mixture of myrrh and aloes about a hundred pounds' weight. ⁴⁰ They took the body of Jesus, and bound it in linen cloths with the spices, as is the burial custom of the Jews. ⁴¹ Now in the place where he was crucified there was a garden, and in the garden a new tomb where no one had ever been laid. ⁴² So because of the Jewish day of Preparation, as the tomb was close at hand, they laid Jesus there.

²⁰ Now on the first day of the week Mary Mag'dalene came to the tomb early, while it was still dark, and saw that the stone had been taken away from the tomb. ² So she ran, and went to Simon Peter and the other disciple, the one whom Jesus loved, and said to them, 'They have taken the Lord out of the tomb, and we do not know where they have laid him.' ³ Peter then came out with the other disciple, and they went toward the tomb. ⁴ They both ran, but the other disciple outran Peter and reached the tomb first; ⁵ and stooping to look in, he saw the linen cloths lying there, but he did not go in. ⁶ Then Simon Peter came, following him, and went into the tomb; he saw the linen cloths lying, ⁷ and the napkin, which had been on his head, not lying with the linen cloths but rolled up in a place by itself. ⁸ Then the other disciple, who reached the tomb first, also went in, and he saw and believed; ⁹ for as yet they did not know the scripture, that he must rise from the dead. ¹⁰ Then the disciples went back to their homes.

Abbreviations

A.L.U.O.S.	*Annual of Leeds Oriental Society*
B.C.	*The Beginnings of Christianity*, ed. F. J. Foakes-Jackson and Kirsopp Lake, 5 vols., London, 1928
B.J.R.L.	*The Bulletin of the John Rylands Library*, Manchester
C.A.H.	*The Cambridge Ancient History*
D.C.C.	*The Oxford Dictionary of the Christian Church*, ed. F. L. Cross, London, 1958
E.J.R.	*The Encyclopedia of the Jewish Religion*, ed. R. J. Zwi Werblowsky and G. Wigoder, London, 1967
E.R.E.	*Encyclopedia of Religion and Ethics*, ed. J. Hastings, 12 vols. and index vol., Edinburgh, 1908–26
E.T.	English Translation
H.D.B.[2]	*Dictionary of the Bible*, ed. J. Hastings, 2nd ed., Edinburgh, 1963
H.Th.R.	*The Harvard Theological Review*
I.E.F.	*Israel Exploration Journal*, Jerusalem, Israel
J.B.L.	*The Journal of Biblical Literature*, Philadelphia (Penn.)
J.J.S.	*The Journal of Jewish Studies*, London
J.Q.R.	*The Jewish Quarterly Review*, Philadelphia (Penn.)
J.R.S.	*The Journal of Roman Studies*, London
J.S.S.	*The Journal of Semitic Studies*, Manchester
J.T.S.	*The Journal of Theological Studies*, Oxford
N.T.	*Novum Testamentum*, Leiden
N.T.S.	*New Testament Studies*, Cambridge
O.C.D.	*The Oxford Classical Dictionary*, Oxford, 1949
P.C.[2]	*Peake's Commentary on the Bible*, 2nd ed., Edinburgh-London, 1962
R.A.C.	*Reallexikon für Antike und Christentum*, hrg. T. Klauser, Bände I–VI (continuing), Stuttgart, 1950–66
R.G.G.[3]	*Religion in Geschichte und Gegenwart*, 3. Aufl., hrg. K. Galling, Bände I–VI, Tübingen, 1957–62
R.H.R.	*Revue d'Histoire des Religions*, Paris
R.V.	Revised Version of the Bible
R.S.V.	American Standard Revised Version of the Bible
S.-B. *Kommentar*	Strack, H. L. und Billerbeck, P., *Kommentar zum Neuen Testament aus Talmud und Midrasch*, 4 Bände, Munich, 1922–8
Schürer, *G.J.V.*	Schürer, E., *Geschichte des jüdischen Volkes im Zeitalter Jesu Christi*, 3 Bände, Leipzig, 1898–1901
Th.L.Z.	*Theologische Literaturzeitung*
Th.Wb.	*Theologisches Wörterbuch zum Neuen Testament*, hrg. G. Kittel, Stuttgart, 1932– continuing
V.C.	*Vigiliae Christianae*, Amsterdam
Z.N.T.W.	*Zeitschrift für neutestamentliche Wissenschaft*, Berlin

References

Chapter One (pages 13–24)

1 It was only during a session (1965) of the Second Vatican Council that the Roman Catholic Church formally exonerated subsequent generations of Jews from responsibility for the murder of Christ; even then the decree met with certain opposition.

2 See Plato's *Apology*, also his *Phaedo*, and Xenophon's *Apology*. Cf. J. B. Bury in *C.A.H.*, V, pp. 382ff.; A. B. Drachmann, *Atheism in Pagan Antiquity* (1922), pp. 64ff.

3 Cf. Geo. Widengren, *Mani and Manichaeism*, E.T., pp. 38–40; L. J. R. Ort, *Mani*, pp. 223–4.

4 Cf. J. Quickerat, *Procès de Condemnation et de Réhabilitation de Jeanne d'Arc* (Paris, 1861, r.ed., 1921).

5 Cf. S. G. F. Brandon, 'The Date of the Markan Gospel', *N.T.S.*, VII (1960–1); *Jesus and the Zealots*, chap. 5; see pp. 68ff.

6 Cf. *R.A.C.* 3, IV, 19; *H.D.B.*², p. 180.

7 I *Cor.* ii:6–8. Cf. ed. Meyer, *Ursprung und Anfänge des Christentums*, III, pp. 350–1.

8 *Gal.* iv:3; *Col.* ii:8, 20. On the *archontes* cf. M. Dibelius, 'Archonten', *R.A.C.*, I, 631–3; W. Grundel, 'Astrologie', *op. cit.*, 817–30; H. Lietzmann, *An die Korinther*, I–II, pp. 11–13; A.-J. Festugière, *La Révélation d'Hermès Trismégiste*, I, pp. 89–96; J. Seznec, *La survivance des dieux antiques*, pp. 35–46; R. Bultmann, *Das Urchristentum im Rahmen der antiken Religionen*, pp. 211–12; S. G. F. Brandon, *History, Time and Deity*, pp. 166–9.

9 Bultmann, pp. 211–12, 219; M. Werner, *Die Entstehung des christlichen Dogmas*, p. 238 (E.T., p. 95); A Grillmeier, *Christ in Christian Tradition from the Apostolic Age to Chalcedon*, p. 15; Brandon, *Man and his Destiny in the Great Religions*, pp. 213–15.

10 Paul becomes the chief figure of *Acts* from chap. xiii to its end (chap. xxviii); Manson, *Studies in the Gospels and the Epistles*, p. 170, n.1.

11 *Acts* is concerned to describe the progress of Christianity, under divine guidance, from its beginnings in Jerusalem to its propagation by Paul in Rome, the capital of the Ancient World. Cf. *B.C.*, II, pp. 177–186; F. F. Bruce, *The Acts of the Apostles*, pp. 29–34; Brandon, *The Fall of Jerusalem and the Christian Church*, pp. 126–36, 208–10.

12 *Gal.* i:6–8; II *Cor.* xi:3–4: on the significance of Paul's terms here cf. *Man and his Destiny*, p. 196, n. 196, and the documentation there cited.

13 Cf. A. D. Nock, *St Paul*, pp. 110–11, 168–9; H. Lietzmann, *Gesch. d. alt. Kirche*, I, pp. 108–9; W. L. Knox, *St Paul and the Church of Jerusalem*, p. 365; M. Simon, *Les premiers Chrétiens*, pp. 79–81; M. Goguel, *La naissance du Christianisme*, pp. 173–6, 320–49; ed. Meyer, *Ursprung u. Anfänge des Christentums*, III, pp. 432–45, 453–9; H. J. Schoeps, *Theologie u. Geschichte des Judenchristentums*, pp. 128ff., 157, 257, 381–4, 420–34, 448–50; T. W. Manson, *Studies in the Gospels and the Epistles*, pp. 170, 216; Brandon, *Jesus and the Zealots*, pp. 152ff.

14 *Gal.* i:19; ii:9. Cf. H. Schlier, *Der Brief an die Galater*, pp. 78–9. On James, see pp. 21, 22, 49ff.

15 This subject is discussed at length, together with a detailed examination of the late legend that the Christian community of Jerusalem fled *en masse* to Pella before the fall of the city, in *Jesus and the Zealots*, pp. 208ff.

16 *H.D.B.*², pp. 600ff.

17 Cf. *Fall of Jerusalem*, pp. 74ff.

18 Cf. *Jesus and the Zealots*, pp. 115ff., 188ff.; see pp. 55–6, 39, 151–2.

19 *Gal.* i:11–17. Cf. Schlier, pp. 43–59; H. G. Wood in *N.T.S.*, I (1954–5), pp. 278–9.

20 *Gal.* ii:7–9. The distinction which Paul draws here between these two 'gospels' seems to be theoretical rather than actual, since it did not prevent him from evangelising Diaspora Jews, nor Peter and other Jerusalem Christians from operating among

Paul's Gentile converts. Cf. *Jesus and the Zealots*, pp. 154, n.1, 163–5.

21 II *Cor.* xi:4. Cf. A. Menzies, *The Second Epistle to the Corinthians*, p. 78; H.-J. Schoeps, *Paulus*, p. 74 (E.T. p. 76); F. F. Bruce in *B.J.R.L.*, 45 (1963), pp. 331–4.

22 The presentation of Jesus as the Messiah of Israel, who would punish the Gentile oppressors of Israel and 'restore the kingdom to Israel' (*Acts* i:6) was not calculated to attract Gentiles. Cf. *Man and his Destiny*, pp. 212ff.

23 II *Cor.* v:13–17. Cf. H. Lietzmann, *An die Korinther, I–II*, pp. 124–5; Nock, *St Paul*, p. 243; J. Klausner, *From Jesus to Paul*, pp. 313–15; A. Loisy, *Les mystères païens et le mystère chrétien*, pp. 242–3; Goguel, *La naissance du Christianisme*, pp. 254, 270–2; A. Schweitzer, *Paul and his Interpreters*, pp. 245–6; Schoeps, *Theologie u. Geschichte des Judenchristentums*, pp. 425–6.

24 Cf. Goguel, pp. 252–9; Bultmann, *Das Urchristentum im Rahmen der antiken Religionen*, pp. 219–22, in *N.T.S.*, I (1955), pp. 13, 16; A. Schweitzer, *The Mysticism of Paul*, pp. 109–30.

25 'Christus nach seiner natürlichen Seite', W. Bauer, *Griechisch-Deutsches Wörterbuch z. d. Schriften d. N.T.²*, 1194; H. Windisch, *Der zweite Korintherbrief*, pp. 186–8; Bultmann, *Theology of the New Test.*, I, pp. 236–8; Manson, *Studies*, pp. 224; W. Schmithals, in *Z.N.T.W.*, 53 (1962), pp. 156–8.

26 Cf. Brandon, *History, Time and Deity*, pp. 159ff.

27 See *Rom.* iii:9, 23–5. Cf. W. Sanday-A. C. Headlam, *The Epistle to the Romans*, pp. 76, 84–6; H. H. Rowley, *The Biblical Doctrine of Election*, pp. 144–6; H. Wildberger, *Jahwes Eigentumsvolk*, pp. 74ff.

28 Cf. Klausner, *From Jesus to Paul*, pp. 444, 467–70.

29 Cf. *E.R.E.*, VII, pp. 199b–200a. It is significant that in the second-century *Dialogue* of Justin Martyr with the Jew Trypho, the latter objects to 'your trust in a mere crucified man' (*op. cit.*, 10), and 'you undertake to prove a thing incredible and almost impossible, that God condescended to be born, and to be made man' (*ibid.*, 68).

30 Cf. *Jesus and the Zealots*, pp. 182ff.

31 *Acts* xxi:27ff.

32 Cf. H. J. Cadbury in *B.C.*, V, p. 338,

also *B.C.*, IV, pp. 349–50; Bruce, *Acts of the Apostles*, pp. 480–1, in *B.J.R.L.*, 46 (1964), pp. 342–5; Manson, *Studies*, pp. 6–7; Brandon, *Jesus and the Zealots*, pp. 186ff.

33 *Fall of Jerusalem*, pp. 152ff., 213ff.

34 *Acts* i:46; iii:1; v:12, 42; xxi:26, 42; x:14; xi:2, 3; xv:1; xxi:21–4; *Gal.* ii:11ff.

35 *Acts* vi:7; xv:5. Cf. Simon, *Les premiers Chrétiens*, pp. 39–41; Brandon, *Jesus and the Zealots*, pp. 118ff.

36 Hegesippus *apud* Eusebius, *Ecclesiastical History*, II, i.2–5, xxiii. Cf. Epiphanius, *Haer*, xxix, lxxviii.6–7; *Fall of Jerusalem*, pp. 52–3; *Jesus and the Zealots*, pp. 122ff.

37 Reference is made to them in *Mk.* xiii:21–22; see pp. 104–126.

38 Cf. Schürer, *G.J.V.*, II, pp. 526–30; S. Mowinckel, *He That Cometh*, pp. 4ff., 280ff.

39 Cf. Schürer, *G.J.V.*, II, pp. 533–44; Mowinckel, pp. 284ff., 340ff.; Klausner, *From Jesus to Paul*, pp. 526–3; M. Black, *The Scrolls and Christian Origins*, pp. 145–63.

40 As Paul eloquently shows in I *Cor.* i:22–3, the idea of a 'crucified Messiah' was a *skandalon* to the Jews. Cf. Klausner, *Jesus of Nazareth*, pp. 301–2, *From Jesus to Paul*, p. 437; Schürer, *G.J.V.*, II, pp. 553–6; Mowinckel, p. 327

41 *Acts* ii: 22–36; v: 30–1. The Jewish Christians found prophetic warranty for a suffering Messiah particularly in the figure of the Suffering Servant of Yahweh; e.g. *Acts* viii:26–38; cf. *Acts* iii:18; *Lk.* xxiv:17–27. Cf. *Fall of Jerusalem*, pp. 76ff.

42 *Acts* i:6. Cf. *Jesus and the Zealots*, pp. 180–1.

43 E.g. *Acts* ii:22–36.

44 *Matt.* xi:2–6; *Lk.* vii:18–23; *John* xi:47. Cf. Bultmann, *Gesch. d. syn. Trad.*, pp. 22, 54; E. Klostermann, *Matthäusevangelium*, p. 94; V. Taylor, *St Mark*, p. 362.

45 Cf. *Jesus and the Zealots*, pp. 108–11.

46 Cf. Goguel, *The Life of Jesus*, p. 463; V. Taylor, *The Formation of the Gospel Tradition*, pp. 44ff.; Manson, *Studies*, pp. 20–2.

47 The first concern of Jewish Christian exegesis was to show how the death of Jesus did not negate his claim to be the Messiah (see n. 40). So far as the early speeches in the *Acts* (e.g. ii:22–36; iii:13–26) may be regarded as reflecting an authentic tradition, the death of Jesus was

interpreted as a martyrdom which had won God's favour so that he had made him both 'Lord and Christ (Messiah), this Jesus whom ye crucified' (ii:36). 'In Acts the Passion of Jesus is identified with the suffering of the Servant, but nowhere is described as giving salvation to men. In the speeches of Peter and Stephen the death of Jesus is regarded as the wicked act of the Jews, parallel to their fathers' persecution of the prophets. If men desire salvation let them repent, and be baptized'—F. J. Foakes Jackson and K. Lake, *B.C.*, I, pp. 391–2. Cf. Bultmann, *Theology of the New Test.*, I, pp. 33–7.
48 See pp. 85ff.
49 See Chapter IV.
50 *Mk.* xiv:57–8. Cf. Taylor, *St Mark*, pp. 565–6.
51 xiv:59.
52 xiv:61–4. See pp. 89ff.
53 xv:1–3. The use of the plural *polla*, 'many things' in describing the chief priests' accusation suggests that they specified more than one instance of sedition. Cf. Taylor, *St Mark*, p. 579. See pp. 92ff.
54 xv:10, 14. See pp. 96ff.
55 xiii:2. Mark, doubtless aware of the tradition of the Sanhedrin trial, is careful not to suggest here that Jesus would himself destroy the Temple and uses a curious impersonal form of statement: 'There shall not be left one stone upon another that shall not be thrown down.' The distinction is not merely academic, because *Jn.* ii:18–19 and *Acts* vi:14 witness to the currency of a tradition in Christian circles that Jesus would destroy the Temple. Cf. Klostermann, *Markusevangelium*, p. 155; Bultmann, *Gesch. d. syn. Trad.*, pp. 126–7, *Ergänzungsheft*, pp. 17–18; M. Simon, *Recherches d'histoire judéo-chrétienne*, pp. 11–12; Brandon, in *N.T.S.*, VII (1961), pp. 134–6, *Jesus and the Zealots*, pp. 234ff.
56 To the Jewish Christians the Temple was the 'house of God'; cf. *Mk.* xi:17; *Matt.* xxiii:21. Taylor (*St Mark*, p. 566), recognises the difficulty here: 'It is not clear why Mark represents the testimony as false. . . . It is more probable that Mark reflects the uneasiness of primitive Christianity regarding the saying on the part of those who continued to observe the Temple worship.' See pp. 42–5.
57 Güsta Lindeskog (in *Abraham Unser*

Vater, pp. 330–1) has recently argued that the Gospel accounts of the trial of Jesus reflect the opposition between the Primitive Church and the Synagogue after the death of Jesus: '*Die konfessionelle Rivalität* färbte auf die Geschichte Jesu ab, die damit unhistorisch wurde' (p. 331). He rightly maintains: 'Dabei müssen wir die Tendenzen postjesuanischen Situation genau bestimmen. Denn diese Tendenzen sind aus historischen Geschichtspunkt a priori als entstellende Faktoren zu betrachten' (p. 331). Unfortunately, in his short article he is unable to indicate the nature and form of these *Tendenzen*. He does not mention the Jewish catastrophe of AD 70 in connection with them.

Chapter Two (pages 25–59)
1 See Chapter III.
2 Jos. *Ant.* xvii:191; *War* i:665; *Matt.* ii:1ff., 19, 22. Cf. E. Lohmeyer–W. Schmauch, *Das Evangelium des Matthäus*, pp. 19–31.
3 The Matthaean dating of the birth of Jesus conflicts with that of *Lk.* ii:1–6, who synchronises the birth with the census of Quirinius in AD 6 (see below). The discrepancy has been much discussed: it is generally agreed that Luke's dating is too late. Cf. E. Klostermann, *Das Matthäusevangelium*, pp. 11–13; Schürer, *G.J.V.*, I, p. 415, n. 167; Ch. Guignebert, *Jésus*, pp. 94–112; F. Schmidtke, 'Chronologie', *R.A.C.*, III, 49–50; F. X. Steinmetzer, 'Census', *R.A.C.*, II, 969–72; G. W. H. Lampe in *Peake's Commentary²*, pp. 720a–c.
4 Cf. A. H. M. Jones, *The Herods of Judaea*, pp. 152–4; A. Momigliano in *C.A.H.*, X, pp. 330–2; S. G. F. Brandon, 'Herod the Great', *History Today*, XII, pp. 240–1.
5 On the divinity of the Roman emperor and its various forms of definition and expression, cf. *O.C.D.*, pp. 783b–4a; A. D. Nock in *C.A.H.*, X, pp. 481–501.
6 Cf. A. Reifenberg, *Israel's History in Coins*, pp. 10–11, 23.
7 See pp. 36, 72.
8 Jos. *Ant.* xvii:221–3; *War* ii:16–18.
9 Jos. *War* ii:53; cf. *Ant.* xvii:267.
10 Judaism logically implied a theocracy: cf. W. O. E. Oesterley, *History of Israel*, II, pp. 383–4; Schürer, *G.J.V.*, I, pp. 453–4;

M. Hengel, *Die Zeloten*, pp. 330–1. See n. 19.

11 Jos. *Ant.* xvii:271–2; *War* ii:56. There is some evidence that this Judas was 'Judas of Galilee', who founded the Zealots: cf. Brandon, *Jesus and the Zealots*, pp. 28–9, 33, n. 3. See p. 28.

12 Jos. *Ant.* xvii:295; *War* ii:75.

13 Jos. *Ant.* xvii:318–320. Cf. Schürer, *G.J.V.*, I, pp. 422–3.

14 Jos. *Ant.* xviii:1–2; *War* ii:117. Cf. Schürer, *G.J.V.*, I, pp. 455–6.

15 Jos. *War* ii:118. On the reasons for calling Judas a rabbi, cf. Brandon, *Jesus and the Zealots*, pp. 31–32, 47, n. 1.

16 Jos. *Ant.* xviii:4–5.

17 Cf. Hengel, *Die Zeloten*, pp. 6–18, 42–50, 78ff., 188–90; Brandon, *Jesus and the Zealots*, pp. 30–42, 46–7, 130.

18 Cf. J. Pedersen, *Israel*, III–IV, pp. 611–727; H. Wildberger, *Jahwes Eigentumsvolk*, *passim*.

19 *Against Apion*, ii:185. Cf. C. Roth, 'The Constitution of the Jewish Republic', in *J.S.S.*, IX (1964); Brandon, *op. cit.*, pp. 32, 48–9.

20 Cf. Brandon, *op. cit.*, pp. 48–9. According to Josephus (*Ant.* xvii:320), the yearly tribute received by Archelaus was 600 talents: this sum would represent the income from Judaea, Idumaea, and Samaria (although Augustus had reduced the Samaritans' contribution by a fourth).

21 The speech of Agrippa II to the Jewish insurgents in 66, as reported by Josephus (*War* ii:356ff.), is significant in this connection.

22 Cf. W. H. C. Frend, *Martyrdom and Persecution in the Early Christian Church*, chap. II; Hengel, *Die Zeloten*, pp. 261–77.

23 Josephus, curiously, does not record the outcome of the revolt, but *Acts* v:37 represents the rabbi Gamaliel as referring to ˈudas of Galilee, who rose up 'in the days of the enrolment, and drew away *some* of the people after him: he also perished, and all, as many as obeyed him, were scattered abroad'. The value of the reference is problematic because the author of *Acts* erroneously puts Judas's movement after that of Theudas' (see below), which may indicate a careless following of Josephus here. Cf. *B.C.*, IV, pp. 60–2; Hengel, *Die Zeloten*, pp. 343–4.

24 Their sentiments are significantly expressed in Jos. *War* ii:410, 411–16. From

the beginning of the Roman rule until the time of Claudius, the high priests were appointed by the Romans(Jos. *Ant.* xx:15); cf. E. M. Smallwood, 'High Priests and Politics in Roman Palestine', *J.T.S.*, XIII (1962). On the priestly aristocracy cf. J. Jeremias, *Jerusalem zur Zeit Jesu*, II, pp. 40–59; J. Klausner, *Jesus of Nazareth*, pp. 216–222.

25 Jos. *Ant.* xvii:3.

26 Cf. Brandon, *Jesus and the Zealots*, pp. 43–5.

27 Cf. W. R. Farmer, *Maccabees, Zealots and Josephus*, pp. 175–82; Hengel, *Die Zeloten*, pp. 277–80.

28 Cf. Brandon, *op. cit.*, pp. 56, 68.

29 Cf. W. Förster, *Palestinian Judaism in New Testament Times*, pp. 192ff.; S. Mowinckel, *He That Cometh*, pp. 284–6, 333–7; Ch. Guignebert, *Le monde juif vers le temps de Jésus*, pp. 176–201.

30 *Matt.* ii:22–3; *Lk.* ii:39. Cf. Schürer, *G.J.V.*, I, pp. 431–49; S. Perowne, *The Later Herods*, pp. 43–57.

31 *Lk.* ii:41–2.

32 Jos. *Ant.* xviii:23; xx:202; *War* ii:118, 433; cf. *Acts* v:37.

33 Cf. Hengel, *Die Zeloten*, pp. 72–3, 77; K. H. Rengstorf, *Th.Wb.*, IV, 889; C. Roth, 'The Zealots in the War of 66–73', *J.S.S.*, IV, pp. 335, n. 2, 336–7, 343, n. 2; G. R. Driver, *The Judaean Scrolls*, p. 245; Brandon, *Jesus and the Zealots*, pp. 43–4.

34 *Ant.* xviii:6–8. Cf. L. H. Feldman, Loeb *Josephus*, IX, pp. 6–9.

35 *Ant.* xviii:6–10, 25; xx:167–72, 256–7; *War* i:10–12; vii:252–74; *Life*, 17ff.

36 E.g. *Matt.* xxvii:24–5; *Lk.* xix:41–44; Eusebius, *Hist. eccl.*, III, iv:2ff.

37 Cf. Brandon, *Jesus and the Zealots*, pp. 208–216. See p. 59.

38 Jos. *War* vii:389–401.

39 Cf. Y. Yadin, *Masada*, pp. 12–13, 201–3.

40 Cf. Y. Yadin, *The Excavation of Masada, 1963/64*, pp. 16–17, 76–9, 91–2; *Masada*, pp. 164–201.

41 Cf. A. Dupont-Sommer, *Les écrits esséniens découverts près de la Mer Morte*, *passim*; M. Burrows, *The Dead Sea Scrolls*, *passim*; *Encyclopedia of the Jewish Religion*, pp. 108–9; *R.G.G.*, V, 740–56.

42 It is generally thought that the name *Kittim* in the Qumrân Scrolls is a synonym for 'Romans': cf. A.Dupont-Sommer, *Les écrits esséniens découverts près de la Mer Morte*, pp. 272, n. 1, 273, notes 1–2; Y. Yadin, *The*

Scroll of the War of the Sons of Light against the Sons of Darkness, pp. 22–6; M. Black, The Scrolls and Christian Origins, pp. 153–4.

43 Fragments of an apocryphal writing, apparently of Qumrân origin, have been found at Masada: cf. Yadin, The Excavation of Masada, 1963/64, pp. 105–108; Masada, pp. 172–4. C. Roth (Historical Background of the Dead Sea Scrolls, pp. 25–35; J.S.S., IV, pp. 338ff.), and G. R. Driver (The Judaean Scrolls, pp. 236, 239–43, 244ff., 251, 266–84, 586–7) have actually identified the Qumrân Covenanters and the Zealots. Cf. R. De Vaux, L'archéologie et les manuscrits de la Mer Morte, pp. 91–4; Brandon, Jesus and the Zealots, pp. 63, n. 4, 327, n. 2. It is interesting to note that a leading Jewish general in the Revolt was John the Essene (Jos. War ii:567; iii:11, 19); a fact of considerable significance, if the Essenes are to be identified with the Qumrân Covenanters, as many scholars think.

44 Cf. Jos. War i:2; see also his tractate Against Apion. Cf. Brandon, op. cit., pp. 144–5; B. Niese in E.R.E., VII, p. 576b.

45 See n. 35.

46 Cf. Brandon, op. cit., pp. 35–7; 'Josephus: Renegade or Patriot?', History Today, VIII (1958).

47 Jos. War ii:118; Ant. xviii:4.

48 See p. 34.

49 War vii:418–19 (trans. H. St. J. Thackeray, Loeb ed. Josephus, III, pp. 621, 623).

50 Cf. Brandon, Jesus and the Zealots, pp. 43–4.

51 War ii:651.

52 War iv:161.

53 Cf. Hengel, Die Zeloten, pp. 42–47, 323; Brandon, pp. 40–1.

54 Cf. Hengel, pp. 47–51.

55 War ii:254–7.

56 Cf. Brandon, pp. 38–40, 45.

57 Cf. Hengel, pp. 151ff.

58 Jos. Ant. xx:102.

59 It is probable that the saying of Jesus: 'If any man would come after me, let him deny himself, and take up his cross, and follow me' (Mk. viii:34) was a well-known Zealot saying. Cf. D. A. Schlatter, Die Geschichte Israels von Alexander dem Grossen bis Hadrian, p. 264; Hengel, p. 266.

60 The Zealots doubtless moved easily between their desert retreats and the villages and towns of Judaea: a case in point is Simon, the Zealot apostle of Jesus (see pp. 40, 65).

61 War ii:427. Cf. Brandon, pp. 56, 132.

62 See pp. 144ff.

63 Ant. xviii:29–35 (the only notable incident recorded is a curious pollution of the Temple by the Samaritans). The War records nothing during these years.

64 See Josephus's presentation of the Emperor Gaius (War ii:184); see pp. 41ff.

65 Jos. Ant. xviii:26.

66 See n. 25.

67 Cf. E. M. Smallwood in J.T.S., XIII (1962), pp. 17–22.

68 Jos. Ant. xviii:35; War ii:169. Josephus generally uses the term epitropos to describe the Roman governors of Judaea. A recently found (1961) inscription at Caesarea shows that Pilate was styled praefectus: cf. J. Vardaman, 'A New Inscription which mentions Pilate as "Prefect"', J.B.L., LXXXI (1962). See Plate 2.

69 Cf. Brandon, Jesus and the Zealots, p. 69.

70 Jos. Ant. xviii:56.

71 See Jos. Ant. xviii:55; Tertullian, Apology, xvi:8; Pliny, Nat. Hist. xiii:3(4), 23; Dionys. Halic., vi:45, 2; Tacitus, Ann., i:39, 7; ii:17, 2. Cf. R. Eisler, $IH\Sigma OY\Sigma$ $BA\Sigma I\Lambda EY\Sigma$ OY $BA\Sigma I\Lambda EY\Sigma A\Sigma$, II, p. 167, n. 2, I, Tafel XXXIV; O.C.D., p. 857b; C. H. Kraeling, 'The Episode of the Roman Standards at Jerusalem', H.Th.R., XXXV, pp. 269–76; A. Dupont-Sommer, Les écrits esséniens, p. 274.

72 Cf. O.C.D., p. 857b.

73 War ii:169; Ant. xviii:56. These accounts seemingly disagree as to whether under former governors the troops had come to Jerusalem without standards, or with standards from which the effigies of the emperor had been removed.

74 Ant. xviii:57–59; War ii:170–4. According to Eusebius (Demonstratio evangelica, viii:2, 122), Philo had recorded Pilate's installation of imperial images in the Temple: see also his Hist. eccl., II, v.7. The passage is not to be found in any of Philo's extant works. Jerome (Comm. in Matt. XXIV.15) also refers to such an event. In view of the silence of Josephus about any violation of the Temple in connection with the standards, it would seem probable that Eusebius and Jerome were confused in their references. The rabbinic Megillath Taanith, xviii, commemorates: 'On the third of Kislev the ensigns were removed from the [temple?] court.' The only occasion on which Roman

standards were erected in the Temple, and sacrifice made to them was in AD 70, according to Josephus (see pp. 72ff.). Cf. Brandon, *Jesus and the Zealots*, p. 71, n. 3.
75 *Ant.* xviii: 55. It is difficult to understand why Pilate should have put his army in Jerusalem for winter-quarters in preference to Caesarea.
76 *Op. cit.*, 57.
77 It has been suggested that Pilate was acting under orders from Sejanus, who was strongly anti-Semitic. Cf. J. Derenbourg, *Essai sur l'histoire et la géographie de la Palestine (d'après les Thalmuds et les autres sources rabbiniques)*, p. 198; H. Graetz, *History of the Jews*, II, p. 139; Schürer, *G.J.V.*, I, p. 492, n. 147; A. D. Doyle, 'Pilate's Career and the Date of the Crucifixion', *J.T.S.*, XLII (1941), p. 192; Philo, *Leg. ad Gaium* (ed. E. M. Smallwood), p. 305.
78 *Ant.* xviii:60–2; *War* ii:175–7.
79 On the water supply of Jerusalem at this time, cf. G. A. Smith, *Jerusalem*, I, chap. 5; Jeremias, *Jerusalem zur Zeit Jesu*, I, p. 14; Perowne, *The Later Herods*, pp. 52–3.
80 In his *Against Apion*, i:167, Josephus translates *Korban* into Greek as *dōron theou* ('God's gift'). Cf. G. Ricciotti, *Flavio Guiseppe*, II, p. 256, note on 175; Feldman, Loeb ed. of *Josephus*, IX, 46, note b.
81 *Ant.* xviii:60, 'who did not like what was done about the water'.
82 *Ant.* xviii:60, *hubrizon eis ton andra*.
83 *Ant.* xviii:61–2; *War* ii:175–7. Cf. Brandon, *op. cit.*, p. 76, n. 3.
84 Josephus does record his action against the Samaritans: *Ant.* xviii: 85–9.
85 Philo, *Leg. ad Gaium*, 276ff. (ed. E. M. Smallwood); see p. 292. Cf. E. R. Goodenough, *The Politics of Philo Judaeus*, p. 17.
86 *Leg. ad Gaium*, 299, 306.
87 *Op. cit.*, 300–1.
88 *Op. cit.*, 302–5.
89 Cf. Smallwood, ed. *Leg. ad. Gaium*, p. 304.
90 Cf. Brandon, *op. cit.*, pp. 71–5.
91 *Jesus and the Zealots*, p. 80.
92 *Ant.* xviii:63–4. Cf. Loeb ed. of *Josephus*, ix, pp. 48–51 and notes; Brandon, *op. cit.*, pp. 359–68.
93 Pp. 151–3.
94 E.g. Suetonius, *Claudius*, 25; Tacitus, *Ann.*, xv:44; *Acts* xvi:6.
95 Pp. 151–2.
96 *Mk.* xv:7.
97 *Mk.* xv:27. Cf. Hengel, *Die Zeloten*,

p. 30; Brandon, *Jesus and the Zealots*, p. 351, n. 1.
98 Cf. Brandon, *op. cit.*, pp. 78, 316, n. 6; J. Blinzler, 'Die Niedermetzelung von Galilaern durch Pilatus', *N.T.*, II, pp. 44–9.
99 According to *Lk.* xxiii:6–7, Pilate sent Jesus to Herod Antipas, on learning that he was a Galilaean. See pp. 120–1.
100 See *Mishnah* (*Yadaim*, 4.8), in H. Danby, *The Mishnah*, p. 785; Epictetus, *Discourses*, IV.vii.6. Cf. Hengel, *Die Zeloten*, pp. 57–61; Klausner, *Jesus of Nazareth*, p. 204; R. Bultmann, *Gesch. d. Synop. Trad.*, p. 57; O. Cullmann, *The State in the New Testament*, p. 14; Kraeling in *H.Th.R.*, XXXV (1942), pp. 286–9.
101 *Mk.* iii:18; *Lk.* vi:15; *Acts* 1:13: Cf. Brandon, *op. cit.*, pp. 42–3. See pp. 144ff.
102 *Matt.* xi:12. The *biastai* could mean Zealots: cf. A. von Gall, *ΒΑΣΙΛΕΙΑ ΤΟΥ ΘΕΟΥ*, p. 205; S. Angus in *E.R.E.*, XII, p. 851a, n. 7; K. Stendahl in *Peake's Commentary²*, p. 684e; H. Windisch, *Der messianische Krieg und das Urchristentum*, p. 35; *Th.Wb.*, IV, 888; T. W. Manson, 'John the Baptist', *B.J.R.L.*, 36 (1954), p. 406, n. 2.
103 *Mk.* xii:14–15, and Synoptic parallels.
104 Pp. 66ff.
105 Cf. M. P. Charlesworth, *C.A.H.*, X, pp. 653ff.
106 Philo, *Leg. ad Gaium*, 203; cf. Jos. *Ant.* xviii:261, *War* ii:184–5; Tacitus, *Hist.*, v. 9.
107 Cf. A. D. Nock, *C.A.H.*, X, pp. 496–7; J. P. V. D. Balsdon, *The Emperor Gaius*, pp. 160–72.
108 Philo, *Leg. ad Gaium*, 200–1. Josephus (*Ant.* xviii:257–61) traces the trouble to Alexandrian anti-Semitism. Cf. Schürer, *G.J.V.*, I, pp. 495–503.
109 Dr Smallwood (*op. cit.*, p. 256, n. on 188) thinks that the statue was to be of Gaius himself in the guise of Zeus.
110 II *Macc.* vi:2; Jos. *Ant.* xii:253; *Dan.* ix:27; xii:11. Cf. M. Noth, *History of Israel²*, pp. 366–7; Farmer, *Maccabees, Zealots and Josephus*, pp. 93–7.
111 Philo, *Legatio ad Gaium*, 197ff.; Josephus, *Ant.* xviii:257ff.; *War* ii:184ff.
112 Cf. Brandon, *Jesus and the Zealots*, pp. 84–7.
113 Jos. *Ant.* xviii:302–9; *War* ii:203.
114 *Ant.* xviii:302; Tacitus, *Hist.*, v. 9. Cf. Goodenough, *The Politics of Philo Judaeus*, p. 18.

115　Jos. *Ant.* xviii:5.

116　*Acts* vi:7; xv:5.

117　E.g. *Acts* v:34–7; xi:28; xii:20–3; xviii:2, 12; xxi:38; xxiv:24; xxv:13.

118　Cf. *B.C.*, II, pp. 177–86; Bruce, *Acts of the Apostles*, pp. 29–34.

119　*Lk.* xix:41–4. The *Acts* forms a sequel to the Lukan Gospel (cf. *Acts* i:1ff.).

120　*Mk.* xiii:1.

121　xiii:2.

122　xiii:3–4.

123　xiii:5ff. Cf. Brandon, *N.T.S.*, 7 (1961), pp. 133ff.

124　See pp. 22–3.

125　See pp. 71ff. Cf. Brandon, *Jesus and the Zealots*, pp. 235ff.

126　See pp. 72–3.

127　*Mk.* xiii:14–20.

128　See n. 110, p. 41.

129　On the significance of the words here in parenthesis see p. 72.

130　Pp. 72ff.

131　Jos. *Ant.* xviii:262. Cf. Brandon, *Jesus and the Zealots*, p. 89, n. 3.

132　Pp. 71–3.

133　Cf. Brandon, *op. cit.*, pp. 87–91.

134　Cf. *ibid.*, pp. 58–9. Cf. Yadin, *The Scroll of the War*, p. 246; Dupont-Sommer, *Les écrits esséniens*, pp. 179ff.

135　Josephus attributed the death of Gaius to the wrath of God (*Ant.* xviii:306). Cf. J. S. Kennard, *Politique et religion chez les Juifs au temps de Jésus et dans l'Église primitive*, p. 12. On 'the elect' cf. N. Walter, *Z.N.T.W.*, 57 (1966), p. 39.

136　*Acts* ii:46.

137　Jos. *Ant.* xix:274–5; *War* ii:206–16.

138　Jos. *Ant.* xix:328, 330–1; *Bikkurim* iii:4; *Sotah* vii:8 (in Danby, *The Mishnah*, pp. 97, 301). Cf. Derenbourg, *Essai*, p. 217; Schürer, *G.J.V.*, I, pp. 554–5.

139　*Acts* xii:1–3. Cf. *B.C.*, III, p. 132.

140　*Acts* xii:4–17. On the possibility that 'another place' was intentionally undefined cf. Brandon, *op. cit.*, pp. 164, 191, 196–8, 297–9.

141　*Acts* xii:19–23. Cf. *B.C.*, III, p. 139.

142　'When he saw it pleased the Jews' (*Acts* xii:3). See p. 49.

143　*Acts* xii:21 describes 'the people' (*ho dēmos*) as shouting: 'the voice of god, not man'. Josephus, in a parallel account (*Ant.* xix:343–350), attributes the blasphemous praise to 'the flatterers' (*hoi kolakes*).

144　*Acts* iv:21; v:28, 40.

145　*Acts* viii:1. Cf. M. Simon, *Les premiers Chrétiens*, pp. 41–2; Brandon, *op. cit.*, p. 155, n. 3.

146　Jos. *Ant.* xix:338–42; *Ant.* xix:326–7; *War* ii:218. Cf. Brandon, *op. cit.*, pp. 95–7.

147　Suetonius, *Claudius*, 25; cf. *Acts* xviii:2; *Dio Cassius*, LX, 6. Cf. A. Momigliano, *L'Opera dell'Imperatore Claudio*, pp. 66, 76; A. D. Nock, *C.A.H.*, X, pp. 500–1; V. M. Scramuzzi in *B.C.*, V, pp. 459–60; W. den Boer, 'Claudius', *R.A.C.*, III, 180–1; E. M. Smallwood, 'Jews and Romans in the Early Empire', *History Today*, XV (1965), pp. 236ff.; F. F. Bruce, *B.J.R.L.* 44 (1962), pp. 311–13, 315.

148　Cf. *Sanhedrin*, 7.4 (in Danby, *The Mishnah*, p. 391). John the Baptist, whom Herod Antipas clearly regarded as politically dangerous, was also beheaded (*Mk.* vi:27; Jos. *Ant.* xviii:118–19). Cf. S.-B. *Kommentar*, I, p. 706.

149　Jos. *Ant.* xix:360–3; *War* ii:220.

150　Jos. *Ant.* xix:97–9; *Acts* v:36; Jos. *Ant.* xx:169–72; *War* ii:261–3 (cf. *Acts* xxi:38). Cf. Brandon, *Jesus and the Zealots*, pp. 99–101, 109ff.

151　Jos. *Ant.* xx:105–113; *War* ii:224–7.

152　Jos. *Ant.* xx:113–17; *War* ii:228–31.

153　*Acts* xxv–xxvi.

154　*Gal.* ii:9. *Stulos* is used as a metaphor for a person holding a key position, providing supporting strength, in *Rev.* iii:12 (cf. I *Tim.* iii:15). Cf. Schlier, *Der Brief an die Galater*, pp. 78–9.

155　*Gal.* ii:11ff. Cf. Brandon, *op. cit.*, pp. 158ff.

156　*Acts* i:11ff.; ii:14ff.; iii:1ff.; v:1ff.

157　*Acts* xii:17.

158　Cf. Brandon, *The Fall of Jerusalem and the Christian Church*, p. 45.

159　*Acts* xv:13ff.

160　*Acts* xxi:18. Cf. A. A. T. Ehrhardt, *The Apostolic Succession*, pp. 22, 28–9, 82; *B.C.*, IV, p. 270; K. L. Carroll, 'The Place of James in the Early Church', *B.J.R.L.*, 44 (1961), pp. 54–5.

161　*Acts* xxi:20ff. Cf. Brandon, *Fall of Jerusalem*, pp. 133–4, 148–50; *Jesus and the Zealots*, pp. 186ff.

162　*Lk.* i:1–4.

163　*Mk.* vi:1–6.

164　*Mk.* iii:21: cf. Klostermann, *Markusevangelium*, p. 36; Taylor, *St Mark*, p. 236.

165　*Mk.* iii:31–5. Cf. Goguel, *La naissance du Christianisme*, pp. 130–3; Brandon, *Jesus and the Zealots*, pp. 274ff.

166　Pp. 75ff.

180   REFERENCES, PAGES 51–57

167   *Mk.* v:37; ix:2; xiii:3; xiv:33; *Matt.* xvii:1; xxvi:37; *Lk.* viii:51; ix:28. Cf. Goguel, *Jesus,* pp. 342–3.
168   *Gal.* ii:9. Cf. O. Cullmann, *Peter: Disciple-Apostle-Martyr,* p. 42, Brandon, *Jesus and the Zealots,* pp. 158–9.
169   Cf. Meyer, *Ursprung und Anfänge des Christentums,* III, pp. 224–5; J. Weiss, *Earliest Christianity,* II, pp. 716–19; Goguel, *La naissance,* pp. 130–4; Schoeps, *Theologie und Geschichte des Judenchristentums,* p. 262; Manson, *Studies in the Gospels and Epistles,* pp. 195–6; Brandon, *op. cit.,* pp. 165–7, 274–6.
170   Brandon, *op. cit.,* pp. 52–3, 166–7.
171   Eusebius, *Hist. eccl.* II, xxiii, 1; cf. III, ix.
172   I *Cor.* xv:7. Cf. Lietzmann, *An die Korinther,* I–II, pp. 78–9. According to a fragment of the lost *Gospel according to the Hebrews,* cited by Jerome, *Vir. ill.* 2 (*Apocrypha* II, ed. E. Klostermann, pp. 6–7), James was converted by the vision of the Risen Jesus. Cf. P. Vielhauer, *Neutestamentliche Apokryphen* (ed. Hennecke–Schneemelcher), I, p. 105; Goguel, *La naissance,* p. 57.
173   Jos. *Ant.* xx:200–1 (trans. L. H. Feldman, Loeb ed. of *Josephus,* IX, pp. 495, 497).
174   Jos. *Ant.* xx:201–3.
175   Cf. Schürer, *G.J.V.,* I, pp. 548–9, 581–2; Goguel, *La naissance,* pp. 144–8, 151–2; Förster, *Palestinian Judaism in New Test. Times,* p. 105, n. 9. See pp. 151ff.
176   See pp. 151–2.
177   Origen, *contra Celsum,* I.47; cf. II.13 fin.
178   Origen, *contra Celsum,* I.47; *Comm. in Matt.* X.17.
179   *War* iv:314–25. Ananus was actually killed by the Idumaeans, allies of the Zealots. Cf. E. M. Smallwood in *J.T.S.,* XIII (1962), pp. 29–30.
180   This could, of course, be inferred from what he says of the reaction of 'the most fair-minded' and those 'strict in observance of the law', if these words remain in their original form. However, his whole statement is curiously ambivalent. Cf. Brandon, *op. cit.,* pp. 115ff.
181   *Ant.* xx:180–1; cf. xx:206–7. Cf. Smallwood, in *J.T.S.,* XIII (1962), p. 27, n. 2.
182   According to Josephus (*Ant.* xx:181), the 'poorer priests were starved to death'.

183   *Acts* vi:7. Cf. P. Winter, 'The Cultural Background of the Narrative in Luke i and ii', *J.Q.R.,* XLV (1954), pp. 160–7.
184   The sentiment expressed in *Lk.* vii:25 doubtless stems from Palestinian tradition. The community of goods in the Jerusalem Church (*Acts* iv:34ff.) is also significant. In view of the social consciousness that finds expression in the so-called Epistle of James (e.g. i:9–11; ii:1–9; v:1–6), it is interesting that the document has been traditionally attributed to him. Cf. F. C. Grant, *The Economic Background of the Gospels,* p. 122, n. 1; W. K. Lowther Clarke, *New Testament Problems,* p. 114.
185   According to *Acts* xv:5, there were Pharisees in the Jerusalem Church, and also those described as 'zealous for the Torah' (xxi:20). Cf. Bruce, *Acts of the Apostles,* p. 391.
186   Cf. Brandon, *Jesus and the Zealots,* pp. 115–21.
187   On Hegesippus see Eusebius, *Hist. eccl.* II, xxiii, 3; IV, viii, 1–2, xxii, 1–9 (Eusebius is our chief source of information about Hegesippus). Cf. F. J. Hort, *Judaistic Christianity,* pp. 164–9; H. Lietzmann, *Geschichte der alten Kirche,* I, p. 192; W. Telfer, 'Was Hegesippus a Jew?', *H.Th.R.,* LIII (1960), pp. 143–53. On Aelia Capitolina cf. M. Join-Lambert, *Jerusalem,* pp. 102–6.
188   In Euseb. *Hist. eccl.* II, xxiii, 5–6. Cf. Brandon, *op. cit.,* p. 122, n. 2.
189   In Euseb. *Hist. eccl.* II, xxiii, 7. Cf. Eisler, *ΙΗΣΟΥΣ ΒΑΣΙΛΕΥΣ,* II, p. 583; H. J. Schoeps, *Theologie und Geschichte des Judenchristentums,* p. 123, n. 1; *Aus frühchristlicher Zeit,* pp. 120–5; Brandon, *op. cit.,* p. 123, n. 1.
190   In Euseb., *op. cit.,* II, xxiii, 18.
191   Cf. Brandon, *op. cit.,* pp. 121–5.
192   In Euseb., *op. cit.,* II, xxiii, 10–18. Cf. Brandon, *op. cit.,* p. 124 and notes. Jewish revolts, attended by atrocities, broke out in 115 in Libya, Egypt, Cyrene, Cyprus, Mesopotamia. After their repression, the Jews of Palestine revolted, led by Bar-Kokhba, and were only subdued after three years of fierce guerilla warfare: cf. Oesterley, *Hist. of Israel,* II, pp. 457–63.
193   E.g. *War* iv:162ff.
194   Cf. Brandon, *Fall of Jerusalem,* chap. 8; *Jesus and the Zealots,* pp. 128–145.
195   Jos. *War* ii:409–410.
196   Jos. *War* ii:411–16. Cf. C. Roth, 'The Debate on the Loyal Sacrifices, AD

66', *H. Th.R.*, LIII (1960), pp. 93–7; Hengel, *Die Zeloten*, p. 111, n. 2; Brandon, *Jesus and the Zealots*, pp. 58, n. 2, 130–1.

197 Jos. *War* ii:425–32.

198 Jos. *War* ii:426–7.

199 See n. 184.

200 In his speech to the Jewish insurgents, Agrippa II contrasts their meagre resources with the mighty power of the Roman Empire (Jos. *War* ii:356ff.).

201 Brandon, *Fall of Jerusalem*, pp. 157ff.

202 Jos. *War* ii:517–42.

203 Cf. Brandon, *Jesus and the Zealots*, p. 135, n. 6.

204 Jos. *War* ii:540–5. Cf. Tacitus, *Hist.* v:10; Suetonius, *Vespasian*, 4; *Orosius*, viii:9 (478). Cf. Brandon, *op. cit.*, pp. 135–7.

205 Cf. Brandon, *op. cit.*, pp. 138–41.

206 Jos. *War* vi:285–7. Josephus tells of a 'false prophet' (*pseudoprophētēs*) who persuaded people that 'God had commanded them to await the 'signs of their salvation' in the Temple.

207 Eusebius, *Hist. eccl.* III, v, 2–3; Epiphanius, *adv. Haer.* xxix.7, xxx.2.2; *de Mens. et Pond.* xv.

208 The Pella-legend is examined at length in *Jesus and the Zealots*, pp. 208–216.

209 *Matt.* xxvi:52: cf. Brandon, *op. cit.*, pp. 307–7. See pp. 77–8.

Chapter Three (pages 60–80)

1 See the survey of opinion on the Fall of Jerusalem down to 1951 in Brandon, *The Fall of Jerusalem and the Christian Church*, pp. 12–14; since that date cf. M. Simon, *Les premiers Chrétiens* (1952), p. 125; W. D. Davies, *P.C.²* (1962), 768a–c; F. V. Filson, *A New Test. Hist.* (1965), pp. 302; J. Daniélou, *Theologie du Judeo-Christianisme* (1958), pp. 68ff.; P. Carrington, *The Early Christian Church*, I (1957), pp. 238ff.; J. Munck in *N.T.S.* VI (1960), pp. 103ff.; W. H. C. Frend, *Martyrdom and Persecution in the Early Church* (1965), pp. 178ff.; Brandon, *Matthaean Christianity* in *The Modern Churchman*, VIII (1965), pp. 152ff.; *Jesus and the Zealots, passim.*

2 One of the reasons for this neglect has doubtless been the rather naive assumption that Paul had effected the break with Judaism long before AD 70: cf. Ed. Meyer, *Ursprung und Anfänge des Christentums*, III, p. 584.

3 From chap. xiii, Paul's activities are the almost exclusive concern of *Acts*.

4 Cf. *Jesus and the Zealots*, pp. 191–8, 289ff.; J. Daniélou–H. Marrou, *The Christian Centuries*, I, p. 45; W. H. C. Frend, *J.T.S.*, XVIII (1967), pp. 23; J. M. Fennelly, *Origins of Alexandrian Christianity* (Ph.D. thesis, Manchester University, 1967).

5 *Gal.* ii:10; I *Cor.* xvi:1–6; II *Cor.* ix:1–15; *Rom.* xv: 25–27. Cf. Lietzmann, *Geschichte der alten Kirche*, I, p. 68; Brandon, *Fall of Jerusalem*, p. 21.

6 Pp. 17ff.

7 Cf. *Fall of Jerusalem*, pp. 138ff.; *Jesus and the Zealots*, pp. 152–4, 183–8, where full references are given.

8 *Acts* xxi:17ff. Cf. *Fall of Jerusalem*, pp. 133ff., 149–152; *Jesus and the Zealots*, pp. 186ff.

9 *Acts* xx:22–30.

10 *Acts* xxi:23ff. Cf. J. Klausner, *From Jesus to Paul*, pp. 399–400.

11 Cf. *Fall of Jerusalem*, pp. 151–3.

12 It is significant that none of Paul's lieutenants such as Timothy and Titus made their mark in the Church.

13 *Gal.* iii:25–29; *Rom.* iii:9.

14 Paul refers to it in *Col.* iv:16. Cf. J. Moffat, *Intro. to Literature of New Testament*, pp. 159, 161

15 Cf. *Fall of Jerusalem*, pp. 214–16, 269.

16 Paul's arrest took place about 55: cf. *B.C.*, V, pp. 470–3.

17 Cf. *Jesus and the Zealots*, pp. 134–5 and refs.

18 E.g. *Gal.* iii:10–13.

19 *Annales*, xv:44. Cf. H. Furneaux, *The Annals of Tacitus*, II, pp. 374–5; Goguel, *Life of Jesus*, pp. 94–7; Ch. Guignebert, *Jésus*, p. 16; Meyer, *Ursprung u. Anfänge des Christentums*, I, p. 209, n. 1; P. de Labriolle, *La réaction païenne*, p. 39; H. Fuchs, 'Tacitus über die Christen', *V.C.*, I, pp. 82–8; B. H. Streeter, *C.A.H.*, X, pp. 254–6. Suetonius, referring to Nero's persecution of the Christians, describes them as 'a type of people who held a new and maleficent superstition' (*Nero*, XLI).

20 Tacitus was born *c.* 55; he died some time after 115: cf. *O.C.D.*, pp. 876–7.

21 Cf. *H.D.B.²*, p. 622a; J. M. Creed, *Gospel of St Luke*, p. 253. Attention has been centred on *Lk.* xix:43, which seems to be a precise reference to the Roman

circumvallation of Jerusalem, described by Josephus (*War* v:491–510): cf. *Fall of Jerusalem*, p. 207.

22 Cf. V. Taylor, *The Formation of the Gospel Tradition*, pp. 35–8; R. Bultmann, *Die Geschichte d. synoptischen Tradition*, pp. 8ff.; *H.D.B.*², pp. 191–2; *R.G.G.*³, II, 1002–3.

23 Cf. B. W. Bacon, *Is Mark a Roman Gospel?*, *passim*; Streeter, *The Four Gospels*, p. 12; Taylor, *Gospel of St Mark*, p. 32; Goguel, *Life of Jesus*, p. 141; Guignebert, *Jésus*, p. 31; T. W. Manson, *Studies in the Gospels and Epistles*, pp. 7, 38–40; R. McL. Wilson, *P.C.*², 696b; *R.G.G.*³, II, 761; F. C. Grant, *The Gospels: their Origin and Growth*, pp. 74, 101–7; Filson, *A New Testament History*, pp. 363ff.; *H.D.B.*², p. 622a; Brandon, *Jesus and the Zealots*, chap. 5.

24 Cf. Streeter, *Four Gospels*, pp. 157–79; C. S. C. Williams, in *P.C.*², 653b–4a; Taylor, *St Mark*, pp. 9ff.; *H.D.B.*², pp. 619–20; *R.G.G.*³, II, 755–60.

25 Cf. J. Bornkamm: 'Erst das Markus-Evangelium ist im eigentlichen Sinne ein Ev., ja man wird den zweiten Evangelisten geradezu als Schöpfer dieser urchristlichen Schriftengattung bezeichnen dürfen', *R.G.G.*³, II, 760. As we shall see, the only part of the original Palestinian tradition that had assumed a connected narrative-form dealt with the trial and crucifixion of Jesus.

26 *Mk.* iii:14–16.

27 *Mk.* iii:18.

28 Cf. iii:17; v:41; vii:3–4, 34; xv:22, 34. Cf. Bacon, *Is Mark a Roman Gospel?*, pp. 55–9.

29 iii:17. Cf. Bacon, p. 56; Taylor, *St Mark*, pp. 231–2.

30 Cf. Hengel, *Die Zeloten*, pp. 72–3, 77; Rengstorf, *Th.Wb.*, IV, 889; Roth, *J.S.S.*, IV, pp. 335, n. 2, 336–7; Driver, *Judaean Scrolls*, p. 245; Brandon, *Jesus and the Zealots*, pp. 42–4, 243ff.

31 *Mk.* xii:13–17. Cf. Brandon, *N.T.S.*, VII, pp. 139–40.

32 xii:13. The impersonal 'they sent' (*apostellousin*: cf. Taylor, *St Mark*, p. 478) is indicative of Mark's attitude here, namely, of setting Jesus over against a hostile collective 'they', who comprise the representatives of official Judaism. See p. 75. Cf. *Jesus and the Zealots*, p. 227, n. 1.

33 The Herodians are associated with the Pharisees in plotting to kill Jesus from the beginning of his ministry (*Mk.* iii:6). Cf. T. A. Burkill, *R.H.R.*, 154, pp. 24–6.

34 See Suetonius, *Titus*, 7: cf. Jones, *The Herods of Judaea*, pp. 257–8. The Markan Gospel shows other signs of antipathy towards the Herodian dynasty: cf. Brandon, *Jesus and the Zealots*, p. 268 and n. 6. On the political significance of the Herodians cf. H. H. Rowley, *J.T.S.*, XLI (1940), pp. 14–27.

35 Mark reinforces the malignity by adding that Jesus saw 'their hypocrisy' (*hypokrisin*), xii:15.

36 Luke (xx:20), following Mark, significantly adds the interpretative comment: 'And they watched him, and sent forth spies . . . that they might take hold of his speech, so as to deliver him to the rule and to the authority of the governor.'

37 *Mk.* xii:14–17.

38 Cf. H. Loewe, *Render unto Caesar*, *passim*; J. Spencer Kennard, *Render to God*, chap. I; A. A. T. Ehrhardt, *Politische Metaphysik von Solon bis Augustin*, II, pp. 25–28.

39 Bultmann (*Gesch. d. syn. Trad.*, p. 25) thinks that verses 14–17 constitute an authentic whole, and that verse 13 has been added by Mark. Cf. *Jesus and the Zealots*, p. 347, n. 1.

40 Cf. Eisler, *ΙΗΣΟΥΣ ΒΑΣΙΛΕΥΣ*, II, pp. 199–201, *Messiah Jesus*, pp. 334–5; Kennard, *op. cit.*, pp. 113–20; Manson, *Jesus and the Non-Jews*, p. 9; Filson, *New Test. History*, pp. 131–2; E. Stauffer, *Christus und die Caesaren*, p. 142–3; Klostermann, *Markusevangelium*, p. 124; Goguel, *Revue historique*, CLXII, pp. 42–3.

41 See pp. 144–6.

42 Cf. Kennard, pp. 121–7; Brandon, *Jesus and the Zealots*, pp. 345–8.

43 *Lk.* xxiii:2.

44 Pp. 144ff.

45 Jos. *War* ii:404; cf. *Jesus and the Zealots*, pp. 128–30.

46 Jos. *War* vii:120–57.

47 Cf. 'Triumphus', *O.C.D.* One of the chief Jewish leaders was executed on this occasion (Jos. *War* vii:153–5).

48 Jos. *War* i:5. Cf. *C.A.H.*, X, chaps. xxiv, xxv; A. Peretti, *La Sibilla babilonese*, pp. 18–20; B. Pin, *Jérusalem contre Rome* (*Un duel pour l'hégémonie en Méditerranée orientale*), p. 13.

49 On the attitude of Babylonian Jewry

and Parthian policy cf. J. Neusner, *History of the Jews in Babylonia*, I, pp. 64–7.

50 Cf. M. P. Charlesworth, *C.A.H.*, XI, pp. 4–6; G. M. Bersanetti, *Vespasiano*, pp. 40–2.

51 Cf. H. St J. Hart, *J.T.S.*, III (1952), pp. 172–98 and plates; A. Reifenburg, *Israel's History in Coins*, pp. 32–3. See Plates 7–10.

52 Jos. *War* vii:116–57 (cf. *Life*, 423). Cf. G. Riciotti, *Flavio Giuseppe*, I, p. 77; IV, pp. 238–52.

53 Jos. *War* vii:139–47.

54 *Ibid.*, 148–151.

55 Cf. L. Curtius–A. Nawrath, *Das Antike Rom*, pp. 39–40, Bilder 40–4; Schürer, *G.J.V.*, I, p. 635, n. 128; T. Mommsen, *Das Weltreich der Caesaren*, p. 390, n.; G. Bendinelli, *Compendio di storia dell'arte etrusca e romana*, pp. 301–4; M. R. Scherer, *Marvels of Ancient Rome*, pp. 75–6, plates 119–23. See Plate 11.

56 *Ibid.*, 122.

57 *Mk.* xv:38. Cf. *Jesus and the Zealots*, pp. 227ff.

58 Cf. Taylor, *St Mark*, p. 596; Bultmann, *Gesch. d. syn. Trad.*, pp. 305–6; T. A. Burkill, *Mysterious Revelation: an Examination of St Mark's Gospel*, pp. 246–8.

59 xv:38–9. Although there is no definite article before 'son' (*huios*), Taylor (*op. cit.*, p. 597) is surely right in saying that 'Mark read much more into the words, regarding them as a parallel at the end of his Gospel to *huios theou* at the beginning (i:1), i.e. as a confession of the deity of Jesus in the full Christian sense'.

60 Jos. *War* vii:162.

61 According to Jos. *War* v:209–19, there were two veils in the Temple: one before the golden doors of the first chamber (*oikos*), the other before the inner chamber, the 'Holy of Holies'. Cf. Jeremias, *Jerusalem*, II, pp. 27–8; S.-B. *Kommentar*, I, 1044.

62 It is well to reflect that before AD 70 Gentile Christians must have felt themselves much inferior to the Jewish Christians, with their expert knowledge of the Jewish scriptures and the Temple cultus.

63 Cf. I *Cor.* v:7; xi:24–5; II *Cor.* iii:6; *Gal.* iii:13. Cf. Bultmann, *Theology of the New Test.*, I, pp. 295ff.

64 It is significant that Mark uses a transliteration of the Latin *centurio*—*kanturiōn*, whereas Matthew and Luke use the Greek *hekatonarchos*; the point would have been

appreciated in Rome. Cf. *Jesus and the Zealots*, pp. 229–30, 279–80.

65 See pp. 22–3, 43–4.

66 Pp. 22–3.

67 Pp. 41–6.

68 *Mk.* xiii:14.

69 Cf. Taylor, *St Mark*, p. 511.

70 Cf. Taylor, *ibid.* See also C. H. Dodd, *J.R.S.*, XXXVII, pp. 534; D. Daube, *The New Test. and Rabbinic Judaism*, pp. 422–36.

71 H. Conzelmann (*Z.N.T.W.*, 50 (1959), p. 220, n. 50), graphically describes the words in parenthesis as 'ein Wink des Evangelisten an seine Leser'.

72 Jos. *War* vi:316.

73 Cf. *O.C.D.*, p. 450; A. D. Nock, *C.A.H.*, X, pp. 483–4. According to Suetonius, *Titus*, v, the army's acclamation and his subsequent wearing of a diadem on a ritual occasion in Egypt caused some suspicion as to his loyalty; but this was immediately dissipated on his arrival in Rome.

74 *Mk.* xiii:8ff. A belief was current at this time in the Roman Empire that a world-ruler would come from Judaea (cf. Jos. *War* vi:312–15; Tacitus, *Hist.*, v. 13; Suetonius, *Vespasian*, 4.5). Cf. Klostermann, *Markusevangelium*, p. 133; H. Conzelmann, *Z.N.T.W.*, 50 (1959), pp. 214–15.

75 See pp. 43–6.

76 Jos. *War* vii:143.

77 *Mk.* xiii:1–3. The artificiality of the *mise en scène* is patent in the idea that one Palestinian Jew would have called the attention of another to the Temple, as though they were visiting it for the first time. The scene is much more credible, if Mark is reminding the Christians of Rome of what they had just seen in the Flavian triumph. Cf. Conzelmann, *Z.N.T.W.*, 50, pp. 212–13.

78 xiii:4–7. The 'signs of the times' had evidently excited much Messianic speculation, as Josephus, Tacitus and Suetonius show (see n. 74 above). It would seem that Mark assumed that his readers knew of some important personage, whose claim to be the prophesied world-ruler from Judaea could be cryptically designated by the words 'I am he!' Since Vespasian was so identified, Mark's reticence here is significant. Cf. *Jesus and the Zealots*, pp. 36, 235, n. 3, 312, 362; Conzelmann, *Z.N.T.W.*, 50, pp. 218; N. Walter,

Z.N.T.W., 57, pp. 41-2, who sees it as evidence of *post* AD 70 date.

79 xiii:9-13: cf. Taylor, pp. 88, 509-10; Conzelmann, *ibid.*, pp. 218-19; Brandon, *op. cit.*, pp. 239-40.

80 xiii:28-31.

81 xiii:7, 32-7. Commenting upon this aspect of Mark's apocalypse, Conzelmann (*ibid.*, p. 215, n. 27) remarks: 'Mir ist es wahrscheinlicher, dass Markus nach 70 geschrieben hat als vor der Zerstörung des Tempels.'

82 Pp. 63, 81.

83 This is, significantly, recognised in *Mk.* xiii:13: 'And ye shall be hated of all men for my name's sake.' Note also Tacitus's description of Christianity as *exitiabilis superstitio* (*Ann.* xv:44), and Suetonius's reference to Christians as *genus hominum superstitionis novae ac maleficae* (*Nero*, XVI); see n. 19. Cf. P. de Labriolle, *La réaction païenne*, pp. 36-45; Frend, *Martyrdom and Persecution in the Early Church*, pp. 161-4.

84 See p. 63. There is some evidence that might indicate that the Romans thought that the Christians were as much attached to the Temple as the Jews. For a discussion of the matter cf. *Jesus and the Zealots*, p. 233, n. 1.

85 *Mk.* xv:10, 14.

86 Pp. 92ff.

87 P. 183, n. 59.

88 Pp. 23-4.

89 *Mk.* viii:27-33; ix:6, 10, 18, 34; x:13-16, 28-32, 35-45. Cf. *Jesus and the Zealots*, pp. 276-9.

90 xv:39. Demoniacs recognise Jesus' divinity (*Mk.* i:24, 34; iii:11-12), for, according to contemporary belief, the insane had supernatural knowledge, through the indwelling demon. Cf. C. Clemen, *Religionsgeschichtliche Erklärung d. N.T.*, pp. 218-19.

91 xiv:10, 11, 20, 21, 43-5.

92 xiv:66-72 (cf. v:29-31).

93 xiv:50.

94 P. 51.

95 Pp. 51-2.

96 Paul would doubtless have made the situation in the Jerusalem Church clear to his Gentile converts during his sojourn in Rome (*Acts* xxviii:15-31); if his stay there had been terminated by his execution, which seems likely, the temporary reassertion there of the authority of the Mother Church was likely to have re-inforced Paul's presentation. The history of Christianity in Rome prior to AD 70 is obscure. It seems originally to have been a Jewish Christian foundation, with which Peter probably had some early association. According to Suetonius (*Claudius*, 25), the Emperor Claudius expelled the Jews from the city, because of disturbances connected with Christianity (impulsore Chresto). Paul's *Epistle to the Romans* suggests that he was preparing to visit the Christian community there, but was doubtful about his reception. According to *Acts* xxviii:22, when Paul eventually came to Rome as a prisoner, the Jews there professed only a vague knowledge of Christianity; this statement is difficult to reconcile with the implication of verse 15 of the existence of a Christian (Gentile?) community there. Cf. Goguel, *La naissance du Christianisme*, pp. 178-89; Brandon, *Fall of Jerusalem*, pp. 145-8.

97 iii:6: cf. *Jesus and the Zealots*, pp. 265-273.

98 xiv:43—xv:11.

99 vi:1-6: cf. *Jesus and the Zealots*, pp. 273-4.

100 xv:29-39.

101 Cf. Frend, *Martyrdom and Persecution in the Early Church*, p. 534, n. 282.

102 See above pp. 63, 74, 81.

103 *Acts* xiii:50; xiv:2, 19; xvii:6, 13; xviii:12ff.; xxiv:1ff.

104 Cf. *Jesus and the Zealots*, pp. 285-300.

105 *Op. cit.*, pp. 164, 191-8, 357.

106 Jos. *War* vii:409-11.

107 Jos. *War* vii:420-1, 433-6. Driver, *Judaean Scrolls*, p. 234, thinks that the Sicarii made for the temple at Leontopolis as being 'the old headquarters of the Zadokite movement'. On the Leontopolis temple and its suppression cf. *Jesus and the Zealots*, pp. 292-3 and notes.

108 Jos. *War* vii:412-19.

109 *Mk.* xiv:47: cf. Taylor, *St Mark*, p. 559: it is 'possible that the same was withheld for prudential reasons'.

110 *Matt.* xxvi:51-4.

111 The saying cannot be regarded as a proverbial condemnation of the profession of arms, since it is manifestly untrue that all soldiers die in armed conflict.

112 Cf. *Jesus and the Zealots*, pp. 305-308.

113 Pp. 109ff.

114 *Lk.* vi:15 (cf. *Acts* i:13). Matthew (x:4) for obvious reasons followed Mark's

lead in leaving Simon designated 'the *Kananaios*'. Luke—Acts were evidently addressed to a Hellenistic Christian community. In view of the divergence of Luke—Acts and Matthew in the location of the post-Resurrection appearances of Jesus, they must represent traditions widely separated in space. Cf. *Jesus and the Zealots*, pp. 285–6.

115 *Lk.* xxii:35–38. It would seem that Luke, aware of the fact that the disciples of Jesus were armed in Gethsemane, endeavoured to account for its contradiction to the ideal of the pacific Christ by declaring that Jesus gave the relevant order to fulfill a prophecy. See pp. 145–8.

116 *Lk.* ii:13–14. Luke also represents the crowd as acclaiming the Messianic entry of Jesus into Jerusalem in terms of peaceable piety (xix:38). See pp. 117ff.

117 *Lk.* xix:41–44. Cf. Creed, *St Luke*, pp. 241–2; Brandon, *op. cit.*, p. 318

118 *Acts* v:30. Cf. *B.C.*, IV, p. 59.

119 Pp. 75–6.

120 *Jn.* i:1–14. Cf. C. H. Dodd, *Interpretation of the Fourth Gospel*, pp. 277–85.

121 *Jn.* xviii:36–7.

122 The use of the word *huperetai* is interesting, because John uses it in xviii:3, 12, 22 in the sense of 'armed retainers'.

123 Pp. 125ff.

124 Cf. viii:44; xiv:30; xvi:10–11. Cf. Dodd, *op. cit.*, pp. 159, 408–9.

125 Cf. M. Simon, *Verus Israel*, pp. 245ff. See pp. 137–9.

126 An *apologia ad Christianos romanos*: see *Jesus and the Zealots*, chap. 5.

127 Cf. S. G. F. Brandon, *The Judgment of the Dead* (London, 1967), pp. 120, 128–30.

Chapter Four (pages 81–106)

1 'Per procuratorem Pontium Pilatum supplicio adfectus erat', *Ann.* xv:44.

2 See pp. 14–16.

3 Pp. 21–4.

4 Cf. V. Taylor, *The Formation of the Gospel Tradition*, pp. 44ff.; Bultmann, *Gesch. d. syn. Trad.*, pp. 297–308; F. W. Beare, *The Earliest Records of Jesus*, pp. 219–221.

5 *Mk.* xiv:56ff.

6 *Mk.* xiv:61–63.

7 xv:1, 3, 15. The *titulus* on Jesus' cross did, by implication, give the cause of his condemnation (xv:26): see p. 104.

8 See pp. 92–3.

9 On the martyr-tradition in Judaism see pp. 29–34. Some reminiscence of the idea of Jesus as the 'faithful witness' may be preserved in *Rev.* i:5; iii:14; I *Tim.* vi:13; cf. *Acts* iv:27.

10 Pp. 21–2.

11 *Mk.* xi:1ff. The ass was the mount for the Messiah-King, according to *Zachariah* ix:9. Cf. H.-W. Kuhn, *Z.N.T.W.*, 50 (1959), p. 88; Mowinckel, *He That Cometh*, pp. 63, 94, 171, 177, 179, 336; Brandon, *Jesus and the Zealots*, p. 349, n. 2. On the political significance of the palm-branches, mentioned in *Jn.* xii:13, cf. W. R. Farmer, *J.T.S.*, III (n.s.), pp. 62–6.

12 *Mk.* xi:10. Cf. Taylor, *St Mark*, pp. 456–7; Mowinckel, p. 292.

13 *Mk.* xi:15–19. Cf. *Matt.* xxi:12; *Lk.* xix:45–6. John (ii:13–22) places the 'Cleansing of the Temple' at the beginning of Jesus' career. He also represents Jesus as uttering, at that time, the threat to destroy the Temple, which Mark describes as the 'false witness' brought against Jesus during the Sanhedrin proceedings. John's dating of the 'Cleansing' not only contradicts the other three Gospels, but it raises insuperable difficulties for understanding the course of Jesus' ministry. Cf. Goguel, *Life of Jesus*, pp. 235–6; C. K. Barrett, *P.C.*[2], 739d; Klostermann, *Markusevangelium*, pp. 128–30; C. H. Dodd, *Historical Tradition in the New Testament*, pp. 300–3; H. W. Montefiore, *Josephus and the New Testament*, pp. 22–9.

14 *Mk.* xi:17. The saying combines the LXX text of *Isa.* xlvi:7 and an adaptation of *Jer.* vii:11; it is evidently an *ad hoc* composition of Mark's and reflects his view of the Temple and its fate: cf. Brandon, *Jesus and the Zealots*, p. 237.

15 Cf. Schürer, *G.J.V.*, II, pp. 266–71; Driver, *Judaean Scrolls*, pp. 32–3; Eisler, *ΙΗΣΟΥΣ ΒΑΣΙΛΕΥΣ*, II, pp. 491–9, *Messiah Jesus*, pp. 489–93; N. Q. Hamilton, *J.B.L.*, LXXXVIII (1964), pp. 369–70.

16 Cf. V. Eppstein, *Z.N.T.W.*, 55 (1964), pp. 43, 45–6; J. Spencer-Kennard, *Render to God*, pp. 62–7.

17 Cf. Jeremias, *Jerusalem*, I, pp. 54–5; S.-B. *Kommentar*, I, pp. 850–2; Winter, *On the Trial of Jesus*, p. 143.

18 *Matt.* xvii:24–6, represents Jesus as paying the Temple tax: cf. H. W. Montefiore, *N.T.S.*, XI (1964), pp. 60–71. The

Passover lamb, consumed at the Last Supper, had probably been purchased and slaughtered in the Temple. According to *Lk.* ii:22–8, a sacrifice of two turtle-doves or pigeons was made in the Temple on behalf of the infant Jesus by his mother at her purification after child birth.

19 *Mk.* xi:18; see also xii:12; cf. Taylor, *St Mark*, pp. 464–5. Mark gives the interesting information (xi:19), that Jesus left the city in the evening, clearly fearing a secret nocturnal arrest.

20 Cf. *Jesus and the Zealots*, pp. 342–3.

21 John (ii:15) even describes Jesus as, single-handed, driving both the traders and the cattle out of the Temple. On the Temple police cf. Jeremias, *Jerusalem*, II, pp. 72–5; Eppstein, *Z.N.T.W.*, 55 (1964), pp. 46–7.

22 According to *Mk.* xi:15, Jesus had entered Jerusalem with his disciples; then they seem suddenly to disappear from the the scene until xi:19, when they accompany him on departing from the city in the evening.

23 We may well ask what happened to the money, when the money-changers' tables were upset? Cf. Klausner, *Jesus of Nazareth*, p. 315.

24 Jos. *War* iv:147–50. Cf. Eisler, *ΙΗΣΟΥΣ ΒΑΣΙΛΕΥΣ*, II, pp. 476–515, *Messiah Jesus*, pp. 480–506, who relates the curious passage in *Lk.* xiii:1 to this operation. According to *Mk.* xi:11, Jesus seems to have reconnoitred the Temple on the previous day. Cf. *Jesus and the Zealots*, pp. 140, 331–6, 338–9.

25 It is significant that the 'Messiah of Aaron' in the Qumrân Scrolls was 'the high priest and head of the entire Congregation of Israel': cf. K. G. Kuhn, 'The Two Messiahs of Aaron and Israel' in *The Scrolls and the New Testament* (ed. K. Stendahl), pp. 54ff.; M. Black, *The Scrolls and Christian Origins*, pp. 145–57.

26 *Mk.* xii:12; cf. Taylor, *St Mark*, p. 477.

27 *Mk.* xiv:10–11. On Judas Iscariot and his motives see p. 148.

28 *Mk.* xiv:32–50.

29 Pp. 148ff. We may notice here Jesus' question to those who arrested him, as reported in *Mk.* xiv:48: 'Have you come out as against a robber (*lēstēn*), with swords and clubs to capture me?' In view of the evidence which we have noted of the use of *lēstēs* for 'Zealot', Jesus' question has a

peculiar significance. Winter, *Trial of Jesus*, pp. 44–8, prefers John's version of the arrest by Romans: see pp. 129–30.

30 *Mk.* xiv:53ff. The high priest, not named by Mark, was Caiaphas, who held office AD 18–36. The traditional site of the 'House of Caiaphas' in the upper city does not seem to be well authenticated; cf. C. Kopp, *The Holy Places of the Gospels*, pp. 352–61.

31 xiv:54, 66–72. Cf. Taylor, *St Mark*, pp. 571–2.

32 Pp. 74–5.

33 *Acts* i:15ff. Cf. O. Cullmann, *Peter: Disciple-Apostle-Martyr*, pp. 33ff. Goguel, *Life of Jesus*, pp. 482–92, after a detailed examination of the relevant data, concludes that the story of Peter's denial is unhistorical. According to Bultmann, 'Die Petrus-Geschichte selbst ist legendarisch und literarisch' (*Gesch. d. syn. Trad.*, p. 290, cf. Ergänzungsheft, p. 40). Cf. Lietzmann, *Kleine Schriften*, II, p. 254.

34 xiv:55–64. According to Taylor (*St Mark*, p. 565), verse 55 'is probably the beginning of a separate narrative inserted between 54 and 66'. Bultmann's solution is very radical: 'Ich halte den ganzen Bericht des Mk für eine sekundäre Ausführung der kürzen Angabe 15.1' (*Gesch. d. syn. Trad.*, p. 290). Cf. Winter, *On the Trial of Jesus*, pp. 23ff., *Z.N.T.W.*, 53 (1962), pp. 260–3, *J.T.S.*, XIV (1963), pp. 94–102.

35 'This passage is probably all that remains of the original reference to the action of the priests in the source into which Mark inserted xiv:55–65' (Taylor, p. 578, cf. p. 646). Cf. Beare, *Earliest Records of Jesus*, pp. 232–3; A. Jaubert, *R.H.R.*, 166 (1964), pp. 146–8 ('Une phrase boiteuse peut être précisément le signe d'une source qui a embarrassé le rédacteur. . . . C'est une raison de penser que cette délibération matinale s'est imposée au rédacteur.').

36 *Mk.* xiv:53, 55–65; xv:1–5 (R.S.V.).

37 xv:61.

38 Pp. 89–90.

39 The location of the Sanhedrin proceedings in the house of the high priest is an inference from xiv:54, 66, which belongs to the interpolated story of Peter's denial. According to Josephus (*War* v:142–147; vi:354), the Council-chamber (*bouleuterion*), was in or adjoining the southern part of the Temple area: cf. Loeb ed. of

Josephus, III, p. 242, note e. Cf. Klausner, *Jesus of Nazareth*, p. 339; J. Blinzler, *The Trial of Jesus*, pp. 112–14; Winter, *On the Trial of Jesus*, pp. 20–2.

40 According to the tractate *Sanhedrin*, 4:1 (in H. Danby, *The Mishnah*, p. 387), trials on capital charges were held in the daytime, and the verdict had also to be reached while it was day. How far this tractate accurately reports Sanhedrin procedure in the first century AD, or represents a later idealised rabbinic 'blue-print', is uncertain. Cf. Klausner, *op. cit.*, p. 340; Guignebert, *Jésus*, p. 566; Blinzler, pp. 135, 145–157; Winter, pp. 20–30; Taylor, pp. 644–6; Jaubert, *R.H.R.*, 166 (1964), pp. 151–3; A. N. Sherwin-White, *Roman Society and Roman Law in the New Testament*, pp. 44–6.

41 *Mk.* xiv:55–64. 'Le passage de Marc cherche à justifier Jésus par rapport *à des juifs* qui pouvaient se scandaliser de cette parole', Jaubert, *R.H.R.*, 166, p. 160.

42 To Mark's readers, Jesus' affirmative answer to the high priests' question (as given by Mark), would have been a statement of truth, and the Sanhedrin's interpretation of it as blasphemy would have been further proof of Jewish obduracy in the face of divine revelation.

43 See Jos. *Ant.* xx:251; cf. Jeremias, *Jerusalem*, II, pp. 17, 59.

44 *Jn.* xi:47–8.

45 Pp. 101ff..

46 Cf. *Mk.* xiv: 55ff., 60, 63. That the chief priests provided the 'false witness' is definitely stated in *Matt.* xxvi:59. On the verb and nouns meaning 'false-witness', cf. W. Bauer, *Wörterbuch z. N.T.²*, 1420. Matthew (xxvi:60–1), evidently bearing the injunction of *Deut.* xix:15 in mind about the joint testimony of two witnesses, makes Mark's indefinite 'many bore false-witness' into two witnesses, who are not designated 'false'. Cf. Blinzler, pp. 99–101; Klausner, pp. 341–2; Bultmann, *Gesch. d. syn. Trad.*, p. 291; M. Simon, *Recherches d'histoire judéo-chrétienne*, pp. 11–13, 15–16; Lietzmann, *Kleine Schriften*, II, pp. 254–5.

47 xiv:59. Jesus' attack on the Temple-establishment doubtless inspired the belief that he had threatened the Temple and its cultus. Josephus similarly charged the Zealots with destroying the Temple (*Ant.* xx:166; *War* ii:391–4, 397–401), despite the fact that they were profoundly attached to it: cf. *Jesus and the Zealots*, pp. 110, 129–130, 140, 142–3. The tradition in *Jn.* ii:18–19, and *Acts* vi:14 possibly derives also from some memory of Jewish accusations and the fact of the Temple's destruction in AD 70. Cf. Simon, *op. cit.*, pp. 11–19; Brandon, *Jesus and the Zealots*, pp. 233ff. See next note.

48 Jos. *War* vi:300–9. G. D. Kilpatrick (*The Trial of Jesus*, pp. 11–13) has argued that 'speaking against the Temple' was probably regarded as blasphemy, and hence a capital offence according to Jewish Law. He cites especially the trial of Stephen in *Acts* vi–vii; for Stephen seems to have been attacked at first because he 'never ceases to speak words against this holy place and the law; for we have heard him say that this Jesus of Nazareth will destroy this place, and will change the customs which Moses delivered to us' (vi:13–14). The Stephen episode is a well-known crux for New Testament scholarship. It seems to indicate the existence in the primitive Christian community in Jerusalem of an anti-cultic party, which was distinguished from the apostles. Stephen's speech, however, is rather a tirade against the Jewish people than against the Temple, and thus raises the question of the anti-Jewish attitude of the author of *Acts*. Despite this episode, *Acts* shows that the Jerusalem Christians continued in their devotion to the Temple. Cf. *Jesus and the Zealots*, pp. 155, n. 3, 157–8.

49 Cf. *Jesus and the Zealots*, pp. 130–1, 140–1.

50 According to *Jn.* xviii:19: 'The high priest then questioned Jesus about his disciples and his teaching.'

51 *Mk.* xiv:60; cf. Klostermann, *Markusevangelium*, p. 173; Taylor, *St Mark*, p. 567; Lietzmann, *Kleine Schriften*, II, pp. 254–5.

52 Pp. 22–4.

53 xiv:61. Cf. S.-B. *Kommentar*, II, p. 51; Taylor, p. 567. According to Mowinckel (*He That Cometh*, pp. 369–70), Jesus would not have been guilty of blasphemy for claiming to be the Messiah; but he would have been guilty if he had claimed to be the Son of Man, as *Mk.* xiv:62 records.

54 Cf. Klausner, *Jesus of Nazareth*, p. 342; Blinzler, pp. 102–11; Goguel, *Life of Jesus*, pp. 510–11; Lietzmann, II, p. 255.

55   See *Mk.* i:1; xv:39; also pp. 70–1. Cf. Winter, *J.T.S.*, XIV (1963), pp. 99–102.

56   'Cette tradition apparaît très ancienne, composée en fonction d'un auditoire juif, et, si l'on peut y discerner un souci apologétique, c'est plutôt celui de justifier Jésus d'une condemnation qu'on ne pouvait évacuer', Jaubert, *R.H.R.*, 166 (1964), p. 161.

57   xiv:62. See note 53.

58   xiv:64. According to Taylor, p. 570, the words 'to be deserving death' (*enochon einai thanatou*), 'appear to express a judicial opinion or verdict rather than a sentence'. He thinks that Mark probably used this phrasing because he was aware that the Sanhedrin was then unable to exact the penalty by stoning. This may be so; but it seems more likely that Mark was concerned to show that the Sanhedrin had really condemned Jesus to death, even though Pilate actually ordered his execution. Winter (*On the Trial of Jesus*, p. 27) thinks that the words in *Mk.* xiv:64b may be a transposition of an expression of condemnation used in the original tradition, 'without explicit indication of the formal passing of a death sentence'.

59   Tractate *Sanhedrin*, 7.4, 5, decrees death for blasphemy only when the culprit has pronounced the Sacred Name itself (Danby, *The Mishnah*, pp. 391–2). According to *Sanhedrin*, 6.4, after death by stoning, the corpse was to be hanged on a beam, set in the ground, with 'a piece of wood jutted from it'; it had to be buried before nightfall (Danby, *The Mishnah*, p. 390). Cf. Klausner, *Jesus of Nazareth*, pp. 344–5; Winter, *On the Trial of Jesus*, pp. 67–74 (a very full discussion of Jewish death penalties).

60   *Jn.* xviii:31. Cf. Blinzler, pp. 157ff.; Winter, pp. 75ff.; S. Zeitlin, *J.Q.R.*, XXI, pp. 344–5, and *Who Crucified Jesus?*, p. 81; Jaubert, *R.H.R.*, 167 (1965), pp. 3–9.

61   Pp. 92ff.

62   *Jn.* xviii:31–32. Cf. Dodd, *Interpretation of the Fourth Gospel*, pp. 427, 433–4.

63   According to a *Baraita* (J. *Sanh.* I.i; VII.2; *Shab.* 15a), 'forty years before the destruction of the Temple, the trial of capital cases was taken away from Israel': cf. S.-B. *Kommentar*, I, p. 1027. [A *Baraita* is general term for all tannaitic teaching not included in the *Mishnah*: cf. *E.J.R.*, p. 57.] Klausner (*op. cit.*, p. 334) interprets this to mean that the Sanhedrin could only carry out a preliminary enquiry preparatory to handing a capital case over to the Roman governor for trial: cf. Blinzler, p. 162.

64   *Jn.* vii:37, 40, 44.

65   *Jn.* viii:59.

66   *Jn.* xii:32, 33. Cf. Winter, *op. cit.*, pp. 88–9.

67   *Acts* xii:30ff. (note especially xxv:9, 20). Cf. Winter, pp. 76–87.

68   Pp. 52–3.

69   Jos. *War* vi:302–5.

70   Jos. *War* ii:117; cf. *Ant.* xvii:2. Cf. Schürer, *G.J.V.*, I, pp. 466–73; A. N. Sherwin-White, *Roman Society and Roman Law in the New Testament*, pp. 8–10.

71   Cf. Schürer, *G.J.V.*, I, pp. 466–73; Klausner, *Jesus of Nazareth*, p. 160; Lietzmann, II, pp. 257–60; Winter, *op. cit.*, pp. 75–100; Sherwin-White, *op. cit.*, pp. 35–43; Förster, *Palestinian Judaism in New Test. Times*, pp. 97–8, 121–4; Blinzler, pp. 157–163; Jaubert, *R.H.R.*, 167 (1965), pp. 3–9; Brandon, *Jesus and the Zealots*, pp. 254–5, 329.

72   So far as the grounds, upon which the Jewish authorites proceeded against Stephen and Paul, can be made out from the narrative of *Acts*, their cases might reasonably be designated as 'religious heresy': neither case seems to have involved a charge of sedition against Rome. On the Jewish conception of heresy and its punishment cf. *E.J.R.*, p. 182.

73   See p. 86.

74   *Mk.* xv:2. 'From this question it is clear that the Jewish hierarchy had decided to base their charge on the political aspect of the claim of Jesus to be the Messiah'—Taylor, *St Mark*, p. 579, who also thinks that the Jewish leaders probably used the phrase *ho basileus Israēl* ('the king of Israel').

75   xv:9, 12, 26.

76   xv:18; see pp. 103–4.

77   xv:32.

78   That Jesus' Messianic kingship was understood realistically by his followers is seen in the request of James and John that they should severally sit on his right and left hand in his kingdom (*Mk.* x:35ff.; *Matt.* xx:20ff.). It is also reflected in the disciples' expectation on the Mount of Olives that the Risen Jesus was about to 'restore the kingdom to Israel' (*Acts* i:6). Cf. J. Spencer Kennard, *Z.N.T.W.*, 53 (1962), pp. 50–1; T. A. Burkill, *V.C.*, XII

(1958), pp. 16–18; Eisler, *IHΣΟΥΣ ΒΑΣΙΛΕΥΣ*, II, pp. 467–75, 530–2; Winter, pp. 107–10; Lietzmann, II, pp. 260–1.

79 Sherwin-White (*op. cit.*, p. 24) does, however, think that the hearing before Pilate, as recounted in the Synoptic narrative, 'fits the Roman framework remarkably well, considering it was written with an entirely different purpose in mind. The trial is *pro tribunali*. . . . Accusations are duly made by *delatores*, the chief-priests and the elders of the people acting as such.'

80 *Mk.* xv:4.

81 xv:5. The word translated (Pilate) 'wondered' (*thaumazein*) has a number of cognate meanings: to be 'astonished', 'surprised', 'astounded' (cf. Bauer, *Wörterbuch z. N.T.*, p. 550).

82 On the question of an implied choice see p. 113.

83 This seems to be the natural inference from xv:5; but Mark possibly intended to suggest that Pilate's 'wonder' was inspired by some numinous element which he sensed in his prisoner. See n. 81.

84 xv:6–9.

85 The curious expression in xv:8 that the crowd 'came up' (*anabas*) suggests that Pilate was in some place to which ascent had to be made. Since it is unlikely that the crowd would have ascended a stairway to Pilate's residence in the Antonia fortress, it would seem probable that the Roman headquarters in Herod's Palace, in the upper city, is the location of the incident. Cf. Blinzler, pp. 173–6; see n. 124.

86 If an *apologia* of the Jerusalem Christians underlies Mark's account of the Roman trial, as we have thought to be probable, it would have been concerned to present Jesus as a victim of Roman injustice, and not to exonerate Pilate. Such touches as Pilate's wonder and his recognition of Jesus' innocence reflect Mark's apologetical concern.

87 Even if the sound of the crowd demanding the amnesty had been heard, it is unlikely that Pilate would immediately have left his tribunal, in the midst of his investigation of Jesus' case, to attend to its demand. If Mark's narrative is accepted, we have also to imagine the Jewish leaders, having been left standing by Pilate's sudden departure, as slipping out from the tribunal and so quickly asserting their control of the crowd, which they had hitherto feared, that they are ready to frustrate Pilate's attempt to use the custom to free Jesus.

88 The suggestion of repeated action by the use of the imperfect tense (*apeluen*) is repeated by the imperfect tense of *epoiei* in xv:8—'as he was wont to do'. Cf. Taylor, p. 582.

89 *Matt.* xxvii:15. Cf. A. H. McNeile, *St Matthew*, p. 410.

90 xv:11. 'Verse 7 is a parenthesis which could follow 8 or 10' (Taylor, p. 581). It is to be noted, for our later consideration, that Mark represents the chief priests as taking the initiative in naming Barabbas (see p. 97, and on the name 'Barabbas' see n. 113).

91 'Mark speaks of the circumstances as if they were well known ("the insurrection"), and, although the incident is not mentioned outside the Gospels, it is in no way incredible' (Taylor, p. 581).

92 xv:10 (*dia phthon*). The naive assumption of insight into Pilate's mind is matched by the naivety of the motive attributed to the Jewish leaders.

93 xv:11–15. On the significance of the scourging of Jesus see n. 123.

94 Commenting upon the surprising control, which, according to Mark, the chief priests suddenly possessed over the crowd, which had so recently supported Jesus, Guignebert pertinently remarks: 'La scène évoque plutôt un effet de théâtre dans une pièce enfantine que la réalité' (*Jésus*, p. 574).

95 A subsidiary issue, which we can only mention but not expect to solve, is that of the language used in this assumed public dialogue between Pilate and the crowd. It is not a serious point, but the tacit assumption that a Roman governor could thus so easily communicate with a Jewish crowd adds to the artificiality of the scene described by Mark.

96 Cf. 'Torture', *O.C.D.*, p. 914.

97 Luke (xxiii:15–16) actually represents Pilate's suggesting this as a solution to the Jewish leaders and people: 'I will therefore chastise him and release him.' See pp. 123ff. Cf. Sherwin-White, pp. 27–8. Albinus had taken similar action with Jesus ben Ananias (see p. 88).

98 The fact that Pilate's term of office (AD 26–36) was one of the longest of the Roman governors of Judaea, before the end of the Jewish state, attests his good record of service in the view of Tiberius.

99 *Acts* xxiii:26–30.

100 The weak, abject figure presented by Mark cannot possibly be identified with the Pilate described by Philo and Josephus: cf. *Jesus and the Zealots*, pp. 68–80, and above pp. 35–41.

101 *Mk.* xi:18; xii:12: see n. 94.

102 This is evident in Mark's anticipatory mention of Barabbas (see above) and Pilate's question in xv:12.

103 *Matt.* xxvii:17–18. See p. 113.

104 See pp. 66ff., 76.

105 Taylor (pp. 582–3), in trying to defend the authenticity of Mark's account of the Barabbas episode, acknowledges that 'Pilate's question is very weak', but defends its genuineness by arguing that 'there does not seem to be any good reason why he cannot have said sarcastically, "What, then am I to do with the King of the Jews?"' Taylor fails to observe that Pilate, according to Mark, obeyed the crowd when they told him, in reply to his sarcasm, to crucify Jesus. It is instructive to see how a competent scholar, when intent on defending a sacred text, fails to see the inherent absurdity of a situation which it describes.

106 Tertullian, *Apology*, v.3: 'Tiberius ergo, cuius tempore nomen Christianum in saeculum introivit, adnuntiata sibi ex Syria Palaestina, quae illic veritatem ipsius divinitatis revelaverant, detulit ad senatum cum praerogativa suffragii sui.' Tertullian even backed up his assertion with the challenge: 'Consult your records' (*Consulite commentarios vestros*)—a supreme piece of bluffing, seeing that his *Apology* is addressed to the magistrates of the Roman Empire; but a safe one since it was unlikely that it would be read by them and was really designed for Christian consumption. Equally significant in this connection is Justin Martyr's (*c.* 100–165) assertion in an *apologia* addressed to the Emperor Antoninus Pius, that he would find the birth of Jesus Christ recorded in the tax-lists of Quirinius, whom he wrongly supposes to have been the first governor of Judaea (*Apol.* i.34). See p. 153.

107 Cf. A. Deissmann, *Licht vom Osten*, pp. 229–31; Taylor, pp. 580–1; Goguel, *Life of Jesus*, p. 519; Guignebert, *Jésus*, pp. 573–4; Blinzler, pp. 205–8, 218–21; Winter, pp. 92–4; E. Stauffer, *Jesus and His Story*, p. 107; Bultmann, *Gesch. d. syn. Trad.*, p. 293, n. 3.

108 Cf. Jos. *Ant.* xii:122–4. It is pertinent to recall that in the affair of the military standards, Josephus emphasised the privilege, granted by former governors, which Pilate violated: see p. 36.

109 On the probability that Barabbas was a Zealot cf. Hengel, *Die Zeloten* pp. 30, 347–8; Cullmann, *The State in the New Testament*, pp. 47–8; Stendahl in *P.C.*², p. 694k; Klausner, *Jesus of Nazareth*, p. 347; Driver, *Judaean Scrolls*, p. 246. Meyer (*Ursprung*, I, p. 195), described Barabbas as 'der politische Agitator und Freiheitsheld'.

110 xv:7 (*en tē stasei*). Cf. Taylor, p. 581; Eisler, II, pp. 462–3. The obvious implication of Mark's statement is that the revolt had been very recent: cf. Meyer, I, p. 195.

111 *Mk.* xv:9, 12.

112 xv:11. In verse 8 the people do not specify any prisoner when asking Pilate to observe the custom.

113 The phrasing used by Mark (xv:7) in introducing Barabbas is curious: 'who was called (*ho legomenos*) Barabbas'. The expression *ho legomenos* is usually preceded by a personal name, and indicates that the person with that name was known by a descriptive title. Consequently, since Barabbas (*Bar Abba*) means 'Son of the Father', it would seem that the personal name has been omitted. In *Matt.* xxvii:16, 17 certain MSS give the reading 'Jesus Barabbas', thus making a contrast, between 'Jesus who is called Barabbas' and 'Jesus who is called Christ' (cf. *Novum Testamentum Graece*, ed. E. Nestle²¹, p. 78). In view of the fact that the idea that a 'robber' was also named 'Jesus' would be distasteful to Christians, many scholars think that the reading 'Jesus Barabbas' could not be a later invention and so preserves an original tradition. Cf. Taylor, p. 581; Goguel, *Life of Jesus*, pp. 516–17; Blinzler, pp. 209–10. Eisler used this similarity of names to explain the Barabbas-episode in terms of a (temporary) confusion of identity between an innocent supporter of the Jewish hierarchy and the rebel-king, Jesus of Nazareth (*ΙΗΣΟΥΣ ΒΑΣΙΛΕΥΣ*, II, pp. 463–9; *Messiah Jesus*, pp. 473–6). The hypothesis of a venerable rabbi, who was accidentally arrested by the Romans, when rounding up rebels, is not convincing. Winter (*On the Trial of Jesus*, p. 99) also invokes a theory of mistaken identity to explain the Barabbas episode:

Pilate released Jesus bar (R) Abba(n) when he realised that he was not Jesus, 'the King of the Jews'.

114 *Lk.* xxiii:19.

115 See also n. 110.

116 See n. 109.

117 Cf. Schürer, *G.J.V.*, I, pp. 458, 464.

118 It is significant that Mark (xv:7) refers to 'the revolutionaries' (*tōn stasiastōn*), who were involved 'in the insurrection' (*en tē stasei*). It would appear that his source had a lively recollection of a notable insurrection in Jerusalem at this time. If a two-pronged attack had been made on the Temple and the Antonia, it would also explain why the Roman garrison in the Antonia did not intervene in the 'Cleansing of the Temple', as they did in the fracas occasioned by Paul's arrest there (*Acts* xxi:30ff.)—they would have been fully engaged with the Zealot attack under Barabbas.

119 See p. 102.

120 According to *Lk.* xxiii:2, the Jewish leaders had accused Jesus of 'perverting our nation, and forbidding us to give tribute to Caesar, and saying that he himself is Christ a king'. Creed (*St Luke*, p. 281) comments: 'A political interpretation is put upon the claim which Jesus had allowed.' However it may have been used, the very fact that the title 'King of the Jews' or 'King of Israel' had been given to Jesus by his followers would have been of decisive significance with Pilate—the attribution of such a title clearly indicated leadership of the recent insurrection. Cf. H. P. Kingdom in *Studia Evangelica*, III (1964), pp. 77ff.

121 *Mk.* xv:27.

122 According to *Lk.* xxiii:40, the 'Penitent Thief' rebuked his companion's railing at Jesus: 'Do you not fear God, since you are under the same sentence of condemnation.' The significance of this saying, long obscured by reading *lēstēs* in *Mk.* xv:27 as 'thief' or 'brigand', becomes manifest when it is realised that *lēstēs* was a derogatory term for 'Zealot'. It is to be noted also that Luke has interpreted Mark's *lēstēs* as *kakourgos* ('malefactor'). Cf. Hengel, *Die Zeloten*, pp. 30, 347–8; Brandon, *Jesus and the Zealots*, pp. 339, n. 1, 351, 358.

123 Cf. Lietzmann, *Kleine Schriften*, II, p. 261.

124 *Mk.* xv:16–20. The preceding action of Pilate, as described by *Mk.* xv:15, first calls for attention: 'Having scourged Jesus, he delivered him to be crucified.' Scourging seems to have been a preliminary to the crucifixion of rebels by the Romans in Judaea: cf. Jos. *War* ii:306; v:449. Cf. Sherwin-White, pp. 26–8; Blinzler, pp. 233–4. The somewhat curious phrase 'he (Pilate) delivered (*paredōken*) him to be crucified' could be due to Mark's reluctance to admit that Pilate actually ordered the execution of Jesus: cf. Taylor, p. 584. The location of the 'Mocking of Christ' constitutes a problem. The *praetorium* suggests that it took place in the palace of Herod, which was the governor's usual residence when in Jerusalem. Christian tradition, however, has come to locate it in the Antonia fortress, where excavation has revealed a *lithostrōton* or 'pavement' corresponding to that mentioned by *Jn.* xix:13. Cf. Blinzler, pp. 234–5; Kopp, *The Holy Places of the Gospels*, pp. 365–73; see n. 78. For the suggestion that the Mocking may have followed a 'dramatic pattern' cf. Winter, *On the Trial of Jesus*, pp. 102–4.

125 Cf. H. St J. Hart, *J.T.S.*, III (n.s.), p. 67, n. 8.

126 Cf. Hart, *ibid.*, pp. 74–5.

127 Cf. C. Daniel, *Numen*, XIII (1966), pp. 93–7. See also Dalman, *Jesus-Jeshua*, p. 12; Hengel, *Die Zeloten*, p. 72.

128 'Et le roi "Zélote" devait être accompagné du signe qui désignait cette secte ou ce parti politique si l'on veut, le roseau' (Daniel, *ibid.*, p. 97). According to Matthew (xxvii:29), the soldiers put a reed in Jesus' right hand, probably as a mock-sceptre with a punning reference.

129 Cf. *Jesus and the Zealots*, pp. 1, n. 4, 103–4, 107, 269.

130 *Mk.* xv:26. Cf. Eisler, *ΙΗΣΟΥΣ ΒΑΣΙΛΕΥΣ*, II, pp. 530–2, *Messiah Jesus*, pp. 514–15; Klostermann, *Markusevangelium*, pp. 164–5; S.-B. *Kommentar*, I, p. 1038; Guignebert, *Jésus*, p. 591; P. Winter, 'Zum Prozess Jesu', *Das Altertum*, 9 (1963), p. 162; W. C. Van Unnik, *N.T.S.*, VIII (1961–2), p. 111.

131 *Mk.* xv:29ff.

132 xv:31–2.

133 Cf. *Jesus and the Zealots*, pp. 100, 110ff., 313, 363, 367–8.

134 See pp. 70–1.

135 *Mk.* xv:29–32, 39.

136 *Mk.* xv:42–6.

137 According to the tractate *Sanhedrin*,

6.5 (Danby, *The Mishnah*, p. 391), two burying-places were kept in readiness by the Sanhedrin for executed criminals. Cf. Goguel, *La naissance du Christianisme*, pp. 42-5; G. Baldensperger, *Le tombeau vide*, pp. 28-9.
138 See pp. 21ff. 'Le "Tombeau vide" doit son origine à une controverse sur la résurrection de Jésus entre les chefs de la chrétienté et les représentants du Judaïsme', Baldensperger, *op. cit.*, p. 131.
139 *Mk.* xvi:1-8. Cf. Goguel, *op. cit.*, pp. 46-50.
140 *Matt.* xxviii:11-15.
141 It is possible that *Mk.* xvi:1-8 represents the first tentative presentation of the story of the Empty Tomb in writing. The concluding statement that the women 'said nothing to anyone, for they were afraid' may be intended to explain the apparent novelty of the story, now given literary permanence in Mark's Gospel.
142 Paul's phrase 'crucified Messiah' (*Christos estaurōmenos*), in I *Cor.* i:23, probably derives from the original Jewish Christian apologetic, which laboured to overcome the *skandalon* by boldly emphasising the implied paradox, for which they found scriptural warranty, while also stressing the martyr-aspect. See p. 21.
143 It should be noted, too, that, according to Mark (xv:13, 14) the very idea that Jesus should be crucified came originally from the Jewish crowd, presumably at the instigation of the chief priests.

Chapter Five (pages 107-139)
1 See pp. 70ff.
2 The *First Epistle of Clement* (*c.* AD 96) shows how the Roman church was in communication with the church at Corinth and sought to compose its troubles. Cf. J. Weiss, *Earliest Christianity*, II, pp. 849ff.; B. H. Streeter, *The Primitive Church*, pp. 184ff.; L. Lietzmann, *Geschichte der Alten Kirche*, I, pp. 201-8.
3 The fact that the Markan Gospel was known to the authors of the Gospels of Matthew and Luke proves that copies were in circulation by AD 80-85. Cf. B. H. Streeter, *The Four Gospels*, pp. 10ff., 338-344; *H.D.B.*², pp. 341-2.
4 It is significant that the Gospels of Matthew and Luke diverge most from each other at just those points where they could

not follow Mark, namely, in their accounts of the Infancy and Resurrection Appearances of Jesus. The Gospel of John presents a different problem here: see below.
5 Cf. C. S. C. Williams in *P.C.*², 653a-d; M. Goguel, *Life of Jesus*, pp. 138-57; Streeter, *Four Gospels*, pp. 395-426.
6 Cf. Streeter, *Four Gospels*, pp. 182-91, 271-92; Williams in *P.C.*², 654b-g.
7 On the problem of Josephus's account of Jesus in this connection see pp. 151-2.
8 Cf. A. Huck, *Synopse der drei ersten Evangelien*, pp. 198-214. See also R. Bultmann, *Geschichte der synoptischen Tradition*, pp. 299-302; E. Lohmeyer-W. Schmauch, *Das Evangelium des Matthäus*, p. 367; E. Klostermann, *Das Matthäusevangelium*, pp. 212-22; N. A. Dahl in *N.T.S.*, II (1955-6), p. 20.
9 See p. 121.
10 Pp. 118ff.
11 Cf. Streeter, *Four Gospels*, pp. 397-401.
12 See pp. 119ff.
13 On the evidence of Luke's Gospel in this connection see pp. 119ff. N. A. Dahl has argued that Matthew and Luke used 'eine neben Markus weiterbestehende oder auf Grund von Markus entstandene Überlieferung' (*N.T.S.*, II (1955-6), p. 21). The few minor agreements of Matthew and Luke against Mark constitute a flimsy basis for this view (*op. cit.*, pp. 31-2).
14 The favourite Gospel in the early Church was Matthew. Of the four Gospels, Mark seems to have been the least valued, since its record appeared to be very meagre compared with those of the other Gospels. Cf. V. Taylor, *Gospel of Mark*, pp. 8-9.
15 Pp. 77ff.
16 *Matt.* xxvi:47-56.
17 Pp. 77-8.
18 Pp. 78ff.
19 Jos. *War* vii:410-19. Cf. Brandon, *Jesus and the Zealots*, pp. 291-4.
20 Cf. *Jesus and the Zealots*, pp. 294-7, 300, 305-10.
21 *Matt.* xxvi:53-4: see p. 78.
22 *Matt.* xxii:1-10. Cf. F. W. Beare, *Earliest Records of Jesus*, pp. 210-11; Klostermann, pp. 173-4.
23 Cf. Streeter, *Four Gospels*, pp. 243-4.
24 xxii:6.
25 xxii:7.
26 xxii:8-10. Cf. Klostermann, *op. cit.*, p. 174; Brandon, *The Fall of Jerusalem and the Christian Church*, pp. 230-1.

27 xxii:11–14. Cf. *Fall of Jerusalem*, p. 231.
28 Cf. *Jesus and the Zealots*, pp. 285–300.
29 *Matt.* xxvi:57; cf. Klostermann, p. 213.
30 xxvi:60–1. Cf. S.-B. *Kommentar*, I, p. 1006; Klostermann, pp. 214–15.
31 xxvi:63. Cf. A. H. McNeile, *St Matthew*, p. 401.
32 xxvi:64. Cf. Lohmeyer-Schmauch, p. 369 ('Jesu Antwort hält sich vielmehr im Stile eines at. lichen Propheten . . .'); Klostermann, p. 215.
33 *Mk.* xiv:62.
34 *Matt.* xxvii:1–2; cf. *Mk.* xv:1. See pp. 86ff.
35 *Matt.* xxvi:57–75.
36 xxvi:65–66.
37 See p. 90.
38 Cf. Klostermann, p. 217; P. Winter, *On the Trial of Jesus*, p. 23.
39 Pp. 105–6.
40 Cf. *Matt.* xxvii:2, 12–13; *Mk.* xv:1, 3: see pp. 92ff.
41 xxvii:11.
42 The variant readings in *Matt.* xxvii:16, 17, giving 'Jesus who was called Barabbas', which appear in certain MSS (cf. *Novum Testamentum Graece*, ed. E. Nestle (1949), p. 78), are accepted as representing the original form of the text here by many scholars. Cf. Klostermann, p. 20; McNeile, p. 411; Lohmeyer-Schmauch, p. 383; Dahl in *N.T.S.*, II, p. 26.
43 *Matt.* xxvii:15–31.
44 See pp. 95ff.
45 xxvii:17; see p. 93. Cf. Dahl in *N.T.S.*, II, p. 26.
46 *sunēgmenōn . . . autōn* (xxvii:17). Equally indefinite is the statement in verse 16: 'And they had then a notorious prisoner'; the pronoun 'they' could refer to either Jews or Romans. Cf. Lohmeyer-Schmauch, p. 384, n. 1.
47 Compare xxvii:12–13 and xxvii:20. See McNeile's laboured attempt to explain how the chief priests succeeded in stirring up the people against Jesus (*op. cit.*, p. 412).
48 xxvii:19. The word *bēma* ('judgment seat') implies that Pilate was again inside the *praetorium*. Cf. Lohmeyer-Schmauch, p. 384, n. 2. On the location of the *praetorium* see p. 191, n. 124.
49 xxvii:20.
50 xxvii:18.
51 See p. 94 on Mark's use of the same reason (xv:10). Cf. G. D. Kilpatrick, *Origins of Gospel of Matthew*, p. 46.

52 xxvii:19. Cf. Klostermann, p. 221; Lohmeyer-Schmauch, p. 384; Dahl in *N.T.S.*, II, p. 26; Bultmann, *Gesch. d. syn. Trad.* p. 305; Ch. Guignebert, *Jésus*, p. 575.
53 See pp. 155ff.
54 Cf. Dahl. in *N.T.S.*, II, p. 26: 'Mit ihren Akklamationen stimmt die Volksmenge dem Urteil ihrer Führer zu; das ist wohl schon der Gedanke des Markus, wird aber bei Matthäus noch klärer herausgestellt.'
55 xxvii:22: see p. 97.
56 xxvii:24. Pilate's concern about a riot here reads rather strangely in the light of Josephus' account of his dealings with the Jews on such occasions: see pp. 35–41.
57 xxvii:24. On Jewish precedents and parallels of such ritual lustration cf. *Deut.* xxi:6ff.; Psalm xxvi:6; S.-B. *Kommentar*, I, p. 1032–3.
58 The phrase 'innocent (*athōos*) from this man's blood' is of Jewish derivation. Cf. Dahl in *N.T.S.*, II, p. 26.
59 xxvii:25. Cf. Klostermann, p. 221; Lohmeyer-Schmauch, pp. 385–6.
60 This penalty is adumbrated in *Matt.* xxiv:29–38.
61 Cf. Lohmeyer-Schmauch, pp. 385–6; M. Simon, *Verus Israel*, pp. 245–63; Winter, *op. cit.*, pp. 57–8. 'Peu de paroles évangéliques ont fait plus de mal que celle-là; et elle n'est qu'une invention du rédacteur!'—Guignebert, *Jésus*, p. 575. Cf. G. Lindeskog, *Abraham Unser Vater*, pp. 328–30.
62 Cf. *Jesus and the Zealots*, pp. 303–4.
63 *Matt.* xxvii:27ff. Cf. Huck, *Synopse*, pp. 208ff.
64 See pp. 105–6.
65 Cf. Dahl in *N.T.S.*, II, p. 27: 'Innerhalb der Passionsgeschichte des Matthäus kommt mehrmals ein ätiologesches Interesse zum Vorschein . . . die Juden seiner Gegenwart stehen für Matthäus unter der Blutschuld, die sie sich zugezogen haben.'
66 The divergences between the Matthaean and Lukan Infancy Stories and Resurrection Narratives indicate a great geographical separation between the places where the traditions developed. Cf. *Jesus and the Zealots*, pp. 285–6. Luke also shows an antipathy towards Alexandrian Christianity: cf. *op. cit.*, pp. 192–5.
67 Cf. J. M. Creed, *Gospel of Luke*, pp. lvi–lxx.
68 *Lk.* i:3; cf. Creed, pp. 2–5.

69 Lk. xxii:53; Klostermann, Das Lukas-evangelium, p. 218.

70 This detachment is seen in another form in Luke's admission that one of Jesus' disciples was a Zealot (see p. 78), and that Jesus ordered the disciples to arm themselves before going to Gethsemane (see p. 78).

71 See Acts i:1–2. Cf. Creed, pp. xi–xiii; H. J. Cadbury in B.C. II, pp. 491ff.

72 The authorship of the Gospel is traditionally ascribed to Luke 'the beloved physician' (Epistle to the Colossians iv:14) and companion of Paul. Cf. Creed, pp. xii–xxi.

73 Pp. 42ff.

74 Cf. Streeter, Four Gospels, p. 219; Creed, p. lxx.

75 Caesarea was founded by Herod the Great as a Hellenistic city. Cf. Schürer, G.J.V., II, pp. 104–8; Brandon, Fall of Jerusalem, pp. 178–9; T. W. Manson, Studies in the Gospels and Epistles, pp. 56, 122.

76 Pp. 46, 49ff.

77 An interesting example of this is Luke's interpretation of the phenomenon of glossolalia ('speaking with tongues') as speaking in foreign languages, so that foreigners in Jerusalem at Pentecost exclaim 'we hear them telling in our own tongues the mighty works of God' (Acts ii:1–13). Cf. K. Lake in B.C., V, pp. 111–121.

78 Lk. xxii:54–62.

79 Pp. 22–3.

80 Lk. xxii:63–5.

81 xxii:63 (auton, referring to Jesus, last mentioned in verse 54). Cf. Klostermann, Lukasevangelium, p. 220.

82 Mk. xxvi:67–8. Cf. Huck, Synopse, pp. 201, 202.

83 Lk. xxii:66–7. Cf. Creed, pp. 276, 278; Klostermann, Lukasevangelium, p. 220.

84 Cf. Winter, pp. 20–3; M. Black in New Testament Studies (ed. A. J. B. Higgins), pp. 22–3; J. Blinzler, The Trial of Jesus, pp. 115–17: 'As Luke 22:66, considered critically as a writing, obviously represents a combination of Mark 14:53b and 15:1a, his details of time are of secondary importance when it is a matter of giving the historical combination of events.'

85 Lk. xxii:67–71.

86 Mk. xiv:63–4. Cf. Klostermann, Lukas-evangelium, pp. 220–1; Blinzler, pp. 116–17.

87 See pp. 92ff.

88 Lk. xxiii:1–5. Cf. Creed, pp. 279–80; Klostermann, p. 222.

89 Cf. Jesus and the Zealots, pp. 32–3, 52–4; see pp. 28ff.

90 P. 117.

91 Pp. 92ff.

92 Pp. 23–4.

93 If this were so, it is significant that he omits all mention of the charge about threatening the Temple. This omission is understandable in view of the fact that he attributes such a threat to Jesus in Acts vi:14.

94 Lk. xxiii:4.

95 xxiii:5.

96 xxiii:6–12.

97 On Herod Antipas cf. Schürer, G.J.V., I, pp. 431–49; A. H. M. Jones, The Herods of Judaea, pp. 176–83, 195–6. Herod Antipas was appointed tetrarch of Galilee after the death of his father, Herod the Great. Luke informs his readers of Herod's position in Galilee in iii:1.

98 xxiii:5. On the possibility that Pilate might have done so cf. A. N. Sherwin-White, Roman Society and Roman Law in the New Testament, pp. 28–31; F. F. Bruce in A.L.U.O.S., V (1966), pp. 15–17.

99 xxiii:11. Pilate interprets Herod's action in returning Jesus as implying that he found no fault in him: xxiii:15.

100 xxiii:10. Cf. Klostermann, p. 223.

101 Reference might be made to Acts xii:21, where 'Herod (i.e. King Agrippa I) put on his royal robes (esthēta basilikēn), and took his seat upon the throne . . .'. Jesus is arrayed in 'shining robe' (esthēta lampran), evidently indicating (mock) royalty. Cf. Creed, p. 282; Klostermann, p. 223.

102 xxiii:12. If we were informed of the relative dates, the incident concerning the shields recorded by Philo might provide an historical cause for the previous enmity between Pilate and Herod Antipas—the latter may have been among the four Herodian princes who petitioned Pilate to remove the offending objects: cf. Jesus and the Zealots, p. 72; see p. 38. Cf. Meyer, Ursprung u. Anfänge des Christentums, I, pp. 201–2.

103 Lk. viii:3; Acts xiii:1. Cf. Klostermann, p. 221.

104 See p. 66.

105 'Noch stärker lässt Lk den Pilatus Jesu Unschuld betonen (23, 4. 14. 20.22;

auch Herodes muss das aussprechen 23.15)'
—Bultmann, *Gesch. d. syn. Trad.*, p. 305.
Cf. Klostermann, p. 221.
106   *Acts* iv:27.
107   *Acts* iv:26. Among those who doubt
the historicity of the incident are Creed, p.
280; Klostermann, pp. 221–2; Meyer, I,
p. 202, n. 1; Bultmann, p. 294; Goguel,
Life of Jesus, p. 515, n. 1; Guignebert, pp.
571–2; Winter, p. 202, n. 4. Black (in *New
Testament Studies*, ed. A. J. B. Higgins, p.
24) argues in favour of the authenticity of
the episode: 'In view of the strong presumption that Luke had access to an alter-
native tradition of the Passion to that of
Mark, this objection to [its omission by
Mark] now falls to the ground.' Its historicity is also accepted by Blinzler, pp.
194–204.
108   *Lk.* xxiii:13.
109   xxiii:13–16.
110   xxiii:16. 'In Luke the term παιδεύσας
is ambiguous, like the English "give him a
lesson". Though commonly translated
"after a beating", it need mean no more
than *cum admoneurim*'—A. N. Sherwin-
White, *Roman Society and Roman Law in
New Testament Times*, pp. 27–8. 'παιδεύσας
ist absichtlich gewählte harmlose Wen-
dung für das auch stilistisch anstössige
φραγελλώσας des Mc Mt'—Klostermann,
p. 225.
111   *Lk.* xxiii:18–25.
112   xxiii:25. 'Lk.'s narrative almost seems
to suggest that it was the Jews who took
Jesus away to be crucified (v. 26)'—Creed,
p. 283.
113   See pp. 94ff.
114   As in *Mk.* xv:16–20.
115   *Lk.* xxiii:11; cf. Klostermann, p. 225.
116   xxiii:18. This Jewish preference for a
'murderer' is featured again in *Acts* ii:14:
'But you denied the Holy and Righteous
One, and asked for a murderer to be
granted to you.'
117   See n. 116.
118   *Lk.* xxiii:26–49. The most notable
additions are the words addressed to the
Daughters of Jerusalem (see n. 119) and the
words from the cross (xxiii:34, 39–43). It
should be noted that the 'Penitent Thief'
rebukes his fellow who rails on Jesus: 'Do
you not fear God, since you are under the
same sentence of condemnation?' He also
asks Jesus, significantly: 'Jesus, remember
me when you come in your kingly power

(*tēn basileian sou*)', xxiii:40, 42. These
statements acquire deeper and more realistic meaning, when it is recalled that those
crucified with Jesus were probably Zealots;
see p. 103. Cf. Klostermann, p. 229.
119   xxiii:27–31; cf. Klostermann, pp.
227–8.
120   Cf. Streeter, *Four Gospels*, pp. 365ff.;
W. F. Howard, *Fourth Gospel in Recent
Criticism and Interpretation* (ed. 1955); F. C.
Grant, *The Gospels*, pp. 154ff.; J. Moffatt,
Intro. to Literature of New Testament, pp.
525ff.; T. W. Manson, *Studies in the
Gospels and Epistles*, pp. 105ff.; C. H. Dodd,
The Interpretation of the Fourth Gospel, pp.
3ff.; A. J. B. Higgins, 'The Words of Jesus
acc. to St John' in *B.J.R.L.*, 49 (1967), pp.
363–5, 370–1.
121   Cf. G. Ogg in *P.C.*², 636b; *H.D.B.*²,
pp. 154–5.
122   *Jn.* ii:13–22. Cf. W Bauer, *Das
Johannesevangelium*, pp. 47–9; C. K.
Barrett in *P.C.*², 739d. *St John*, p. 163. On
the significance of the context of John's
theology cf. Dodd, pp. 300–3; D. A.
Schlatter, *Der Evangelist Johannes*, pp. 74–
83.
123   Cf. Dodd, *Interpretation of Fourth
Gospel*, pp. 444–53; *Historical Tradition in
the Fourth Gospel*, pp. 24, 97–8, 120;
Barrett, *St John*, pp. 17–18, 117–18.
124   *Jn.* vi:15. Cf. Winter, *On the Trial of
Jesus*, p. 139; Goguel, *Jesus*, pp. 369ff.
H. W. Montefiore (*N.T.S.*, VIII (1961–2),
pp. 135ff.) has seen in the Feeding of the
Five Thousand some indication of a
'Revolt in the Desert'. See pp. 145ff.
125   *Ibid.* J. Blinzler (*N.T.*, II, pp. 44–9)
suggests that the Galilean crowd, after
Jesus' withdrawal, went on to keep the
Passover at Jerusalem, and that Pilate,
alarmed at their Messianic fervour, attacked
them. He thinks that *Lk.* xiii:1 refers to the
incident and Jesus' reaction on hearing of it.
Cf. Barrett, *St John*, pp. 231–2.
126   vi:22–51; cf. Barrett, *St John*, pp. 239–
240.
127   Cf. *Jesus and the Zealots*, pp. 100,
108–9.
128   Cf. *op. cit.*, pp. 110–11.
129   *Jn.* xii:12–15. John, only, gives the
significant acclamation 'King of Israel';
Luke (xix:38) comes nearest with 'the
King who cometh in the name of the Lord'.
The mention of palm branches is also
notable as symbolising the victorious king

or hero. Cf. Bauer, pp. 160-1; Dodd, *Interpretation*, p. 370.

130 xii:16. Cf. Barrett, *St John*, pp. 346-7, 349.

131 xii:19. Cf. Dodd, *Interpretation*, p. 371.

132 xi:47-49. Cf. Dodd, *Historical Tradition*, pp. 24, 95, 97-8; Barrett, *St John*, pp. 337-8.

133 The R.S.V., quoted here, by translating *hēmōn . . . ton topon* (xi:48) as 'our holy place' adds the adjective 'holy' to 'place' (*topon*), thereby interpreting 'place' to mean the Temple. Winter (*On the Trial of Jesus*, p. 40) reasonably interprets the statement as: 'The Romans will deprive us both of our office and of our status as a nation.'

134 Cf. Schlatter, p. 257; Bauer, p. 156; Barrett in *St John*, p. 338; but see also n. 133.

135 *Jn.* xi:49-53.

136 xi:52: cf. Schlatter, p. 260; Barrett, *St John*, p. 339. According to Winter, *op. cit.*, p. 38, 'The contrast between the stark realism in the high-priest's words and the interpretation given to them points to the conclusion that Jn. 11 47a.48 preserves some element of a tradition (or 'source') which was in existence before the author of the Fourth Gospel undertook his work.'

137 Cf. Goguel, pp. 477-80; Lindeskog, *Abraham Unser Vater*, p. 333.

138 *Jn.* xi:57.

139 xii:19.

140 xviii:2-3: cf. Bauer, p. 209. On the identity of the soldiers see p. 129.

141 xviii:10: cf. Schlatter, pp. 328-9.

142 xviii:13-14.

143 Cf. xi:49.

144 xviii:15ff.

145 Annas is to be identified with the high priest Ananus, whose appointment to the high priesthood in AD 6 by Quirinius, the legate of Syria, is recorded by Josephus, *Ant.* xviii:26. Ananus (Annas) held office from AD 6 to 15, when he was deposed by the procurator Valerius Gratus. His tenure as high priest was one of the longest under the Romans, and doubtless gave him great status even after his deposition. Cf. E. M. Smallwood, *J.T.S.*, XIII n.s. (1962), pp. 15, 16; L. H. Feldmann, Loeb ed. *Josephus*, ix, p. 22, n. *e*. It is difficult to see the force of Winter's argument (*op. cit.*, p. 33), that the Annas mentioned here by John cannot

be Ananus, because his 'term of office had expired some years before Kaiaphas succeeded him, and long before Jesus started his public activity'. A period of about fifteen years only is involved. Cf. Blinzler, *Trial of Jesus*, pp. 81-4, 86-9.

146 xviii:24.

147 xviii:28. A MS (Syr. S.) re-arranges the order of verses in xviii:12-27 by inserting verse 24 between 13 and 14, 15; and 16-18 follow 19-23. This order makes Caiaphas the high-priest who examines Jesus: cf. *Novum Test. Graece*, ed. Nestle, p. 286.Cf. Streeter, *Four Gospels*, pp. 381-2.

148 Cf. Bauer, pp. 213-14; M. Black in *New Testament Essays* (ed. A. J. B. Higgins), pp. 26-7.

149 Cf. Goguel, p. 507, n. 1; Barrett, *St John*, pp. 437-8.

150 See n. 147. The re-arrangement of the text in MS Syr. S was probably motivated by the desire to remove this anomaly.

151 Cf. Winter, pp. 31-43; Guignebert, p. 566.

152 See notes 147 and 150 for what seems to be the only MS evidence of a departure from the traditional text and the motive that prompted the amendment.

153 See pp. 85ff., 110ff., 118ff.

154 *Jn.* xviii:15-18, 25-27.

155 The words *speira* and *chiliarchos* in xviii:3, 12 mean, respectively, a 'cohort' and a 'tribune', both Latin military terms. The subject has been discussed at length by Winter (pp. 44-49), who concludes that both Roman soldiers and Temple police took part in the arrest of Jesus. Cf. Bauer, p. 209; Blinzler, *Trial of Jesus*, pp. 63-9; Barrett, *St John*, pp. 433, 437.

156 *Mk.* xiv:43; *Matt.* xxvi:47. See p. 85. On the possibility that Mark suppressed the Roman part in the arrest cf. Goguel, pp. 468-9; Guignebert, pp. 563-4.

157 xviii:3, 10, 12.

158 Cf. Winter, pp. 137-8.

159 xviii:19-21.

160 The striking of Jesus after his reply to the high priest (xviii:22-3), is interpreted by Winter (p. 106) as 'a third-degree interrogation'.

161 xviii:13, 19-24.

162 xviii:28-32.

163 xviii:28.

164 The reference to the Passover here means that Jesus was crucified on the Day of the Preparation for the Passover (cf.

xix:14), i.e. on the fourteenth day of the month Nisan, and not on 15 Nisan, according to the Synoptic Gospels, which show the Last Supper as the Passover (e.g. *Mk.* xiv:12-25). The point has been much debated by scholars. Since evidence has been found at Qumrân of the use of a sectarian calendar which differed slightly from the accepted Pharisaic calendar, a solution of the difference between John and the Synoptics has been suggested along these lines by some scholars. Cf. G. Dalman, *Jesus-Jeshua*, pp. 86ff.; Bauer, pp. 214-15; Black in *New Testament Essays* (ed. A. J. B. Higgins), pp. 26-32; *The Scrolls and Christian Origins*, Appendix D, who suggests that Judas may have carried evidence from the Last Supper (*Jn.* xiii:26-30) of Jesus' illegal celebration of the Passover to the chief priests (*op. cit.*, 201); K. G. Kuhn in *The Scrolls and the New Testament* (ed. K. Stendahl), pp. 82-93. Cf. A. Jaubert in *N.T.S.*, VII (1960-1), pp. 22-30, in *R.H.R.*, 166 (1964), pp. 149ff., 167 (1965), p. 33, in *N.T.S.*, XIV (1968), pp. 145-64. So far as this conflict of dating concerns our subject, it is to be noted as further evidence of the general uncertainty that invests the Gospel accounts of the last days of Jesus.

165 xviii:29ff.

166 See pp. 129ff.

167 xviii:30. Cf. Bauer, p. 215. '30 shows a hardly credible insolence, and throws doubt upon John's editing of his Marcan material', Barrett, *P.C.*[2], 775h.

168 xviii:31.

169 Blinzler, p. 188, tries to get out of the difficulty by assuming that: 'The procurator is thinking, or at least pretending to think, of a crime which is not a capital one, and he therefore invites the Jews to judge the accused according to their own law; for of course they can judge noncapital cases independently themselves.' Such an assumption, in order to defend the authenticity of John's account, reveals how weak the case is.

170 See pp. 90-2.

171 xii:32-3. 'Das ist stilisierte Darstellung aber nicht irgendwie wägbare historische Relation'—H. Lietzmann, *Kleine Schriften*, II, p. 274.

172 xviii:33-38.

173 See pp. 92ff.

174 *Mk.* xv:3; *Jn.* xviii:30.

175 *Jn.* xviii:34. Cf. Schlatter, pp. 339-40.

176 Confirmation of this inference is given in xix:12.

177 xviii:35a. 'Einen Anspruch Jesu an Pilatus gibt es nicht. Das ist durch die völlige Trennung gänzlich ausgeschlossen, die den Juden von allen anderen Völkern trennt'—Schlatter, p. 40.

178 xviii:35b.

179 xviii:36a.

180 xviii:36b. 'Das apologetische Motiv ist deutlich (Justin *Ap.* I.11) und war schon 6.15 in gleicher Richtung hervorgetreten' —Bauer, p. 216. It is significant that John implies that Jesus had sufficient forces to resist his being handed over to the Jews, if he chose. The word *hypēretai*, used for servants in verse 36, is used for armed retainers in xviii:3, 12, 22. Cf. Brandon, *Jesus and the Zealots*, pp. 318-20.

181 xviii:28-9.

182 xix:16.

183 Pp. 138ff.

184 *Jn.* xii:31; xvi:11; cf. Bauer, p. 163, 197.

185 viii:44. Cf. Bauer, pp. 127-130; Schlatter, pp. 215-17; Dodd, *Interpretation*, pp. 159, 201ff.; Winter, *On the Trial of Jesus*, pp. 114-15.

186 Cf. H. W. Huppenbauer, *Der Mensch zwischen zwei Welten*, *passim* (see particularly p. 53); Black, *The Scrolls and Christian Origins*, pp. 134, 171.

187 *Jn.* xviii:37.

188 xviii:38a. 'Die Frage des Pilatus 38 ist nicht von Wissensdurst diktiert, sondern Ausdruck skeptischer Stimmung'—Bauer, p. 217. 'In this Pilate stands for the unbelieving world'—Dodd, *Interpretation*, p. 436.

189 xviii:38-40.

190 Cf. Bauer, p. 217 (40).

191 xix:1-3.

192 E.g. see J. Combe, *Jerome Bosch* (Paris 1946), Plate 43.

193 xix:4-22.

194 xix:10. 'Pilatus beruft sich auf die ihm zustehende Amtsbefugnis. Vgl. Digesten 50, 17, 37: *Nemo, qui condemnare potest, absolvere non potest*, ähnlich 42, 1, 3'— Bauer, p. 219.

195 xix:12. On the title 'friend of Caesar' cf. Bauer, p. 219 (12). Cf. Blinzler, pp. 236-7; Goguel, p. 525. E. Bammel (*Th.L.Z.*, 77, 209) makes the pertinent

observation on verse 12: 'Der Nachsatz bringt die Prämisse, die den Vordersatz begründet.'

196 See p. 189, n. 98. The assumed enmity between Pilate and the Jewish leaders is scarcely borne out by Caiaphas's long tenure of office under Pilate. As Dr Small-wood pertinently remarks: 'Presumably Caiaphas had been a congenial High Priest to Pilate, who had found him in office on his arrival in 26, and, far from exercising his right of appointment, had kept him there through the whole of his ten-year procuratorship'—J.T.S., XIII (1962), p. 22. Indeed the evidence of the long cooperation between Pilate and Caiaphas increases the probability that the action taken to suppress Jesus was a joint undertaking.

197 See the re-interpretation of the Barabbas episode pp. 101-4, 147ff.

198 Pp. 98-9.

199 xviii:38; xix:4, 6; cf. Bauer, p. 218 (6).

200 xix:6. There is much inconsistency about whom Pilate deals with in this episode. The transaction starts with the Jewish leaders in xviii:28; changes to the Jews in xviii:38; returns to leaders in xix:6; changes to Jews in xix:7; continues with Jews in xix:12; changes to chief priests in xix:15.

201 See n. 185.

202 xix:16. Cf. Barrett, St John, pp. 442-454.

203 Pp. 125ff.

204 xix:15. Cf. Schlatter, p. 347.

205 See p. 33.

206 xix:19-20. Cf. Bauer, 222; Schlatter, pp. 348-9. Winter, p. 106, rightly observes that, in John's account, the words of the titulus,'instead of being an indication of the cause of pronouncing a judicial verdict, are understood to have a prophetic signifi-cance'.

207 xix:23, 32ff.

208 xix:38.

209 xix:31.

210 'The Jews of the Fourth Gospel are praeter-natally the enemies of the World Saviour, determined to destroy him. . . . In this respect, the Fourth Gospel only gives a bizarre exaggeration to a notion that is present already in the Marcan outline: *the Jews are ab initio the enemies of Jesus*'—Winter, pp. 114-15.

Chapter Six (pages 140-150)

1 Luke represents the Risen Christ as in-structing the disciples: '"Was it not necessary that the Christ [Messiah] should suffer these things and enter into his glory." And beginning from Moses and all the prophets, he interpreted to them in all the Scriptures the things concerning himself' (xxiv:26-7). This passage signifi-cantly reveals the process by which the original Jewish Christians explained the Crucifixion as attesting the Messiahship of Jesus.

2 See pp. 21ff.

3 Pp. 22-4, 92.

4 Pp. 75-6, 79-80.

5 Pp. 8off.

6 Pp. 14ff.

7 This, as we have seen, is actually what Pilate did according to the Gospel writers, despite their intention to make him a witness to Jesus' innocence.

8 *Mk.* i:9ff.; *Matt.* xiv:12; *Jn.* iii:22ff.

9 Cf. J. Klausner, *Jesus of Nazareth*, pp. 243ff.

10 *Matt.* iii:1ff.; *Lk.* iii:2ff. Cf. *H.D.B.*, p. 509.

11 *Mk.* vi:14-19: cf. V. Taylor, *St Mark*, pp. 310-17.

12 Jos. *Ant.* xviii:116-19: see the notes of L. H. Feldman in the Loeb ed. of *Josephus*, vol. ix, pp. 82-4. Cf. C. Daniel in *Numen*, XIII (1966), pp. 93-5.

13 John's denunciation of the marriage might have provided the immediate cause of John's arrest and execution. Mark's romantic account of the matter reflects the hostility he shows towards the Herodian dynasty: cf. Brandon, *Jesus and the Zealots*, p. 268, n. 6.

14 *Lk.* xiii:31ff. (cf. J. M. Creed, *St Luke*, pp. 186-7); *Mk.* vi:14-16. On the subject generally see M. Goguel, *Life of Jesus*, pp. 264-78, 346-58; Meyer, *Ursprung u. Anfänge des Christentums*, I, pp. 82-94; T. W. Manson in *B.J.R.L.* 36 (1954), pp. 398ff.; Klausner, *op. cit.*, pp. 239ff.; F. F. Bruce, *A.L.U.O.S.*, V (1966), pp. 10-15; W. H. Brownlee, in *The Scrolls and the New Testament* (ed. K. Stendahl), pp. 33-53; A. J. B. Higgins in *B.J.R.L.*, 49 (1967), pp. 381-5.

15 *Mk.* i:14-15. Cf. Ch. Guignebert, *Jésus*, pp. 394-5; Goguel, *Jesus*, pp. 311-12; Taylor, *St Mark*, pp. 165-7.

16 Cf. Schürer, *G.J.V.*, II, pp. 533–44; S. Mowinckel, *He That Cometh*, pp. 169–81, 403–410.

17 *Matt.* iii:11–17; *Lk.* iii:15–17; *Jn.* i:19ff.

18 E.g. *Mk.* viii:27–30; xiv:61–2.

19 Cf. S.-B. *Kommentar*, I, pp. 162–5. The conflict, recorded in the Gospels, with the Pharisees and scribes over observance of the minutiae of the ritual law doubtless means that Jesus, in the prophetic tradition, emphasised the basic spiritual principles of the Torah.

20 Cf. Goguel, pp. 579–85; Guignebert, *Jésus*, pp. 449–74; T. W. Manson, *The Teaching of Jesus*, pp. 285ff.

21 Of the flouting of Jewish sacred law by Herod Antipas cf. Jos. *Ant.* xviii:38, 119, *Life*, 65; *Mk.* vi:18.

22 See p. 30. On Galilee in this connection cf. Klausner, *op. cit.*, pp. 143, 153, 156, 173.

23 Cf. Klausner, p. 173. See also R. H. Lightfoot, *Locality and Doctrine in the Gospels*, pp. 114–25.

24 It is significant that the Galileans strongly supported Antigonus, the last king of pure Maccabean stock, against Herod (the Great): cf. Jos. *Ant.* xiv:413–30. See pp. 27ff.

25 See p. 35, 40, 67, 78.

26 *Matt.* xvi:17. Cf. R. Eisler, *IHΣOYΣ BAΣIΛEYΣ*, II, pp. 67–8; O. Cullmann, *Petrus²*, pp. 23–4 (E.T., p. 22), *The State in the New Testament*, pp. 16–17; M. Hengel, *Die Zeloten*, p. 55.

27 *Mk.* iii:17 (cf. *Lk.* ix:54). Cf. Taylor, *St Mark*, pp. 231–2; Klausner, p. 260; G. Dalman, *Jesus-Jeshua*, p. 12; Brandon, *Jesus and the Zealots*, pp. 203–5.

28 It is significant that, whereas Zacchaeus, a tax-collector, is recorded to have recognised the incompatibility of his profession on his conversion, *Lk.* xix:1–10, nothing is said of the incompatibility of Simon's Zealotism with his discipleship to Jesus.

29 See pp. 28ff.

30 See pp. 67ff.

31 It is significant that in *Lk.* xxii:35–8 the disciples are already armed.

32 See the discussion of this issue in *Jesus and the Zealots*, pp. 340–1.

33 *Matt.* xi:2–6; *Lk.* vii:18–23; *Jn.* xi:47: cf. *Jesus and the Zealots*, p. 313, n. 2.

34 *Jn.* vi:15 (see p. 126ff).

35 Cf. H. W. Montefiore in *N.T.S.*, VIII (1961–2), pp. 135–41. *Mk.* xv:26; cf. Eisler, *op. cit.*, II, pp. 530–2; Klostermann, *Markusevangelium*, pp. 164–5; P. Winter in *Das Altertum*, 9 (1963), p. 162; W. C. Van Unnik, in *N.T.S.*, VIII (1961–2), p. 111.

36 *Mk.* iii:22 (see pp. 75–6).

37 See pp. 30–1, 40.

38 Pp. 35, 40, 65.

39 Pp. 39–41.

40 See pp. 84ff.

41 *Mk.* xii:13–17.

42 *Lk.* xxiii:2, 5.

43 See pp. 67ff.

44 *Mk.* x:33–4; cf. *Matt.* xx:17–19; *Lk.* xviii:31–4.

45 'In its precision the third prophecy [i.e. *Mk.* x:33–4] is a *vaticinium ex eventu*'— Taylor, *St Mark*, p. 437.

46 On the probable date of the Crucifixion cf. Goguel, *Jesus*, pp. 226–8 (Goguel accepts the year 28 as most likely); Guignebert, *Jésus*, pp. 520–2 (about the year 30); *H.D.B.²*, p. 157 (about AD 29); G. Ogg in *P.C.²*, 636c (AD 33); L. Koep in *R.A.C.*, III, 50 (29?); H. Conzelmann, *R.G.G.³*, III, 626 (AD 30).

47 Cf. Goguel, *Jesus*, pp. 343–6; Guignebert, *Jésus*, pp. 360–79; Winter, *On the Trial of Jesus*, pp. 111–35.

48 *Mk.* viii:34.

49 Cf. *Jesus and the Zealots*, pp. 57, 269.

50 *Mk.* xi:1–7.

51 'Auf Grund von Sach 9.9, war schon bei den Tannaiten der Esel zu dem Messiastier geworden'—H.-W. Kuhn in *Z.N.T.W.*, 50 (1959), p. 88; cf. S.-B. *Kommentar*, I, pp. 842–4. Cf. Taylor, pp. 451–3; Klostermann, *Markusevangelium*, p. 126; Meyer, *op. cit.*, I, p. 163; Klausner, 309–10; Eisler, *op. cit.*, II, pp. 459–63; H. P. Kingdom in *Studia Evangelica*, III, p. 83; Brandon, *Jesus and the Zealots*, pp. 349–50.

52 *Matt.* xxi:10. Cf. Eisler, *op. cit.*, II, pp. 462–3.

53 *Matt.* xxi:12ff.; *Lk.* xix:45ff. *Mk.* xi: 11, 15ff. (which suggests that Jesus reconnoitred the Temple situation on the day of his Triumphal Entry).

54 Pp. 84–5, 102.

55 It is significant that *Matt.* x:34 attributes the following saying to Jesus: 'Do not think that I have come to bring peace on the earth; I have not come to bring peace, but a sword.' The coming of the Messiah was expected to be an 'age of the sword':

cf. S.-B. *Kommentar*, I, p. 585; M. Black, *An Aramaic Approach to the Gospels and Acts*, p. 116.

56 See pp. 102ff.

57 Pp. 103ff.

58 See p. 191, n. 118.

59 Cf. A. Reifenberg, *Israel's History in Coins*, pp. 13, 30–1; Brandon, *Jesus and the Zealots*, p. 49, Plates III and IV. See Plates 5–6.

60 *Mk.* xv:7.

61 *Mk.* xi:18. See p. 85.

62 E.g. *Mk.* xi:27ff.; xii:12; xiv:1–2.

63 *Mk.* xiv:12–16; cf. Taylor, pp. 537–8.

64 *Mk.* xiv:26, 32; *Jn.* xviii:1. See Map 2.

65 *Mk.* xiv:34–6; *Lk.* xxii:41–4. The dramatic Gospel accounts of the Agony in Gethsemane fail to explain the nature of the choice then confronting Jesus. Cf. T. Lescow in *Z.N.T.W.*, 58 (1967), pp. 215–223.

66 *Mk.* xiv:28. Cf. Klostermann, *Markusevangelium*, pp. 149–51; Brandon, *Jesus and the Zealots*, pp. 340, n. 6, 342.

67 *Lk.* xxii:35–8; see n. 32.

68 *Mk.* xiv:10–11; *Matt.* xxvi:14–16; *Lk.* xxii:3–6.

69 Cf. Goguel, *Jesus*, pp. 440–42, 495–8; Guignebert, *Jésus*, pp. 528–30, 547–58; Klausner, pp. 324–6; *H.D.B.*², pp. 535–6; K. Lüthi, *Judas Iskarioth in der Geschichte der Auslegung von der Reformation bis zur Gegenwart, passim*.

70 Cf. F. Schulthess, *Das Problem der Sprache Jesu*, pp. 41, 54–5; Cullmann, *The State in the New Testament*, pp. 15–16.

71 Cf. *Jesus and the Zealots*, p. 204, n. 1.

72 See refs. in n. 69.

73 *Mk.* xiv:43; *Matt.* xxvi:47. It is interesting that Jesus is recorded to have asked: 'Have you come out as against a robber (*lēstēs*=Zealot?), with swords and clubs to capture me?' (*Mk.* xiv:48).

74 See above p. 129.

75 *Mk.* xiv:44.

76 *Mk.* xiv:50.

77 The haste with which the Jewish enquiry is conducted, according to the Gospel records (including Matthew) clearly belies the statement in *Matt.* xxvi:3–5, that the Jewish leaders delayed action against Jesus until after the feast. A possible explanation is that Judas's defection suddenly presented them with an opportunity, the success of which depended on presenting the people quickly with a *fait accompli*. However, like

so much of the Gospel record, such a statement is inconsistent with other evidence.

78 See p. 88.

79 See pp. 87, 89–90.

80 Pp. 106, 119ff. The charge of attempting to destroy the Temple may also have been included.

81 Pp. 102–4.

82 As we have seen, unless Pilate had strong reason for acting otherwise, this would have been his obvious course: see pp. 141ff.

83 See p. 104.

84 Pp. 103ff. 'Das Wesentliche ist, dass der römischen Prokurator Jesus als "Judenkönig" zum Tode verurteilt und ans Kreuz schlagen lässt. Das war die gewöhnliche Todesart für Landfriedensbrecher'— Lietzmann, *Kleine Schiften*, II, p. 261.

85 Cf. *Jesus and the Zealots*, pp. 108–9, 110–113, 368, n. 1; see pp. 104, 126.

86 See pp. 57–9. On the subsequent fate of the remnants of Jewish Christianity, and their rejection as heretics by Catholic Christianity cf. H. J. Schoeps, *Theologie und Geschichte des Judenchristentums*; G. Strecker, *Das Judenchristentum in den Pseudoklementinen*; M. Simon, *Verus Israel*; J. Daniélou, *Théologie du Judéo-Christianisme*; G. Hoennicke, *Das Judenchristentum im ersten und zweiten Jahrhundert*.

Chapter Seven (pages 151–160)

1 On Josephus see generally H. St John Thackeray, *Josephus: the Man and the Historian*; B. Niese, 'Josephus', *E.R.E.*, VII; F. J. Foakes Jackson, *Josephus and the Jews*; S. G. F. Brandon, 'Josephus: Renegade or Patriot?', *History Today*, VIII (1958).

2 As the passage cited below shows, Josephus appears to suggest that Jesus was superhuman, that he was the Messiah, and rose from the dead.

3 Cf. Brandon, *Fall of Jerusalem*, p. 110, n. 1.

4 *Jesus and the Zealots*, pp. 359–68.

5 Eusebius, *Historia Ecclesiastica*, I.xl, 7–8; cf. *Demonstratio Evangelica*, III, pp. 3, 105–6.

6 Cf. *Jesus and the Zealots*, pp. 361–2.

7 *Ant.* xviii:63–4. For text and translation: cf. L. H. Feldman, Loeb ed. of *Josephus*, vol. ix, pp. 48–51; Eisler, *ΙΗΣΟΥΣ ΒΑΣΙΛΕΥΣ*, I, pp. 84–7, *Messiah Jesus*, pp. 58–62; *Flavii Josephi Opera*, ed. B.

Niese, iv, pp. 151–2 (text); G. Mathieu–L. Herrmann, *Oeuvres complètes de Flavius Josephus* (ed. T. Reinach), iv, pp. 145–6 (trans.); G. Ricciotti, *Flavio Giuseppe*, I, p. 174 (trans.).

8   *War* vi:312–15.

9   Cf. *Jesus and the Zealots*, pp. 59–60.

10   Pp. 104, 126.

11   Cf. *Jesus and the Zealots*, pp. 47, n. 1, 59–60, 363.

12   Cf. Liddell and Scott, *Greek-English Lexicon*[9], I, p. 558, *sub. nom.*

13   Eusebius (*op. cit.*, I, xi.9) cites the passage to refute the *Acta Pilati* circulated by the Emperor Maximin; see p. 153.

14   Cf. Eisler, *ΙΗΣΟΥΣ ΒΑΣΙΛΕΥΣ*, I, pp. xxix–xxxii, *Messiah Jesus*, pp. 13–15, 591–2; Sherwin-White, *Roman Society and Roman Law in the New Testament*, p. 105, n. 5.

15   See pp. 100, 155.

16   Eusebius, *Eccl. Hist.*, I, ix.3; ix.v; vii.i. Cf. P. de Labriolle, *La réaction païenne*, pp. 327–8; F. Scheidweiler in *New Testament Apocrypha* (ed. E. Hennecke), I, pp. 444–7.

17   Cf. A. Alföldi, *The Conversion of Constantine and Pagan Rome*, pp. 36ff.

18   Cf. Eisler, *ΙΗΣΟΥΣ ΒΑΣΙΛΕΥΣ*, I, pp. xxxii–xxxv, 8; *Messiah Jesus*, pp. 15–16.

19   See the interesting evidence collected by Eisler of the Christian censorship of pagan and Jewish works regarded as detrimental to Christianity: *ΙΗΣΟΥΣ ΒΑΣΙΛΕΥΣ*, I, pp. 44–5, 402ff., 534ff., *Messiah Jesus*, pp. 11ff., 594–5.

20   According to de Labriolle (*op. cit.*, p. 328): 'Il paraît probable que, dès le second siècle, des pièces de ce genre, forgées par quelque main trop zélée, coururent dans les milieux chrétiens.'

21   It is to be noted that these apocryphal accounts draw most obviously upon the Gospels of Matthew and John.

22   Cf. M. R. James, *Apocryphal New Testament*, p. 95; Scheidweiler in *op. cit.*, I, pp. 449–50. The composition is also known as the *Gospel of Nicodemus*.

23   James, pp. 98–9, 101; Scheidweiler, I, pp. 450–1, 456.

24   James, pp. 96–7; Scheidweiler, I, pp. 451–3.

25   James, p. 100: Scheidweiler, I, p. 455.

26   James, p. 100; Scheidweiler, I, pp. 455–456.

27   James, p. 103; Scheidweiler, I, p. 458. See pp. 115ff.

28   Trans. James, p. 103; cf. Scheidweiler, I, p. 459. Much is made in these apocryphal writings of the two malefactors.

29   James, p. 105; Scheidweiler, I, p. 460.

30   James, pp. 105ff.; Scheidweiler, I, pp. 460ff.

31   James, pp. 153–4; Scheidweiler, I, pp. 481–2.

32   *Lk.* iii:1–2. Archelaus is evidently taken from *Matt.* ii:22, in ignorance of the fact that this Herodian prince had been deposed in AD 6.

33   Trans. James, pp. 154–5; cf. Scheidweiler, I, pp. 483–4.

34   Justin Martyr, *First Apology*, 35, 48.

35   Tertullian, *Apology*, xxi:24 ('Pilatus, et ipse iam pro sua conscientia Christianus').

36   *Apol.* v:2–3.

37   Origen, *Commentary on John*, xxviii:13–14; *Commentary on Matthew*, x:21.

38   Cf. R. M. Grant, *The Earliest Lives of Jesus*, p. 95.

39   James, *op. cit.*, pp. 90–1; cf. Ch. Mauer, *New Testament Apocrypha* (ed. E. Hennecke), I, pp. 179–83.

40   Cf. *Dictionary of the Christian Church* (ed. F. L. Cross), p. 1072a; *R.G.G.*[3], V, 383. Pilate is commemorated as a martyr in the Coptic Church on 25 June. His wife is also given the fuller name of Claudia Procula. As a holy figure, Pilate grew in popularity among the Copts in the sixth and seventh centuries; in middle Egypt his name was frequently used as a baptismal name. The Ethiopian Christians adopted his cult from the Copts; a Coptic history of Pilate, dating from the fourth century, was translated in Ethiopic from an Arabic translation. The 'apotheosis' of Pilate reaches its fullest development in an Ethiopic *Martyrium Pilati*, which describes his crucifixion by the Jews as a disciple of Jesus. Pilate is saved from death by divine intervention. Although he subsequently restores the dead son of Tiberius to life by laying him in the tomb of Jesus, Pilate is eventually beheaded, after crucifixion, on the orders of Tiberius. In this extraordinary writing, Herod (Antipas) is held as chiefly responsible for crucifixion of Jesus. Pilate is also a witness of Christ's resurrection. Cf. M.-A. Van den Oudenrijn, *Gamaliel: äthiopisch Texte zur Pilatusliteratur*, pp. xliii–xliv, liv, 29, 55, 121, 127–38, 145–69.

41   Cf. Winter, *On the Trial of Jesus*, pp. 57–61.

42   *Eccl. Hist.* II, vii. Eusebius adds the curious and inexplicable note: 'Those who record the Olympiads of the Greeks with the annals of events relate this.'

43   Cf. James, pp. 157–9. See also Schürer, *G.J.V.*, I, p. 492, n. 151; *Michelin Guide Book to Switzerland*, 4th ed. (1965), p. 145.

44   Cf. *R.G.G.*³, IV, 47–49.

45   Cf. T. Klauser, *Jahrbuch für Antike und Christentum*, I (1958), pp. 20–1; A. Grabar, *The Beginnings of Christian Art*, pp. 67ff. Examples of Christian painting are also found in the so-called 'Christian House' at Dura-Europos, on the Euphrates.

46   Cf. L. Hertling–E. Kitschbaum, *The Roman Catacombs*, chap. xii.

47   See the list of subjects given by Klauser, *op. cit.*, IV (1961), p. 134.

48   Cf. Klauser, *op. cit.*, IV, pp. 133–6; Hertling–Kirschbaum, pp. 202–5; Grabar *op. cit.*, 102–5; P. du Bourguet, *Early Christian Painting*, pp. 28–34.

49   I *Timothy* vi:13. Cf. W. H. C. Frend, *Martyrdom and Persecution in the Early Church*, pp. 14, 81, 83, 89–91.

50   Cf. Hertling–Kirschbaum, pp. 227–9; M. Gough, *The Early Christians*, pp. 88ff.

51   Cf. H. Lerclercq, *La vie chrétienne primitive*, plate XLIX, p. 85, who dates it for the first half of the third century. The *graffito* was found in 1856, in the ruins of the Palatine palace, Rome, traced on the wall of a room in the school for Imperial pages. An accompanying Greek inscription reads: 'Alexamene adores (his) God.' Cf. Gough, p. 83, fig. 9; Hertling–Kirschbaum, p. 229; P. du Bourguet, *Early Christian Painting*, p. 21.

52   Cf. P. du Bourguet, *Early Christian Painting*, p. 16 and fig. 53; Grabar, *Beginnings of Christian Art*, p. 115; Hertling–Kirschbaum, p. 227; F. Grossi Gondi, *I Monumenti cristiani*, p. 24 (22): these scholars are doubtful about the identification of the scene. Lerclercq (*op. cit.*, p. 79, plate XVII) regards the identification as the Crowning with Thorns as being well based; he also dates the picture from the first half of the second century.

53   Cf. Grossi Gondi, *op. cit.*, pp. 91–101; Grabar, *op. cit.*, pp. 237–68; E. Panofsky, *Tomb Sculpture*, pp. 39–44, figs. 139–67.

54   The sarcophagus came from San Paoli fuori le Mura: it is No. 55 in the Lateran Museum sequence. Cf. Grabar, p. 243, ill. 271; F. Van der Meer–C. Mohrmann, *Atlas of the Early Christian World*, fig. 170, who dates it from 330–40.

55   In the *Epistle to the Hebrews* (xi:17–19), the sacrifice of Isaac is related to that of Christ. The theme is developed by the Christian Fathers: cf. *D.C.C.*, p. 703.

56   The portraying of this incident also reflects the popularity of the Matthean Gospel, where only it is described (see p. 115).

57   Cf. Grabar, p. 246, fig. 273; Panofsky, fig. 157.

58   In these scenes Pilate is invariably represented as looking away from Jesus, and an attempt seems to be made to indicate his doubt and perplexity by the position of his hand. It is to be noted that in these early depictions, Jesus is shown as a beardless youth.

59   See Grabar, fig. 264.

60   Cf. Grossi Gondi, pp. 103, 104, 108, 121, 122.

61   Cf. Grabar, pp. 249–52, figs. 276, 278; Panofsky, fig. 147; Gough, *The Early Christians*, fig. 38, p. 258.

62   Cf. Van der Meer–Mohrmann, ills. 466, 467, p. 143; Gough, fig. 39, p. 258; Grabar, p. 265, figs. 295, 297.

63   This form of division was frequently used on both pagan and Christian sarcophagi, and it does not necessarily denote separate episodes.

64   The motif of the sleeping soldiers is obviously derived from *Matt.* xxviii:13 and they become a constant feature in subsequent representations of the Resurrection in Christian Art on into the Renaissance period. It is interesting to note that, according to the apocryphal *Acts of Pilate*, the soldiers witnessed the Resurrection (cf. James, *Apocryphal New Testament*, p. 106, see also p. 92).

65   Cf. Hertling–Kirschbaum, pp. 227–9.

66   Pilate's hand-washing could, of course, be more easily portrayed than any incident of the Sanhedrin trial. However, there can be little doubt that the Roman trial dominated the imagination of the early Christians.

67   See note 58.

68   Cf. Van der Meer–Mohrmann, ill. 198; Grabar, p. 274, fig. 308.

69   The scene is represented with greater

realism than on the sarcophagi. Jesus is shown as being firmly held by two soldiers.

70 Cf. Gough, figs. 55, 56, pp. 260–61.

71 Gough interprets the action of the centurion as piercing the side of Jesus (*Jn.* xix: 34–7), but no weapon can be discerned.

72 Cf. Van der Meer–Mohrmann, ill. 476; Grabar, *Byzantium*, p. 261, fig. 299; *R.G.G.*[3], IV, 47.

73 See Plates 18, 19, 21 and 22. The mosaics were commissioned by the Gothic king Theodoric, i.e. before 526.

74 The nimbus or halo was gradually adopted into Christian art during the third and fourth centuries. Cf. *D.C.C.*, p. 605.

75 The number three is puzzling. Two figures, Annas and Caiaphas, are intelligible, as on the Brescia *lipsanotheca* (see p. 158).

76 The fact that Theodoric built Sant' Apollinare Nuovo as an 'Arian cathedral' seems to be irrelevant in this connection. Cf. E. Hutton, *The Story of Ravenna*, pp. 209ff.

77 Cf. Grabar, *Byzantium*, fig. 232, p. 402; Van der Meer–Mohrmann, ill. 388.

78 The gesture of Pilate's right hand is eloquent.

79 Cf. Brandon, *History, Time and Deity*, chap. vi; *The Judgment of the Dead*, chap. v.

80 B. Blumenkranz (*Le Juif médiéval au miroir de l'art chrétien*, p. 135) shows that the medieval artist by depicting the Jews in contemporary dress represented the Passion of Christ as 'un crime éternellement répété auquel son voisin juif se trouve toujours participer'. Cf. A. Malraux, *The Metamorphosis of the Gods*, pp. 287–300; K. Clark, *The Nude*, pp. 221–35, 243–50; E. Mâle, *Religious Art*, pp. 78, 112–21, 186–187. See also *Medieval English Verse* (trans. B. Stone), pp. 33–41.

81 E.g. see 'The Resurrection' in the York Pageant of the Carpenters, in *Everyman and Medieval Miracle Plays*, ed. A. C. Cawley, pp. 173–88; see also the interesting medieval Cornish drama 'The Death of Pilate', in *op. cit.*, pp. 235–63. Cf. M. D. Anderson, *Drama and Imagery in English Medieval Churches*, pp. 51, 112.

82 Cf. R. G. Collingwood, *The Idea of History*, pp. 129ff.; A. Schweitzer, *The Quest of the Historical Jesus, passim*; H. Zahrnt, *The Historical Jesus, passim*; H. Conzelmann in *R.G.G.*[3], III, 619–53.

83 'What is truth? said jesting Pilate: and would not stay for an answer', Francis Bacon, *Essays*, 'Of Truth'.

84 'Le procurateur de Judée', in *L'Étui de Nacre* (1892).

Bibliography of Ancient and Modern Writers

Alföldi, A. *The Conversion of Constantine and Pagan Rome*, E. T., Oxford, 1948
Anderson, M. D. *Drama and Imagery in English Medieval Churches*, Cambridge, 1963
Bacon, B. W. *Is Mark a Roman Gospel?*, Harvard University Press, 1919
Baldensperger, G. *Le tombeau vide; la légende et l'histoire*, Paris, 1935
Balsdon, J. P. V. D. *The Emperor Gaius (Caligula)*, Oxford, 1934
Bammel, E. 'φίλος τοῦ καίσαρος', in *Th.L.Z.*, 77 (1952)
Bauer,W. *Griechisch-Deutsches Wörterbuch zu der Schriften des Neuen Testament*, 2. Aufl., Giessen, 1928
—— *Das Johannesevangelium*, 3. Aufl., Tübingen, 1933
Barrett, C. K. *The Gospel according to St John*, London, 1960
Beare, F. W. *The Earliest Records of Jesus*, Oxford (Blackwell), 1962
Bendinelli, G. *Compendio di storia dell'arte etrusca e romana*, Milan, 1931
Bersanetti, B. M. *Vespasiano*, Rome, 1941
Black, M. *An Aramaic Approach to the Gospels and Acts*, Oxford, 1946
—— *The Scrolls and Christian Origins*, London–Edinburgh, 1961
Blinzler, J. *The Trial of Jesus*, E.T., Cork, 1959
—— 'Das Synedrium von Jerusalem und die Strassprozessordnung der Mischna', in *Z.N.T.W.*, 52 (1961)
—— *Zum Prozess Jesu*, ed. W. Koch, Weiden, 1967
—— 'Die Niedermetzelung von Galiläern durch Pilatus', in *N.T.*, II (1958)
Blumenkranz, B. *Le Juif médiéval au miroir de l'art chrétien*, Paris, 1966
den Boer, W. 'Claudius', in *R.A.C.*, III (1957), 180–1
Bornkamm, J. 'Evangelien, synoptische', in *R.G.G.³*, II (1958)
du Bourguet, P. *Early Christian Painting*, E.T., London, 1965
Brandon, S. G. F. *The Fall of Jerusalem and the Christian Church*, 1951, 2nd ed., 1957, repr. 1968, London
—— 'Josephus: Renegade or Patriot?', in *History Today*, vol. VIII (1958)
—— 'The Date of the Markan Gospel', in *N.T.S.*, vol. VII (1960–1)
—— *Man and his Destiny in the Great Religions*, Manchester University Press 1962
—— 'Herod the Great', in *History Today*, vol. XII (1962)
—— *History, Time and Deity*, Manchester University Press, 1965
—— 'Matthaean Christianity', in *The Modern Churchman*, vol. VIII (1965)
—— *Jesus and the Zealots*, Manchester University Press, 1967
—— *The Judgment of the Dead*, London, 1967
—— 'The Death of James the Just: a New Interpretation', in *Studies in Mysticism and Religion* (Presented to Gershom G. Scholem), ed. R. J Zuri Werblowsky, Jerusalem, 1967-8 'Pontius Pilate: in History and Legend', in *History Today*, vol. XVIII (1968)
Brownlee, W. H. 'John the Baptist in the New Light of the Ancient Scrolls', in *The Scrolls and the New Testament*, ed. K. Stendahl
Bruce, F. F. *The Acts of the Apostles*, London, 1951
—— 'Christianity under Claudius', in *B.J.R.L.*, vol. 44 (1962)
—— 'When is a Gospel not a Gospel', in B.J.R.L vol. 46 (1964)
—— 'St Paul in Rome', in *B.J.R.L.*, vol. 46 (1964)
—— 'Herod Antipas, Tetrarch of Galilee and Peraea', in *A.L.U.O.S.*, völ V (1966)
Bultmann, R. *Die Geschichte der synoptischen Tradition*, 3. Aufl Göttingen, 1957: Ergänzungsheft, Göttingen, 1958
—— *Urchristentum im Rahmen der antiken Religionen*, Zürich, 1949

Bultmann, R. 'History and Eschatology in the New Testament', in N.T.S., vol. I (1954–5)
—— The Theology of the New Testament, E.T., vol. I, London, 1959
Burkill, T. A. Mysterious Revelation: an Examination of St Mark's Gospel, Cornell University Press, New York, 1963
—— 'L'antisémitisme dans l'évangile selon saint Marc', in R.H.R., 154 (1958)
—— 'The Trial of Jesus', in V.C., XII (1958)
Burrows, M. The Dead Sea Scrolls, London, 1956
Carrington, P. The Early Christian Church, 2 vols., Cambridge, 1957
Carroll, K. L. 'The Place of James in the Early Church', in B.J.R.L., vol. 44 (1961)
Cawley, A. C. (ed.), Everyman and Medieval Miracle Plays (Everyman Library), London, 1956
Clark, K. The Nude: A Study of Ideal Art, London, 1960
Clarke, W. K. L., New Testament Problems, London, 1929
Clemen, C. Religionsgeschichtliche Erklärung des Neuen Testaments, Giessen, 1924
Collingwood, R. G. The Idea of History, Oxford, 1946
Conzelmann, H. 'Geschichte und Eschaton nach Mc 13' in Z.N.T.W., 50 (1959)
—— 'Jesus Christus', in R.G.G.³, III (1959), 619–53
Creed, J. M. The Gospel according to St Luke, London, 1929
Cullmann, O. The State in the New Testament, E.T., London, 1957
—— Petrus: Jünger-Apostel-Märtyrer, 2. Aufl., Zürich–Stuttgart, 1960. E.T., Peter: Disciple-Apostle-Martyr, London, 1953
Curtius, L. and Nawrath, A. Das Antike Rom, Wien, 1944
Dahl, N. A. 'Die Passiongeschichte bei Matthäus, in N.T.S., II (1956)
Dalman, G. Jesus-Jeshua, E.T., London, 1929
Daniel, C. 'Esséniens, zélotes et sicaires et leur mention par paronymie dans le N.T.', in Numen, XIII (1966), Leiden
Daniélou, J. Théologie du Judéo-Christianisme, Tournai, 1958
Daniélou, J. and Marrou, H. The Christian Centuries, vol. I, E.T., London, 1964
Daube, D. The New Testament and Rabbinic Judaism, London, 1956
Davies, W. D. 'The Jewish State in the Hellenistic World', in P.C.² (1962)
Deissmann, A. Licht vom Osten, 4. Aufl., Tübingen, 1923
Derenbourg, J. Essai sur l'histoire et la géographie de la Palestine (d'après les Thalmuds et les autres sources rabbiniques), Paris, 1857
Dibelius, M. 'Archonten', in R.A.C., I (1950), 631–3.
Dodd, C. H. 'The Fall of Jerusalem and the "Abomination of Desolation" ', in J.R.S., vol. XXXVII (1953–4)
—— Interpretation of the Fourth Gospel, Cambridge, 1954
—— Historical Tradition in the New Testament, Cambridge, 1963
Doyle, A. D. 'Pilate's Career and the Date of the Crucifixion', in J.T.S., vol. XLII (1941)
Drachmann, Atheism in Pagan Antiquity, London, 1922
Driver, G. R. The Judaean Scrolls, Blackwell, Oxford, 1965
Dupont-Sommer, A. Les écrits esséniens découverts près de la Mer Morte, Paris, 1959
Ehrhardt, A. A. T. The Apostolic Succession, London, 1953
—— Politische Metaphysik von Solon bis Augustin, 2 Bände, Tübingen, 1959
Eisler, R. ΙΗΣΟΥΣ ΒΑΣΙΛΕΥΣ ΟΥ ΒΑΣΙΛΕΥΣΑΣ (Die messianische Unabhängigkeitsbewegung vom Auftreten Johannes des Taufers bis zum Untergang Jakobs des Gerechten. Nach der neuerschlossen Eroberung von Jerusalem des Flavius Josephus und den christlichen Quellen), 2 Bände, Heidelberg, 1929–30
—— The Messiah Jesus and John the Baptist (According to Flavius Josephus' recently discovered 'Capture of Jerusalem' and other Jewish and Christian sources). English edition by A. H. Krappe, London, 1931
Epiphanius, Adversus (Octoginta) Haereses, Patrologia Graeca, tomes, XLI, XLII, Paris, 1858
—— De Mensuris et Ponderibus, Patrologia Graeca, tome XLIII, Paris, 1864
Eppstein, V. 'The Historicity of the Gospel Account of the Cleansing of the Temple', in Z.N.T.W., 55 (1964)

Eusebius, *Demonstratio Evangelica*, ed. Dindorf, vol. III, Leipzig, 1867
—— *Ecclesiastical History*, text and trans. K. Lake, Loeb Classical Library, 2 vols., London, 1926
Farmer, W. R. 'The Palm Branches in John 12:13' in *J.T.S.*, vol. III (1952)
—— *Maccabees, Zealots and Josephus*, Columbia University Press, New York, 1957
Fennelly, J. M. *Origins of Alexandrian Christianity*, Ph.D. thesis (1967), deposited in the Arts Library, Manchester University
Festugière, A.-J. *La Révélation d'Hermès Trismégiste*, 4 tomes, Paris, 1950–4
Filson, F. V. *A New Testament History*, London, 1965
Förster, W. *Palestinian Judaism in New Testament Times*, E.T., Edinburgh, 1964
Frend, W. H. C. *Martyrdom and Persecution in the Early Church*, Oxford (Blackwell), 1965
—— 'The Gospel of Thomas: is Rehabilitation Possible?', in *J.T.S.*, vol. XVIII (1967)
Fuchs, H. 'Tacitus über die Christen', in *V.C.*, vol. I (1950)
Goguel, M. *The Life of Jesus*, E.T., London, 1933
—— *La naissance du Christianisme*, Paris, 1946
—— 'Jésus et le Messianisme politique: Examen de la théorie de M. Robert Eisler' in *Revue historique*, vol. LXII (1929), Paris
Goodenough, E. R. *The Politics of Philo Judaeus*, with a general bibliography of Philo, by H. L. Goodhart and E. R. Goodenough, Yale University Press, 1938
Gough, M. *The Early Christians*, London, 1961
Grabar, A. *The Beginnings of Christian Art*, E.T., London, 1967
—— *Byzantium: From the Death of Theodosius to the Rise of Islam*, E.T., London, 1966
Graetz, H. *History of the Jews*, E.T., vol. II, London, 1891
Grant, F. C. *The Economic Background of the Gospels*, Oxford, 1926
—— *The Gospels: the Origin and Growth*, London, 1965 (1957)
Grant, R. M. *The Earliest Lives of Jesus*, London, 1961
Grillmeier, A. *Christ in Christian Tradition from the Apostolic Age to Chalcedon (451)*, E.T., London, 1965
Grossi Gondi, F. *I Monumenti cristiani*, Roma, 1923
Grundel, W. 'Astrologie', in *R.A.C.*, I (1950), 817–31
Guignebert, Ch. *Le monde juif vers le temps de Jésus*, Paris, 1935
—— *Jésus*, Paris, 1947 (1933)
Hamilton, N. Q. 'Temple Cleansing and Temple Bank', in *J.B.L.*, vol. LXXXVIII (1964)
Hart, H. St J. 'Judaea and Rome: the Official Commentary', in *J.T.S.*, vol. iii (1952)
Hengel, M. *Die Zeloten*, Leiden, 1961
Hennecke, E. and Schneemelcher, W. (ed.), *New Testament Apocrypha*, E.T., R. McL. Wilson, vol. I, London
Hertling, L. and Kirschbaum, E. *The Roman Catacombs and their Martyrs*, E.T., London, 1960
Higgins, A. J. B. 'The Words of Jesus according to St John', in *B.J.R.L.*, 49 (1967)
Hoennicke, G. *Das Judenchristentum im ersten und zweiten Jahrhundert*, Berlin, 1908
Hort, F. J. *Judaistic Christianity*, London, 1894
Hutton, E. *The Story of Ravenna*, London, 1926
Isorin, J. *Le vrai procès de Jésus*, Paris, 1967
James, M. R. *The Apocryphal New Testament*, Oxford, 1926
Jaubert, A. 'Jesus et le calendrier de Qumrân', in *N.T.S.*, vol. VII (1960–1)
—— 'Les séances du Sanhédrin et les récits de la Passion', in *R.H.R.*, vols. 166 (1964), 167 (1965)
—— 'Le mercredi où Jésus fut livré', in *N.T.S.*, vol. XIV (1968)
Jeremias, J. *Jerusalem zur Zeit Jesu*, I, II. Teil, 2. Aufl., Göttingen, 1958
Join-Lambert, M. *Jerusalem*, E.T., London, 1966
Jones, A. H. M. *The Herods of Judaea*, Oxford, 1938
Josephus *The Jewish War; Against Apion*, text and trans., H. St John Thackeray, in Loeb Classical Library, 3 vols., London, 1926–8. Italian trans., with notes, G. Ricciotti,

La guerra guidaica, vols. II–IV, Turin, 1937 (see Ricciotti, G.). German trans. *De Bello Judaico: Der Judische Krieg*, hrg. O. Michel und O. Bauernfeind, I. Band, Bad Homburg, 1960

—— *Jewish Antiquities*, text and trans. of Books xv–xvii, R. Marcus and A. Wikgren, vol. VIII; Books xviii–xx, L. H. Feldman, vol. IX (in Loeb Classical Library), London–Cambridge (Mass.), 1963, 1965. Text. B. Niese, *Flavii Josephi Opera*, vol. IV (*Ant.* xvi–xx and *Vita*), Berlin, 1890. French annotated trans. G. Mathieu and L. Hermann in *Oeuvres complètes de Flavius Josephus* (sous la direction de Th. Reinach), t. IV, Paris, 1929

Justin Martyr *Works*, trans. G. J. Davie, Oxford, 1861

Kennard, J. Spencer *Politique et religion chez les Juifs au temps de Jésus et dans l'Église primitive*, Paris, 1927

—— *Render to God*, New York, 1950

——'The Jewish Provincial Assembly', in *Z.N.T.W.*, 53 (1962)

Kilpatrick, G. D. *The Trial of Jesus*, published by the Friends of Dr Williams' Library, London, 1953

Kingdom, H. P. 'Messiahship and the Crucifixion', in *Studia Evangelica*, III, ed. F. L. Cross, Berlin, 1964

Klausner, J. *Jesus of Nazareth*, E.T., London, 1929

—— *From Jesus to Paul*, E.T., London, 1942

Klauser, T. 'Studien zur Entstehungsgeschichte den christlichen Kunst, I', in *Jahrbuch für Antike und Christentum*, I (1958), Tübingen

Klein, G. *Zum Prozess Jesu*, ed. W. Koch, Weiden, 1967

Klostermann, E. *Das Matthäusevangelium*, 2. Aufl., Tübingen, 1927

—— *Das Markusevangelium*, 2. Aufl., Tübingen, 1927

—— *Das Lukasevangelium*, 2. Aufl., Tübingen, 1929

Knox, W. L. *St Paul and the Church of Jerusalem*, Cambridge, 1925

Koch, W. (ed.), *Zum Prozess Jesu*, Weiden, 1967

Koep, L. 'Chronologie' in *R.A.C.* III (1962), 60–97

Kopp, C. *The Holy Places of the Gospels*, E.T., Edinburgh–London, 1963

Kraeling, C. H. 'The Episode of the Roman Standards at Jerusalem', in *H.Th.R.*, vol. XXXV (1942)

Kuhn, H.-W. 'Das Reittier Jesu in der Einzugsgeschichte des Mc-Evangeliums', in *Z.N.T.W.*, 50 (1959)

Kuhn, K. G. 'The Two Messiahs of Aaron and Israel', in *The Scrolls and the New Testament* (ed. K. Stendahl), London, 1958

De Labriolle, P. *La réaction païenne: étude sur la polémique antichrétienne du Ier au VIe siècle*, Paris, 1942 (1934)

Lampe, G. W H. 'Luke', in *P.C.*²

Lerclercq, H. *La vie chrétienne primitive*, Paris, 1928

Lescow, T. 'Jesus in Gethsemane bei Lukas und im Hebräerbrief', in *Z.N.T.W.*, 58 Band (1967)

Lietzmann, H. *An die Korinther*, I–II, 2. Aufl., Tübingen, 1923

Lietzmann, H. *Geschichte der alten Kirche*, I. Band, Berlin–Leipzig, 1937

—— 'Der Prozess Jesu', in *Kleine Schriften*, II (*Texte und Untersuchungen zur Geschichte der altchristlichen Literatur*, 68. Band=V. Reihe, Band. 13. Berlin, 1958 (originally published in *Sitzungsberichte der Preussischen Akademie der Wissenschaften phil.-hist. Klasse*, 1931, XIV, Berlin 1934)

Lightfoot, R. H. *Locality and Doctrine in the Gospels*, London, 1938

Lindeskog, G. 'Der Prozess Jesu im judisch-christlichen Religionsgespräch', in *Abraham Unser Vater: Juden und Christen im Gespräch über die Bibel. Festschrift für Otto Michel zum 60. Geburtstag*, hrg. O. Betz, M. Hengel, P. Schmidt. Leiden/Köln, 1963

Loewe, H. '*Render unto Caesar*: Religious and Political Liberty in Palestine*, Cambridge, 1940.

Lohmeyer, E. and Schmauch, W. *Das Evangelium des Matthäus*, Göttingen, 1958

Loisy, A. *Les mystères païens et le mystère chrétien*, Paris, 1914

Lüthi, K. *Judas Iskarioth in der Geschichte der Auslegung von der Reformation bis zur Gegenwart*, Zürich, 1955

Mâle, E. *Religious Art: from the Twelfth to the Eighteenth Century*, E.T., New York, 1958

Malraux, A. *The Metamorphosis of the Gods*, E.T., London, 1960

Manson, T. W. *The Teaching of Jesus*, Cambridge, 1935

——'John the Baptist', in *B.J.R.L.*, vol. 36 (1954)

—— *Jesus and the Non-Jews*, University of London (Athlone Press), 1955

Manson T. W. *Studies in the Gospels and the Epistles*, Manchester University Press, 1962

McNeile, A. H. *The Gospel according to St Matthew*, London, 1952 (1915)

Medieval English Verse, ed. B. Stone, Harmondsworth, 1964

Menzies, A. *The Second Epistle to the Corinthians*, London, 1912

Meyer, Ed. *Ursprung und Anfänge des Christentums*, 3 vols., Stuttgart–Berlin, 1921–3

di Miscio, G. *Il processo di Cristo*, Milan, 1967

Mishnah, The, trans. H. Danby, Oxford, 1933

Moffatt, J. *An Introduction to the Literature of the New Testament*, 3rd revised ed., Edinburgh, 1933

Momigliano, A. *L'Opera dell 'Imperatore Claudio*, Florence, 1932

—— 'Rebellion within the Empire', ch. xxv, in *C.A.H.*, vol. X (1934)

Mommsen, T. *Das Weltreich der Caesaren*, Wien–Leipzig, 1933

Montefiore, H. W. 'Revolt in the Desert?', in *N.T.S.*, vol. VIII (1961–2)

—— *Josephus and the New Testament*, London, 1962

——'Jesus and the Temple Tax', in *N.T.S.*, vol. XI (1964)

Mowinckel, S. *He That Cometh*, E.T., Oxford (Blackwell), 1958

Munck, J. 'Jewish Christianity in Post-Apostolic Times', in *N.T.S.*, vol. VI (1960)

Nardi, C. *Il processo di Gèsu, re dei Guidei*, Bari, 1966

Neusner, J. *History of the Jews in Babylonia*, vol. I, Leiden, 1965

Neutestamentliche Apokryphen (hrg. E. Hennecke, and W. Schneemelcher), I. Band, Tübingen, 1959

New Testament, *Novum Testamentum Graece*, hrg. E. Nestle, 19. Aufl., Stuttgart, 1949

—— (Gospels) A. Huck, *Synopse der drei Evangelien*, Tübingen, 1928

Niese, B. 'Josephus' in *E.R.E.*, vol. VII (1914)

Nock, A. D. 'Religious Developments from the Close of the Republic to the Death of Nero', ch. xv, in *C.A.H.*, vol. X (1934)

—— *St Paul*, London, 1938

Noth, M. *A History of Israel*, E.T., London, 1960

Oesterley, W. O. E. *A History of Israel*, vol. II, Oxford, 1932

Ogg, G. 'The Chronology of the New Testament', in *P.C.*²

Origen, *contra Celsum*, ed. C. H. E. Lommatzsch, Berlin, 1834

—— *Commentarium in Mattheum*, ed. C. H. E. Lommatzsch, Berlin, 1834

Ort, L. J. R. *Mani: a Religio-Historical Description of his Personality*, Leiden, 1967

Panofsky, E. *Tomb Sculpture*, London, 1964

Pedersen, J. *Israel: its Life and Culture*, I–IV, in 2 vols., Copenhagen and London, 1926, 1940

Peretti, A. *La Sibilla babilonese nella Propaganda ellenistica*, Florence, 1943

Perowne, S. *The Later Herods*, London, 1958

Philo, *Legatio ad Gaium*, ed. and trans. E. M. Smallwood, Leiden, 1961

Pin, B. *Jerusalem contre Rome (Un duel pour l'hégémonie en Méditerranée orientale)*, Paris, 1938

Reifenberg, A. *Israel's History in Coins*, London, 1953

Rengstorf, K. H. 'λῃστής', in *Th.Wb.*, IV, 262–7

Ricciotti, G. *Flavio Guiseppe. Lo Storico giudeo-romano*, Turin (see under Josephus)

Roth, C. *Historical Background of the Dead Sea Scrolls*, Blackwell, Oxford, 1958

——'The Zealots in the War of 66–73', in *J.S.S.*, vol. IV (1959)

—— 'The Debate on the Loyal Sacrifices', in *H.Th.R.*, vol. LIII (1960)

—— 'The Constitution of the Jewish Republic of 66–70', in *J.S.S.*, vol. IX (1964)

Rowley, H. H. 'The Herodians', in *J.T.S.*, vol. XLI (1940)

Rowley, H. H. *The Biblical Doctrine of Election*, London, 1950
Sanday, W. and Headlam, A. C. *The Epistle to the Romans* (International Critical Commentary), Edinburgh, 1900
Scramuzza, V. M. 'The Policy of the Early Roman Emperors towards Judaism', in *B.C.*, vol. V (1933)
Scherer, M. R. *Marvels of Ancient Rome*, New York–London, 1956
Schlatter, A. *Der Evangelist Johannes*, Stuttgart, 1930
Schlatter, D. A. *Die Geschichte Israels von Alexander dem Grossen bis Hadrian*, Stuttgart, 1925
Schlier, H. *Der Brief an die Galater*, Göttingen, 1962
Schmidtke, F. 'Chronologie', in *R.A.C.*, III (1957), 49–50
Schmithals, W. 'Paul und historische Jesus', in *Z.N.T.W.*, 53 (1962)
Schoeps, H. J. *Theologie und Geschichte des Judenchristentums*, Tübingen, 1949
—— *Aus frühchristlicher Zeit: religionsgeschichtliche Untersuchungen*, Tübingen, 1950
—— *Paulus: die Theologie im Lichte der jüdischen Religionsgeschichte*, Tübingen, 1959. E.T., *Paul: the Theology of the Apostle in the Light of Jewish Religious History*, London, 1961
Schürer, E. *Geschichte des judischen Volkes im Zeitalter Jesu Christi*, 3 Bände, Leipzig, 1898–1901
Schweitzer, A. *The Quest of the Historical Jesus*, E.T., London, 1910
—— *Paul and his Interpreters*, E.T., London, 1912
—— *The Mysticism of Paul*, E.T., London, 1931
Seznec, J. *La survivance des dieux antiques*, The Warburg Institute, London, 1940
Simon, M. *Verus Israel: étude sur les relations entre Chrétiens et Juifs dans l'Empire romain (135–425)*, Paris, 1948
—— *Les premiers Chrétiens*, Paris, 1952
—— *Recherches d'histoire judéo-chrétienne*, Paris–La Haye, 1962
Smallwood, E. M. 'High Priests and Politics in Roman Palestine', in *J.T.S.*, vol. XIII (1962)
—— 'Jews and Romans in the Early Empire', in *History Today*, vol. XV (1965)
Smith, G. A. *Jerusalem*, 2 vols., London, 1907
Stauffer, E. *Christus und die Caesaren*, Hamburg, 1952
—— *Jesus and His Story*, E.T., 1960
Steinmetzer, F. X. 'Census', in *R.A.C.*, II (1954), 969–72
Stendahl, K. 'Matthew', in *P.C.*²
Strack, H. L. and Billerbeck, P. *Kommentar zum Neuen Testament aus Talmud und Midrasch*, 4 Bände, Munich, 1922–8
Strecker, G. *Das Judenchristentum in den Pseudoklementinen*, Berlin, 1958
Streeter, B. H. *The Four Gospels*, London, 1924
—— 'The Rise of Christianity', ch. vii, in *C.A.H.*, vol. XI (1936)
Suetonius, *Lives of the Caesars*, ed. C. L. Roth, Leipzig, 1891
Tacitus, *Annales, Historiae*, ed. C. Halm, 2 vols., Leipzig, 1891
—— *The Annals of Tacitus*, ed. H. Furneaux, 2nd ed., Oxford, 1934
Taylor, V. *The Formation of the Gospel Tradition*, London, 1945
—— *The Gospel according to St Mark*, London, 1952
Telfer, W. 'Was Hegesippus a Jew?', in *H.Th.R.*, vol. LIII (1960)
Tertullian, *Apology*, Loeb Classical Library, ed. and trans. T. R. Glover, London, 1960
Thackeray, H. St John, *Josephus: the Man and the Historian*, New York, 1929
Van den Oudenrijn, M.-A. *Gamaliel: äthiopische Texte zur Pilatusliteratur*, Freiburg, 1959
Van der Meer, F. and Mohrmann, C. *Atlas of the Early Christian World*, E.T., London–Edinburgh, 1958
Vardaman, J. 'A New Inscription which mentions Pilate as "Prefect"', in *J.B.L.*, vol. LXXXI (1962)
Van Unnik, W. C. 'Jesus the Christ', in *N.T.S.*, vol. VIII (1961–2)
De Vaux, R. *L'archéologie et les manuscrits de la Mer Morte* (Schweich Lectures, 1959), London, 1961

Walter, N. 'Tempelzerstörung und synoptische Apokalypse', in *Z.N.T.W.*, 57 (1966)

Werner, M. *Die Entstehung des christlichen Dogmas*, 2. Aufl., Bern–Tübingen, 1941

—— *The Formation of Christian Dogma*, E.T., by S. G. F. Brandon, London, 1957

Widengren, Geo. *Mani and Manichaeism*, E.T., London, 1965

Wildberger, H. *Jahwes Eigentumsvolk*, Zürich, 1960

Wilson, R. Mcl. 'Mark', in *P.C.*[2]

Windisch, H. *Der messianische Krieg und Urchristentum*, Tübingen, 1909

—— *Der zweite Korintherbrief*, Göttingen, 1924

Winter, P. *On the Trial of Jesus*, Berlin, 1961

—— 'Zum Prozess Jesu', in *Das Altertum*, 9 (1963)

—— 'The Cultural Background of the Narrative in Luke i and ii', in *J.Q.R.*, vol. XLV (1954)

—— 'Markus 14:53b, 55–64 ein Gebilde des Evangelisten', in *Z.N.T.W.*, 53 (1962)

—— 'The Marcan Account of Jesus' Trial by the Sanhedrin', in *J.T.S.*, vol. XIV (1963)

—— *Zum Prozess Jesu*, ed. W. Koch, Weiden, 1967

Wood, H. G. 'The Conversion of St Paul: its Nature, Antecedents and Consequences', in *N.T.S.*, vol. I (1954–5)

Yadin, Y. *The Scroll of the War of the Sons of Light against the Sons of Darkness*, Oxford, 1962

—— *The Excavation of Masada, 1963/64*. Preliminary Report, *Israel Exploration Journal*, Jerusalem, vol. XV (1965). *Masada*, E.T., London, 1966

Zahrnt, H. *The Historical Jesus*, E.T., London, 1963

Zeitlin, S. *Who Crucified Jesus?*, New York, 1942

—— 'The Crucifixion of Jesus Re-examined', in *J.Q.R.*, vol. XXXI (1940–1)

Index of Ancient Sources

The figures in brackets indicate notes

Index of Modern Authors

The figures in brackets indicate notes

Index of Names and Subjects

The figures in brackets indicate notes